Essential GCSE ICT

for WJEC

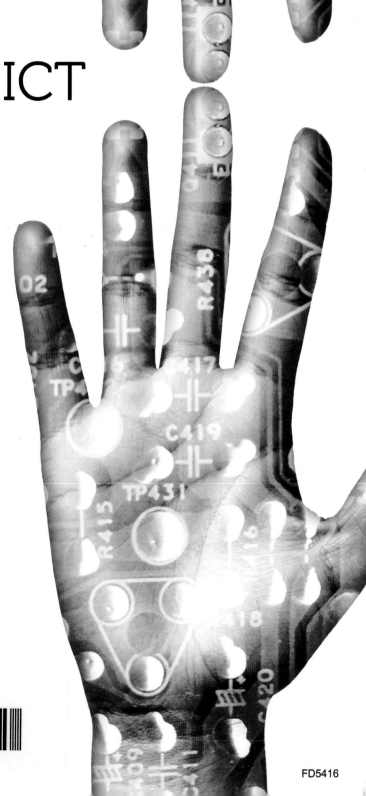

WJEC
CBAC

Stephen Doyle

FD5416

© 2010 Folens Limited, on behalf of the author.

United Kingdom: Folens Publishers, Waterslade House,
Thame Rd, Haddenham, Buckinghamshire HP17 8NT.

www.folens.com

Ireland: Folens Publishers, Greenhills Road, Tallaght, Dublin 24.

Email: info@folens.ie

This material has been endorsed by WJEC and offers high quality support for the delivery of WJEC qualifications. While this material has been through a WJEC quality assurance process, all responsibility for the content remains with the publisher.

Editor:	Geoff Tuttle
Project development:	Adrian Moss (Instructional Design Ltd) with Rick Jackman (Jackman Publishing Solutions Ltd)
Concept design:	Patricia Briggs
Layout artist:	Greengate Publishing Services
Illustrations:	Greengate Publishing Services
Cover design:	Jumpto! www.jumpto.co.uk
Cover image:	Courtesy of Chris Harvey/Fotolia.com

First published 2010 by Folens Limited

Every effort has been made to contact copyright holders of material used in this publication. If any copyright holder has been overlooked, we should be pleased to make any necessary arrangements.

British Library Cataloguing in Publication Data.

A catalogue record for this publication is available from the British Library.

ISBN 978-1-85008-541-6

Contents

Introduction to WJEC GCSE

What the book covers

This book covers both the GCSE (Single Award) and the GCSE (Short Course) in ICT.

- To obtain a GCSE (Short Course) in ICT you need to study Units 1 and 2.
- To obtain a GCSE (Single Award) in ICT you need to study Units 1–4.

Units

The specification for GCSE ICT is arranged in Units. There are four units for the Single Award GCSE and two units for the Short Course GCSE.

Unit 1   Understanding ICT
Unit 2   Solving Problems with ICT
Unit 3   ICT in Organizations
Unit 4   Developing Multimedia ICT Solutions

The way the book is organized

The book covers the content needed for Units 1–4. This means that if you are taking the GCSE (Single Award), you will need to cover all the material in this book. If you are taking the GCSE (Short Course), you will only need to cover some of the material in this book.

The book is organized in topics:

- Topics 1–12 cover the material for the Unit 1 examination.
- Topics 13–27 cover the material for the Unit 3 examination.

Unit 1: Understanding ICT

Single Award 20%; Short Course 40%
External Assessment: 1½ hours

This examination paper assesses the requirements to the Key Stage 4 Programme of Study for Information Technology and the functional elements of ICT in a home and school context.

Unit 2: Solving Problems with ICT

Single Award 30%; Short Course 60%
Controlled Assessment: 22½ hours

This controlled assessment requires you to produce a portfolio of work. For this you have to obtain and interpret different types of information: using, developing and communicating information to meet the purpose of your studies and to present the results of your work. This controlled assignment will test the practical aspects of the functional elements of ICT.

Unit 3: ICT in Organizations

Single Award 20%
External Assessment: 1½ hours

This examination paper will assess the 'application' content of ICT in a business and industry context.

Unit 4: Developing Multimedia ICT Solutions

Single Award 30%
Controlled Assessment: 22½ hours

This controlled assessment gives you the opportunity to develop a piece of work using multimedia software following a single task brief issued by WJEC.

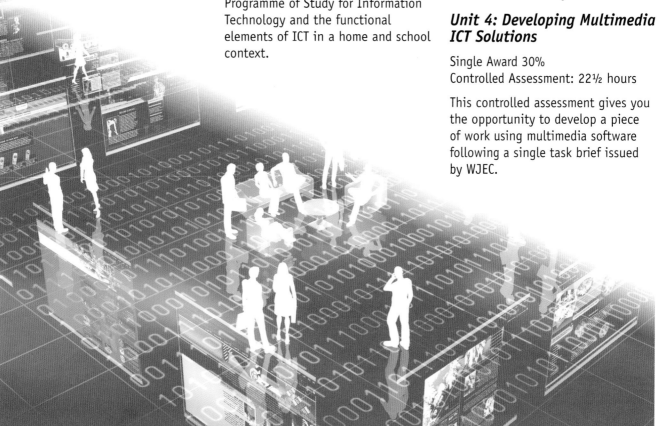

Introduction to WJEC GCSE *continued*

The organization of Unit 1

Understanding ICT

The material for Unit 1 is divided into topics, which are:

Topic 1	Data and quality of data*	Topic 8	Information handling software
Topic 2	Home entertainment	Topic 9	Email
Topic 3	Home and personal communication systems	Topic 10	Spreadsheet software
		Topic 11	DTP software
Topic 4	Home business	Topic 12	Web and presentation software*
Topic 5	Organizations: school, home and environment*	Topic 24	Staying safe online
		Topic 25	Data protection issues
Topic 6	ICT and learning	Topic 26	Health issues
Topic 7	Applications software		

The organization of Unit 3

ICT in Organizations

The material for Unit 3 is divided into topics, which are:

Topic 13	Web software	Topic 19	Networks
Topic 14	Presentation software	Topic 20	Human–computer interfaces (HCIs)
Topic 15	Multimedia	Topic 21	Organizations
Topic 16	Digital imaging	Topic 22	Social and environmental impact
Topic 17	Animation	Topic 23	Legal and ethical issues*
Topic 18	Sound and music	Topic 27	Emerging technologies

Note some of the material in the topics is examined in the other unit. For example, if a topic in Unit 1 has an asterisk next to it, it means that some of the content of the topic is examined in Unit 3. There is also once occurrence in Topic 23 in Unit 3 where some of the material is examined in Unit 1.

Unit 1	Material examined in Unit 3
Topic 1 Data and quality of data	Encoding of data (page 4)
	The advantages and disadvantages of using ICT for storing data (page 5)
	Verification (parity check, double keying and visual check (page 8)
	Validation (batch total and hash totals) (pages 8–9)
	How errors can occur (page 6)
Topic 5 Organizations: school, home and environment	Advantages and disadvantages of control systems (pages 58–59)
Topic 12 Web and presentation software	Data compression techniques (page 136)
	Advantages and disadvantages of data compression techniques (page 136)
Topic 23 Legal and ethical issues	Issues concerning copyright misuse (page 262)

Introduction to the features in the student book

The philosophy behind the student book

This student book has been based on extensive research from schools and colleges on the different ways ICT is taught and this book has been developed with all the findings in mind. As this is a new specification, many students and teachers/lecturers will be finding their way and the aim of the book is to provide a depth of coverage for the material for Units 1–4.

This book builds on the material students will have covered at Key Stage 3 and seeks to cover the material needed for the WJEC GCSE Short Course and Single Awards in ICT.

This book should be used by the teacher/lecturer in conjunction with the teacher support materials. Of course this book can be used stand-alone, but if you are a teacher then there are many resources in the teacher support materials to help your students succeed and maximize their marks. The Teacher Resource Guide CD-ROM contains the following non-digital resources: Answers to the Questions, Worksheets, Activities, Case studies and multiple-choice questions.

The Teacher Resource Guide CD-ROM also includes a wealth of digital materials such as PowerPoint presentations, multiple-choice questions, matching questions and so on. These will all help your students consolidate their understanding of the topics.

The structure of the student book

There are two units for the GCSE Short Course and four units for the GCSE Single Award. The student book covers all four units. Units 1 and 3 are assessed by examination and Units 2 and 4 are assessed by controlled assessment.

The material for Units 1 and 3 is divided into topics, with each topic being further divided up into double-page spreads. This allows division of each topic into bite-size easily digested chunks of material. For consistency and to make the student book easy to use, all topics are structured in the same way.

Material for Units 2 and 4 use some of the material in Units 1 and 3 but this time in a practical context.

Students will have used many of the tools and techniques in their Key Stage 3 work and their work in other subjects.

Topic introduction pages

The first page of each topic consists of an introduction to the material in the topic and includes the following features:

Topic introduction: just a couple of paragraphs introducing students to the subject matter in the topic.

Key concepts: this lists the key concepts covered in the topic. These key concepts are identical to those in the GCSE WJEC specification.

Contents: the contents lists the spreads used to cover the topic and each spread covers key concepts.

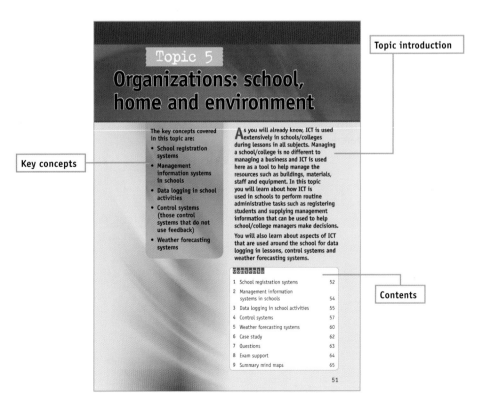

Introduction to the features in the student book *continued*

Topic spreads

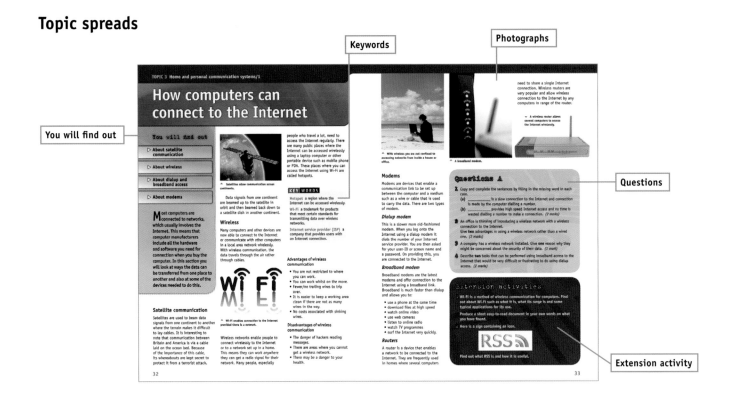

Keywords

Photographs

You will find out

Questions

Extension activity

Questions and Extension activities

Questions are usually included at the end of each content spread and are used to consolidate learning. Some **Extension activities** are also included within the content spreads. This allows you to look at the spreads and then practise the questions. The answers to all the questions are available in the teacher support materials, which are available separately on CD-ROM and complement the student text.

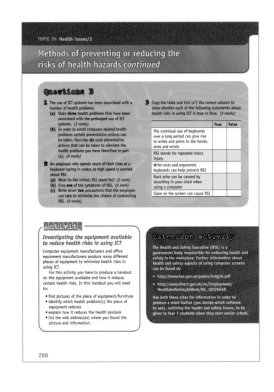

Questions spreads

Examination style questions: are designed to be similar to GCSE examination questions and have marks to give you the opportunity to understand how answers are marked. The answers to the questions are included on the Teacher Resource Guide CD-ROM.

Test yourself: consists of a series of statements with a blank space in which to insert the missing word or words that appear in a list. Students can either write the missing words as a list or they can write the complete sentence with the missing word inserted. The answers to these are available on the Teacher Resource Guide CD-ROM.

Activities: offer interesting things for you to do that will help add to and reinforce the material in the spreads and give you practice with ICT skills.

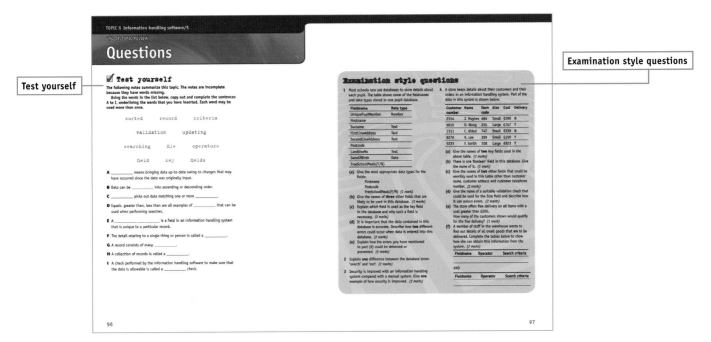

Test yourself

Examination style questions

Case study spreads

Case studies: real-life case studies are included in some of the topics that relate directly to the material in the topic. Case studies give a context in which you can answer the examination questions. Often examination questions on ICT ask not only for a definition or explanation but also an example. Case studies build up your knowledge of how the theory you learn about is used in practice.

Case study questions: will give you practice at answering questions that relate to real-life situations. The questions have been carefully constructed to be similar to the examination questions you could be asked and relate directly to the case study and other material contained in the content spreads. If your teacher has the Teacher Resource Guide, they will have the answers to these case study questions.

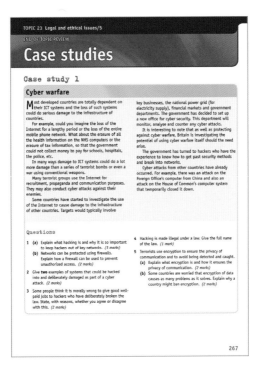

Introduction to the features
in the student book *continued*

Exam support

Worked example: is an important feature because it gives you an insight into how the examination questions are marked. At GCSE, you can have the knowledge but still fail to get a good mark because you have failed to communicate what you know effectively. It is essential that you understand just what is expected of you when answering questions for GCSE.

Student answers: you can see an examination question with examples of two different student answers. For each student answer there is a corresponding sample Examiner's comment.

Examiner's comment: offers you an insight into how examiners mark student answers. The main thing here is to be able to see the mistakes that can be made and ensure that you do not make similar mistakes. By analysing the way answers are marked, you will soon be able to get more marks for the questions that you answer by not making common mistakes.

Examiner's answers: offers some of the many possible answers and an indication of how the marks are distributed between the answers. It should be borne in mind that there are many possible correct answers to some questions and that any mark scheme relies on the experience of the markers to interpret the mark scheme and to give credit for answers that do not appear in the mark scheme.

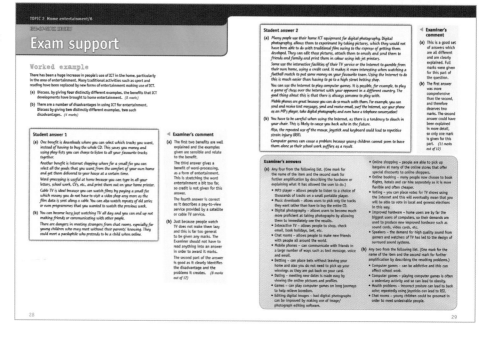

Summary mind maps

Mind maps are great fun to produce and a very good way of revising. They are included at the end of each topic to summarize the material contained in the topic. Sometimes there will be only one mind map and other times there will be several – it all depends on how the material in the topic is broken down.

As well as using these mind maps to help you revise, you should produce your own.

Why not produce them using the computer? There are many good pieces of mind-mapping software.

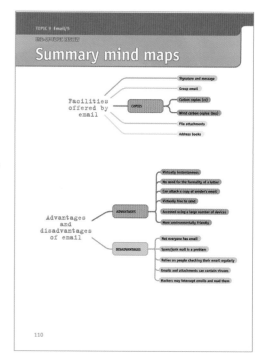

Topic 1
Data and quality of data

The key concepts covered in this topic are:

- **Evaluating data for fitness for purpose, accuracy and bias**
- **Data and information**
- **Data validation**

In this topic you will learn about what data is and why it is important as the raw material for any ICT system. You will learn about the need for data to be fit for purpose, accurate and unbiased. It is no good processing data that has errors in it.

Also in this topic you will find out about terms such as information and knowledge and the methods used to prevent inaccurate data being processed by the ICT system.

Contents

Evaluating data for fitness for purpose, accuracy and bias

You will find out

▷ **About what data is and how it arises**

▷ **About information and knowledge**

▷ **About the evaluation of data for fitness for purpose, accuracy and bias**

In this section you will learn about the importance of ensuring that the data being collected is collected properly. If the data is collected incorrectly, no amount of processing by a computer will make it right.

What exactly is data?

Data consists of raw facts and figures (e.g., readings from sensors, survey facts, etc.). These raw facts and figures are meaningless because they lack relevance. If you look at data, it is either no use to you or not in a form that you can use.

There are a number of forms that data can take. Data can be:

- numbers
- words
- images
- sound
- video.

Take a look at the following figures:

£72,000, £110,000, £128,000

The above set of numbers is data. It tells us nothing because there is no context. We do not know if they are a Premiership player's weekly wage, the price of a car or the value of sales of own brand baked beans sold in a week.

If we are told that these three numbers are a Premiership footballer's average weekly wage for the years 2008, 2009 and 2010, we now have information.

The raw data (i.e. the numbers) can be processed in many ways:

- A graph could be drawn to show the trend.
- We could work out the percentage by which the average increased for each year.
- We could work out the average wage over the three years.

All this processing will produce information and will give us knowledge.

Information

Information is data that has been processed by the computer. Processed can mean:

- Having calculations performed on it.
- Converting it to give it meaning.
- Organizing it in some way (putting it into numerical order, alphabetical order, into a database structure, etc.).

▶ Data can arise in the following ways.

Knowledge

Knowledge is obtained from information by applying rules to it. You can see that there is a considerable increase in the average wage of the footballers and this is knowledge we have gained from the information.

GIGO (garbage in garbage out)

ICT people often use the term GIGO, meaning garbage in garbage out. This means that if the data is inaccurate then no amount of processing will produce any useful information. The output from the computer will be incorrect. It is therefore essential that the data put into a computer system is good quality data.

Ways in which data can arise

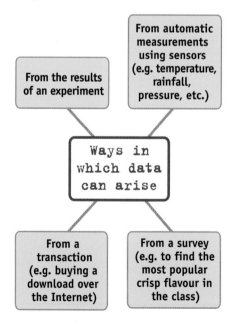

From the results of an experiment

From automatic measurements using sensors (e.g. temperature, rainfall, pressure, etc.)

Ways in which data can arise

From a transaction (e.g. buying a download over the Internet)

From a survey (e.g. to find the most popular crisp flavour in the class)

GIGO abbreviation for garbage in garbage out. It means that if you put rubbish into the computer then you get rubbish out.

Data raw facts and figures, e.g. readings from sensors, survey facts, etc.

Processing performing calculations or arranging the data into a meaningful order.

Transaction a piece of business, e.g. an order, purchase, return, delivery, transfer of money, etc.

Information data that has been processed by the computer.

Knowledge derived from information by applying rules to it.

Evaluation of data for fitness for purpose, accuracy and bias

Evaluating data for fitness for purpose

Fitness for purpose means that the data is suitable for doing the job for which it was collected.

Here are two ways data may not be fit for purpose:

- Too few items of data – for example, data could be collected to determine which polystyrene cup was the best at keeping a cup of coffee hot. If the person took only two readings, the data would be unfit for purpose as you cannot plot a graph using so few readings.
- Not collecting the right data – another example would be if you wanted to find out what 16–18 year olds did in their free time. If some of the people you interviewed were not in this age group the data would not be fit for purpose. It would be pointless using this data to produce any meaningful information.

Evaluating data for accuracy

The data collected may not be accurate. For example, temperature readings taken by a person reading a thermometer rely on them being able to read the thermometer properly.

Here are some ways that data could be inaccurate:

- Making data up – a person recording traffic flow manually may get fed up after a few hours and decide to make up some of the readings. This data will no longer be accurate.

- Some data missing – for example, a company that sells trainers might want to know who the best salesperson is for each month. The data they would need would be the value of each order a particular salesperson has made. There will be lots of these orders so totals need to be worked out. If some of the orders had not been included in the figures then it would be impossible to rank the sales staff and the data. The data used is inaccurate.
- Mistakes when collecting data – numbers could be written down incorrectly.

Evaluating data for bias

It is so easy to bias data in some way. Bias means that there is a tendency or preference towards a particular result. Here are some ways you can bias data:

- Not taking a representative sample – for example, going along to the local Labour club to collect data that can be used to find out how the whole population is likely to vote in the next election is not a good idea. Clearly the majority of people will vote Labour. By collecting the data in this way the person has biased the data.
- Prompting a certain answer – asking the questions in a way that you might be prompting a person to give a certain answer. For example, 'You don't like Manchester United football team do you?' clearly tells the person that you don't like them. They are more likely to agree with you, so an argument does not develop.

Questions A

1 Complete the sentences below by filling in the missing word in each case.
  (a) Raw facts and figures such as readings from sensors are called _____.
  (b) Data that has been processed by the computer is called _____.
  (c) _____ is derived from information by applying rules to it.
  (3 marks)

2 Students in a school conduct a survey to find out who the favourite teacher is.
  (a) The teacher in charge of the survey has said that the survey should produce good quality data. Describe **three** features of good quality data. *(6 marks)*
  (b) Mr Jones is a teacher at the school. One of the questions is 'Do you agree that Mr Jones is the best teacher in the school?' Give **one** thing that is wrong with this question and give a reason for your answer. *(2 marks)*

3 (a) Give **three** different types of data. *(3 marks)*
  (b) By giving a suitable example, explain how data is processed to produce information. *(3 marks)*

Extension activity

Using what you have learnt in this topic, produce a survey form that could be used to determine who the favourite teacher is in your school.

Explain how your survey will ensure accuracy, unbiased data and fitness for purpose.

Encoding and the storage of data

You will find out

▷ **About the encoding of data**

▷ **About the advantages and disadvantages of encoding data**

▷ **About the problems processing inaccurate data can cause**

When a large amount of data needs entering into a computer system, it makes sense to encode it. Encoding means putting the data into a code and reducing its size.

This section also looks at the advantages and disadvantages of storing data using ICT systems.

Encoding of data

Data is often coded when it is collected on input into an ICT system. The reasons for this are:

- Coded data is quicker to type in.
- It takes up less storage space on disk.
- It is easier to check a code using validation checks.
- It is faster to access data that is coded.
- It is quicker to send the data over a network.

There are many examples of encoding data and here are a few:

Sex:
M = Male
F = Female

Date:
19/08/10 = 19 August 2010

Country of origin for cars:
GB = Great Britain
D = Germany
IRL = Ireland
CH = Switzerland

Sizes of clothes:
S = Small
M = Medium
L = Large
XL = Extra large

Airport codes:
LHR = London Heathrow
MAN = Manchester
RHO = Rhodes

All these examples show there is less to type in when data is encoded.

▲ Size labelling in clothes is a form of encoding.

▲ All flights have a code. The codes are shown on the departure board.

▲ This car number plate tells you where the car is from and its year. The arrangement of letters and digits is unique for a particular car.

The advantages and disadvantages of using ICT for storing data

ICT offers lots of advantages when storing data but there are a few disadvantages as well.

Advantages

- Less storage space is needed – possibility of lots of portable devices, smaller offices required, as no bulky filing cabinets.
- Data is easily copied – data can be copied very quickly.
- Easier to back up – backups can be performed quickly and transferred off-site using the Internet or copied onto removable media such as CD. Ensures the security of data.
- Easily transferred – data can be transferred using networks.
- Fast access to stored data – it is easy and fast to access stored data. You can perform detailed searches.
- Data can be put into a secret code when stored (i.e. encrypted).

▲ This collection of music CDs takes up a lot of space.

▲ This MP3 player can store the entire music collection in the previous diagram.

Disadvantages

- Copying data – means copyright holders lose out on money when music, games and videos are copied.
- Data can be copied quickly – means personal data can be stolen.
- Reliance on networks – means if the network fails, you cannot access the data.
- Training needed – people need to know how to access the stored data.
- Security problems – data needs to be protected from viruses, hackers, etc.

Problems processing inaccurate data causes

Errors in data can cause all sorts of problems such as:

- Incorrect decisions being made, resulting in loss of money, goods being sent to the wrong address, people being refused credit, etc.
- Having to spend time sorting out mistakes.
- Loss of goodwill.
- Loss of trust.
- Being prosecuted under the Data Protection Act 1998 for not keeping accurate personal data.

Questions B

1. Explain what encoding is and give a suitable example. *(3 marks)*

2. When data is collected it is often encoded. Describe **two** reasons why data is encoded. *(2 marks)*

3. There are both advantages and disadvantages in storing data using ICT. Give **two** advantages and **two** disadvantages in using ICT systems for the storage of data. *(4 marks)*

Extension activity

The following subjects are taken at GSCE at Grange Hill School:

Mathematics   English language   English literature

Science   History   Geography

PE   ICT   Cookery

Chemistry   Biology   Law

Business studies   Spanish   French

Physics   Design technology

The school uses a computer system to store information about students and each student has a record that shows their timetable. At the moment each student takes around nine GCSE subjects and the subjects are typed in for each student. This is a very time-consuming job.

You have been asked by the deputy to come up with a simple coding system for the above subjects. You will need to bear in mind that there are classes in Years 11, 12 and 13 who can take any combinations of the subjects.

Produce your coding system and clearly explain how it works. You should also outline the advantages that your coding system offers.

Data validation

You will find out

▷ **About how errors can occur**

▷ **About the types of validation**

You have already learnt that if incorrect data is processed, it will produce incorrect information. In many cases the information is used to make decisions and these decisions will probably be wrong. It is therefore necessary to take as many precautions as possible to make sure that the data being processed is accurate.

In this section you will learn about the techniques used to reduce the errors in data.

Register As a New User

Please enter the following information. Areas marked with * are required

Title:*	
First Name:*	
Last Name:*	
How Do You Prefer to be Addressed?: (optional)	
Organisation: (optional)	
House Number/Name:*	
Address Line 1:*	
Address Line 2: (optional)	
Town or City:*	
County/State/Region:*	
Postcode/Zipcode:*	
Country:*	United Kingdom
Email Address:*	
Choose a Username:* (4 - 20 characters)	
Choose a Password:* (4 - 20 characters)	
Confirm Password:*	
Resource Code: (optional - if you have already purchased a product with a resource code)	
School Type:*	Primary
Sign up to our monthly email: (Your email address will be kept confidential and be used only for the purposes of this newsletter.)	☐
Keep informed about Folens products: (Tick if you wish to be contacted about our products.)	☐

Our Privacy Statement gives detailed information regarding our use of personal data collected from the site.

Register with Folens

▲ Here is an online form that customers fill in when they want to purchase some books. Notice that there are presence checks where the user must enter data. Notice also that the user has to verify the password they choose.

How errors can occur

Errors in data can occur during:

- transcription (using the wrong form, mishearing words, etc.)
- input (e.g., keyboarding errors, etc.)
- processing (e.g., mistakes in formulas in spreadsheets, programming errors, etc.)
- transmission (e.g., data is corrupted as it travels through wires, cable, through air, etc.).

Types of error

When inputting data using a keyboard there are two types of error:

- **Transcription errors** – errors introduced when transferring data from a form (e.g., application form, order form, etc.) to a computer. They can also be caused by mishearing what a person says over the telephone and entering it into the computer.
- **Transposition errors** – easily made when typing quickly and involves typing letters or numbers in the wrong order.

Here are some examples:

- 'fro' instead of 'for'
- the account number 100065 instead of the correct account number 100056
- the flight number AB376 instead of BA376.

Data validation

Validation is a check performed by a computer program during data entry. Validation is the process that ensures that data accepted for processing is sensible and reasonable. For example, a living person's date of birth could not be before 1890 as in 2010 this would make them 120 years old (the current oldest person is 115).

Validation is performed by the computer program being used and consists of a series of checks called **validation checks**.

ISBN 978-1-85008-280-4

9 781850 082804

▲ The 13-digit number shown underneath the bars is encoded in the bars, which means the bars can be scanned to give the number rather than have to type it in.

When a developer develops a solution to an ICT problem, they must create checks to reduce the likelihood of the user entering incorrect information. This is done by restricting the user as to what they can enter, or checking that the data obeys certain rules.

Types of validation check

Validation checks are used to restrict the user as to the data they can enter. There are many different validation checks, each with their own special use including:

- **Data type checks** – these check that data being entered is the same type as the data type specified for the field. This would check to make sure that only numbers are entered into fields specified as numeric.
- **Presence checks** – some database fields have to be filled in, whilst others can be left empty. A presence check would check to make sure that data had been entered into a field. Unless the user fills in data for these fields, the data will not be processed.
- **Range checks** – are performed on numbers. They check that a number being entered is within a certain range. For example, all the students in a college are aged over 14, so a date of birth being entered which would give an age less than this would not be allowed by the range check.
- **Format checks** – are performed on codes to make sure that they conform to the correct combinations of characters. For

example, a code for car parts may consist of three numbers followed by a single letter. This can be specified for a field to restrict entered data to this format.

- **Check digits** – are digits that are added to important numbers such as account numbers, International Book Numbers (ISBNs), Article numbers (the numbers under the barcode), etc. These numbers are placed at the end of the block of numbers and are used to check that the numbers have been entered correctly into the computer.

When the large number is entered, the computer performs a calculation using all the numbers to work out this extra number. If the calculation reveals that the extra number (called the check digit) is the same as that calculated by the other numbers, it means that all the numbers have been entered correctly.

Questions C

1 **(a)** What is meant by a check digit? *(3 marks)*
   (b) Give **two** different examples where check digits are used. *(2 marks)*

2 Here are some dates of birth that are to be entered into an ICT system:
   12/01/3010
   01/13/2000
   30/02/1999

   Assume that all the dates are in the British format dd/mm/yyyy. For each one, explain why they cannot be valid dates of birth. *(3 marks)*

3 When an employee joins a company they are given an employee code.
   (a) Here is an example of an employee code:
   LLLNNNNNN   where L is a letter of the alphabet and N is a number.
   Explain **one** type of validation that could be used with this field. *(2 marks)*
   (b) Employees are given an annual salary.
   Explain **one** type of validation that could be used with this field. *(2 marks)*

4 A computer manager says, 'data can be valid yet be incorrect'. By giving **one** suitable example, explain what this statement means. *(3 marks)*

Data verification

In many cases data is input into a computer using a form or other document as the source of the data. It is important that data being entered is exactly the same as the data on the form. In other words the person doing the typing has not introduced errors through misreading. In this section you will learn about the different methods of data verification.

Data verification

Verification means checking that the data being entered into the ICT system perfectly matches the source of the data. For example, if details from an order form were being typed in using a keyboard, then when the user has finished, the data on the form on the screen should be identical to that on the paper form (i.e., the data source). Also if data was sent over a network, the data needs to be checked when it arrives to make sure no errors have been introduced.

Here are some methods of verification:

- **Visual check/proof reading** – involves one user carefully reading what they have typed in and comparing it with what is on the data source (order forms, application forms, invoices, etc.) for any errors, which can then be corrected.
- **Double entry of data** – involves using the same data source to enter the details into the ICT system twice and only if the two sets of data are identical will they be accepted for processing. The disadvantage of this is that the cost of data entry is doubled.

  Double entry of data is often used when creating accounts over the Internet. They may ask you to create a password and enter it twice. This ensures there are no mistakes that would prevent you from accessing the account.
- **Parity checking** – involves checking data after it has been sent through a wire or wirelessly. Parity checks check that the data has not been corrupted (i.e. altered) in any way.

Further methods of validation

When large numbers of input documents are used for data entry, it is necessary to check that all the documents have been input and processed properly. There are two checks that can be performed:

- hash totals
- batch totals.

Hash totals

Hash totals are meaningless totals used for a check. For example, if each survey form is numbered (e.g., 000001, 000002, 000023, etc.) then the total of all the numbers could be calculated and input to compare with the answer the computer calculates. If the hash totals are equal it shows that all the survey forms have been input.

▲ **Parity checking checks for errors when data is sent over networks.**

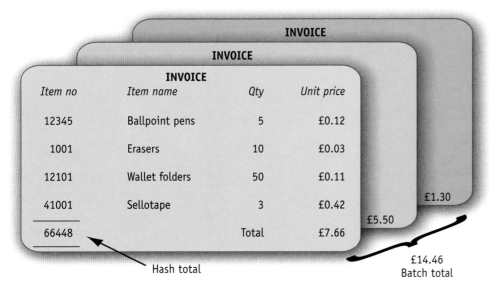

INVOICE

Item no	Item name	Qty	Unit price
12345	Ballpoint pens	5	£0.12
1001	Erasers	10	£0.03
12101	Wallet folders	50	£0.11
41001	Sellotape	3	£0.42
66448		Total	£7.66

Hash total

£1.30

£5.50

£14.46
Batch total

▲ Hash and batch totals are used to make sure all invoices have been processed.

Batch totals

Batch totals are like hash totals except the totals have meaning. For example, adding up all the totals of a batch of invoices could be used to check that all the invoices had been input. The total would be the total amount owed for those invoices processed in the batch. The amounts could be worked out manually and then compared with the answer the computer calculates. Any discrepancies could then be checked.

▲ Batch totals have meaning.

Batch total a meaningful total that is used to check that the computer has input all the data.

Hash total meaningless total of numbers, such as order numbers, used to check that all the data has been entered.

Parity check check to make sure that the data sent is the same as that received when data is transmitted from one computer to another.

Verification checking that the data being entered into the ICT system perfectly matches the source of the data.

Questions D

1 The school secretary types student information, from forms given to parents before the child joins the school, into the computer system. When these details are typed in, transcription errors and transposition errors can occur. Describe the difference between these two types of error. *(2 marks)*

2 An online form for ordering DVDs uses a presence check for some of the fields.
  (a) Explain what a presence check is and why some fields have them whilst others don't. *(3 marks)*
  (b) Give **one** field that might have a presence check and **one** field that would not need a presence check. *(2 marks)*

Extension activity

Using the Internet and other sources of information, find out how a parity check actually works. Use several sources and produce an illustrated explanation of your answer.

Questions

 Test yourself

The following notes summarize this topic. The notes are incomplete because they have words missing.

Using the words in the list below, copy out and complete sentences A to K, underlining the words that you have inserted. Each word may be used more than once.

data   GIGO   processing   code

evaluating   information   knowledge

transposition   transcription

verification   validation   quality

A _____ consists of raw facts and figures (e.g., reading from sensors, survey facts, etc.).

B Data processed by a computer is called _____.

C _____ is the term ICT people use to describe that if you put rubbish into an ICT system, you get rubbish out.

D _____ is obtained from information by applying rules to it.

E Checking data for fitness for purpose, accuracy and bias is called checking the _____ of the data.

F _____ means performing calculations or organizing the data.

G Encoding means putting data into a _____, which makes input quicker and it takes up less storage space.

H An error made when typing in data using a document as a source is called a _____ error.

I Swapping characters around while typing is called a _____ error.

J _____ checks are used to restrict the data a user can enter.

K _____ means checking that the data being entered perfectly matches the source of the data.

Examination style questions

1 (a) Explain the meaning of the term GIGO. *(2 marks)*
   (b) It is important that data entered into the computer is accurate.
        Explain **three** consequences of processing inaccurate data. *(3 marks)*

2 When Year 7 students join the senior school, a form in filled in by their parents. The details on the form are then typed into a computer. The details are verified after typing. Explain briefly, how the details may be verified. *(2 marks)*

3 In a database system a user has to type data into certain fields using a keyboard.
   Give **three** different types of mistake the user could make. *(3 marks)*

4 A person's date of birth is entered into a database. State **three** things the validation program could check regarding this date as part of the validation. *(3 marks)*

5 When a new member joins a fitness club they are given a membership number. The membership number is made up in the following way:
   Customer date of birth as six numbers.
   The final two figures of the year in which the customer joins the fitness club.
   A letter which is either J or S depending on whether they are a junior or senior member.
   (a) Write down the membership number for a junior member who joined the club in 2010 and was born on 21/05/98. *(1 mark)*

   (b) When the membership number is entered into the database, it is validated.
        Explain what is meant by data validation. *(2 marks)*
   (c) Two examples of data validation are:
             range check
             format check.
        Explain how these two methods could be used on the **membership number** field described above. *(2 marks)*
   (d) It would be better if the membership number were unique to a particular member.
        (i)   Explain why the method described might not result in a unique membership number. *(1 mark)*
        (ii) Explain **one** problem not having a unique membership number might cause. *(2 marks)*

6 Supermarkets use point of sale (POS) terminals at the checkout. This system makes use of a laser scanner to read the bar codes on the goods.
   (a) The bar code contains a check digit. Explain how this can be used to detect an error in reading the bar code. *(3 marks)*
   (b) Describe **two** different applications that would use bar codes. *(2 marks)*
   (c) Explain how each of the following checks can be used to validate data. *(4 marks)*
        (i)   Format check
        (ii) Presence check
        (iii) Parity check
        (iv) Range check.

END-OF-TOPIC REVIEW

Exam support

Worked example

(a) Define the terms data, information and knowledge. *(3 marks)*

(b) Give **two** reasons for encoding data. *(2 marks)*

Student answer 1

(a) Data is information before it is processed.

Information is data that has been processed.

Knowledge is what you know about the information.

(b) To make it harder for people to understand as you need to decipher it.

Putting data into a code summarizes it so there is less to type in.

◄ **Examiner's comment**

(a) The definition of data is true but it is not really appropriate to explain it this way.

The definition of information is fine.

The definition of knowledge is vague and gains no marks.

(b) For the first answer the student is confusing coding with encrypting.

The second answer is fine.

(2 marks out of 5)

Student answer 2

(a) Data consists of raw facts and figures at the collecting stage, before they are processed.

Information is either data that has a context or data that has been processed in some way (e.g., sorted, presented clearly, had calculations performed, etc.).

Knowledge is the rules that are used to interpret and apply information.

(b) The amount of data that needs to be entered can be reduced using encoding. For example Female and Male can be encoded as F and M and this means faster data input.

Because coded data is shorter, it takes up less disk space, which means the processing of the data is faster.

◄ **Examiner's comment**

(a) The first two definitions are correct and expressed clearly, but knowledge is not the rules, it is the result of interpreting information.

(b) Both are valid reasons for encoding, so full marks.

(4 marks out of 5)

Examiner's answers

(a) One mark each for suitable definitions similar to the following:

- Data – raw facts or figures or a set of values, measurements or records of transactions
- Information – consists of processed data or data with a context
- Knowledge – is derived from information by applying rules to it

(b) One mark each for two reasons such as:

- Less time is spent typing the data in, so data entry costs are lower
- The fewer the keystrokes made, the less chance of making transcription/keyboarding errors
- Less memory is needed to store the shortened data

Summary mind maps

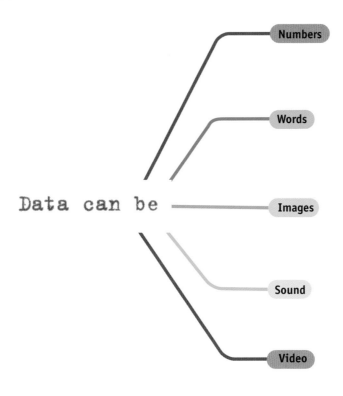

Data can be
- Numbers
- Words
- Images
- Sound
- Video

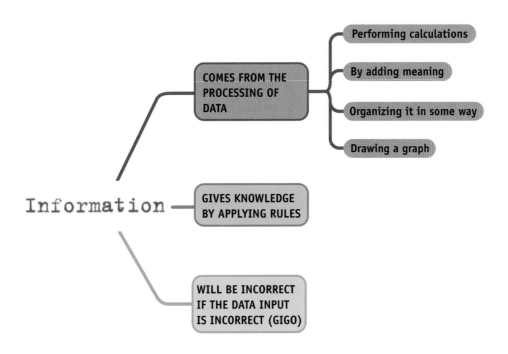

Information
- COMES FROM THE PROCESSING OF DATA
  - Performing calculations
  - By adding meaning
  - Organizing it in some way
  - Drawing a graph
- GIVES KNOWLEDGE BY APPLYING RULES
- WILL BE INCORRECT IF THE DATA INPUT IS INCORRECT (GIGO)

Summary mind maps *continued*

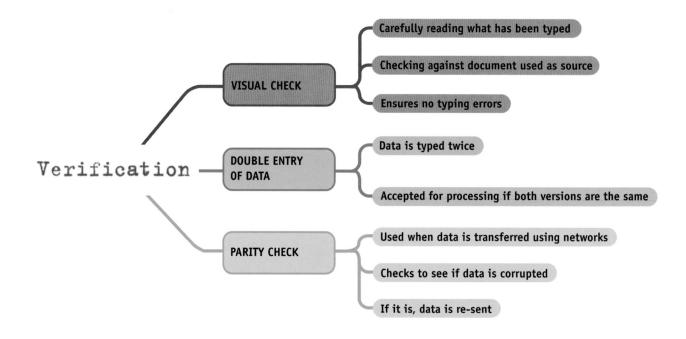

Verification

VISUAL CHECK
- Carefully reading what has been typed
- Checking against document used as source
- Ensures no typing errors

DOUBLE ENTRY OF DATA
- Data is typed twice
- Accepted for processing if both versions are the same

PARITY CHECK
- Used when data is transferred using networks
- Checks to see if data is corrupted
- If it is, data is re-sent

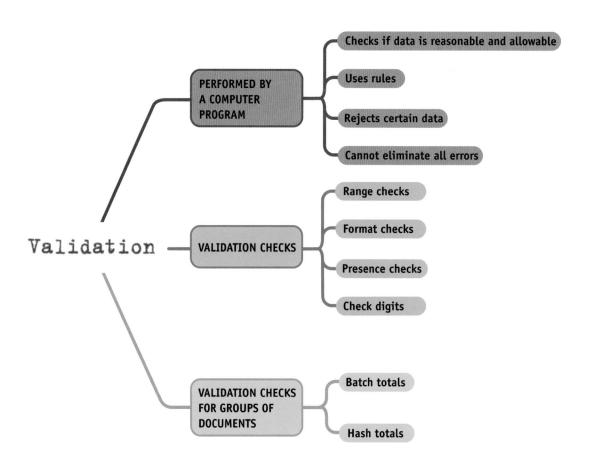

Validation

PERFORMED BY A COMPUTER PROGRAM
- Checks if data is reasonable and allowable
- Uses rules
- Rejects certain data
- Cannot eliminate all errors

VALIDATION CHECKS
- Range checks
- Format checks
- Presence checks
- Check digits

VALIDATION CHECKS FOR GROUPS OF DOCUMENTS
- Batch totals
- Hash totals

Home entertainment

The key concepts covered in this topic are:

- **Interactive TV services**
- **Gaming**
- **Digital photography**
- **Webcam services**
- **Social networking**
- **Music**
- **Mobile phones**

In this topic you will learn about the important use of ICT systems for home entertainment. Digital TV is now with us and many of us use subscription services such as cable and satellite services. Most people use ICT in some form for their home entertainment and the way we entertain ourselves has totally changed with new developments in ICT. Generally the improvements involve the reduction in size, making more devices portable, and the speed of data communication, which gives us faster Internet connection.

Contents

Interactive digital television

You will find out

▷ **About the use, services, input and output devices used with interactive TV**

Home entertainment used to be centred on the television but more people spend time using the Internet. This is changing with the introduction of digital TV, which offers many more facilities and brings the services normally associated with computers and the Internet into your lounge.

In this section you will learn about interactive TV and interactive services that are available.

Services available through interactive digital television

Digital TV offers a lot more besides the improvement in picture quality and greater choice of channels. Digital TV offers many interactive features such as:

- joining in with programmes by sending in comments
- viewing extra new stories and sports coverage
- booking cinema and holiday tickets
- playing games
- shopping
- placing bets
- using email
- placing votes for programmes – there are plans to use this service for voting in parliamentary elections
- interactive advertisements.

Many of the services that we currently use the Internet for, we will be able to access using our TV.

Disadvantages of satellite/cable

- cost of subscriptions
- bad weather disrupting the satellite signals.

Pay-to-view services

Pay-to-view TV services are subscription-based services where you pay a monthly or one-off fee for digital TV services that include:

- satellite channels and other services
- cable TV and other services
- digital terrestrial TV and other services (like ordinary TV but with an encrypted signal).

One-off fees are payable to watch:

- a specific film
- a specific sporting event (e.g., Premiership football match, boxing match, etc.).

Interactive services (e.g., betting, voting and dating)

There are a large number of interactive services available using the Internet and some of the cable/satellite systems. Here are a few of them.

▲ The thrill of gambling on horse races can lead to serious addiction for some people.

Online betting

If you go onto any sports website on the Internet you will notice the large number of online betting sites. Some of these sites concentrate on casino-style games such as poker and roulette and others offer betting on sporting events such as football, horse racing, boxing, tennis, golf and almost any other event.

Advantages of online betting

- You do not have to leave the house – handy for older or disabled people.
- Special Internet offers – there are special offers to tempt you to gamble more.
- No need to pick up your winnings – they are simply added to your credit or debit card.
- Quicker – you do not need to travel to a high street betting shop.

Disadvantages of online betting

- A credit or debit card is needed – you have to create an account using a card before you are allowed to bet.
- It can become addictive – for most people gambling is just a bit of fun but others can lose their family and home through excessive gambling.
- People may gamble more than they would when using cash – the use of credit cards may encourage people to bet larger amounts.

Dating

There are a huge number of dating sites on the Internet and many people choose to date this way because it offers them convenience in their busy lives. By looking at people's pictures and learning about their interests, you may feel that you know more about them than you would just chatting in a bar.

▲ Internet dating sites offer an alternative way of meeting partners.

Advantages of online dating:

- Some people are shy and find it hard to meet people. They can get to know someone using chat rooms or email first.
- Many people are busy and like a faster way to meet others.
- You can find out what their job and interests are before deciding to meet.

Disadvantages of online dating

- You need to be extremely careful. People are not always what they seem.
- They may send you a picture that is not of them.
- They may be meeting lots of other people – so can they be trusted?

Online voting

One problem that governments have is that many young people are turned off politics and therefore do not vote. Maybe it is just too hard for younger people to vote. If they could vote using the Internet, then many more of them may vote. Putting crosses on bits of paper in a church hall or a school may not appeal to them.

"For a good relationship, I need someone who shares the same taste in music, movies, and TV...so I've started dating my iPod."

Advantages of online voting

- Encourages more people to vote, as not as much effort is needed.
- People would not be needed to count the votes, so it could be cheaper.
- Results would be obtained faster.
- People who are away would not need to use postal votes.

Disadvantages of online voting

- Not everyone has a computer and the Internet.
- Good security systems would be needed to prevent vote rigging.
- It is likely to have very high initial costs.

Questions A

1. Give **three** interactive services offered by digital TV. *(3 marks)*

2. There are plans in many countries for voting in elections to be done using the Internet.
   (a) Describe what equipment a person would need in their home in order to be able to vote using the Internet. *(2 marks)*
   (b) Describe **two** advantages in people voting using the Internet. *(2 marks)*
   (c) Describe **two** disadvantages in people voting using the Internet. *(2 marks)*

3. Digital TV has the facility of interactive online betting.
   (a) Explain the meaning of 'interactive online betting'. *(2 marks)*
   (b) Describe an advantage and a disadvantage in using the betting service. *(2 marks)*

Extension activity

The types of service offered by digital TV are changing all the time. New uses are being thought up. For this activity you are required to research the services and write a list of each one with a brief description of the advantages they offer the user.

Gaming and digital photography

You will find out

▷ **About gaming**

▷ **About basic digital photography**

Many people use ICT for playing computer games. Sometimes the games are played using special consoles and other times ordinary computers are used. In some cases the games can be played online and there are also games that can be played where you compete against others.

Many people have become interested in digital photography because of the ease with which photographs can be taken using cameras and phones. You can also have fun editing them. In this section you will also be looking at the basics of digital photography.

Gaming

Many computers are used by all ages to play games, which vary from traditional games such as chess, cards, backgammon to flight/racing car simulations to fast-moving arcade-type games.

Games are important drivers in the computer industry and many home computers used to play games have more processing power than many computers used in a business setting.

For fast action computer games it is necessary to use:

- a fast processor
- a large screen
- a large amount of RAM
- a disk drive with plenty of storage capacity
- a high quality graphics card
- a high quality sound card
- large powerful speakers
- specialist input devices such as joysticks, game controllers, steering wheels, etc.

Input devices used in gaming:

▲ A games controller.

▲ A steering wheels acts as an input device for a driving game.

Advantages of computer games

- Young children can learn from them.
- They can make learning fun.
- Some games are played online as a team, so it encourages teamwork.
- They can lead to well-paid employment as a games designer, programmer, etc.

Disadvantages of computer games

- They can be addictive.
- They are often a sedentary activity where little physical activity takes place and this can lead to obesity.

▶ A joystick.

- They can be very violent and some people think that this can cause teenagers to act violently.
- They waste time – schoolwork can suffer through the time spent playing games.
- Health problems – repeated use of input devices such as a joystick or mouse can lead to repetitive strain injury (RSI), also incorrect posture when sitting can lead to back ache.

Basic digital photography

Most people own a digital camera or a mobile phone with a camera and store their photographic images on their home computer. Many people like the flexibility offered by digital images. For example:

- They can be shared by attaching them to emails.
- They can be sent via mobile phones.
- They can be passed to social networking sites such as Facebook, MySpace, etc.
- They can be edited.

Photo editing software

Using photo editing software and a digital image you can:

- copy part of an image
- add text
- re-size
- crop (i.e., only use part of the image)
- remove red eye
- alter the file format
- apply filters (i.e., alter the colours in an image).

Input devices used in digital photography

An image sensor picks up the light from the image. The image sensor is made up of a silicon chip consisting of millions of photosensitive diodes. Each diode is capable of capturing a pixel of light.

The pixels form the whole picture. The whole map of the pixels is converted to a binary code and this is compressed before storing.

▼ **This is the image sensor in a camera.**

Megapixels

The number of pixels a digital camera can detect is measured in megapixels. Generally, the more megapixels there are, the better the quality of the picture. However, increasing the number of megapixels in an image decreases the number of photographs you can store on the memory card.

Storing digital photographs

Most digital cameras use memory cards, which are solid state devices that are able to store digital information. These memory cards use what is often called flash memory, which is a type of memory that can be written to and erased many times over.

Several different kinds of memory cards are used in digital cameras; examples include

- Secure Digital (SD) cards
- CompactFlash (CF) cards
- Memory Sticks.

KEY WORDS

Megapixel one million pixels (i.e., dots of light).

Pixel a dot of light forming a digital image.

▲ **A Memory Stick.**

▲ **Several different kinds of memory cards are used to store photographs in digital cameras.**

Gaming and digital photography *continued*

Output devices used in digital photography

The main output device is the LCD screen where you view the image. If it is blurred, someone has their eyes shut or is pulling a strange face, you can delete it and take it again.

Other output devices include:

- a computer screen
- a printer (ink-jet printers are the best type for printing photographs)
- a TV (some TVs have memory card readers)
- the screen of a mobile phone
- a digital photo frame.

▲ Digital photo frames are output devices.

Copyright 2005 by Randy Glasbergen.
www.glasbergen.com

"I HAVE TO STAY HOME TONIGHT AND HELP MY DAD WITH HIS NEW CAMERA PHONE. WE NEED TO DELETE 750 PICTURES OF HIS HAND."

Extension activity

You have to research buying the latest digital camera. You have to decide what you need to look for in terms of features and you have a budget of £100.

Select the features that are important and produce a table showing the three best cameras and show the features they have.

Questions B

1 A digital camera is advertised as a 10-megapixel camera. Explain what is meant by a megapixel and why it is an important quantity when purchasing a digital camera? *(3 marks)*

2 A popular use for ICT in the home is digital photography.
 (a) Sharing of photographs between friends and family is made easy with digital photography. Explain the methods by which digital photographs can be shared. *(3 marks)*
 (b) A memory card contains hundreds of digital photographs. Describe **two** methods by which the digital photographs can be output. *(2 marks)*

3 Many people use their computers and digital cameras for digital photography.
 (a) Give **three** reasons why digital photography has become a popular use of computers for home users. *(3 marks)*
 (b) Many of these home users will use digital image editing software with their digital images. Give **three** features of image editing software and describe why each of them is useful to a home computer user. *(3 marks)*
 (c) Discuss the specialist input and output requirements for digital photography. *(4 marks)*

4 It has been suggested by a computer expert that the home games market has driven recent advances in ICT.
 (a) Describe, by giving **two** relevant examples, how the human–computer interface can be improved by the use of specialist input devices for games. *(4 marks)*
 (b) Describe **two** health problems that the prolonged playing of computer games could cause. *(2 marks)*

Webcam services and social networking sites

You will find out

▷ **About webcam services**

▷ **About social networking sites**

Web cameras are included with most new personal computers and laptops and they enable people to see each other when chatting using a range of services. In some cases they can be used just like a phone except you can see the person you are talking to. In this section you will be looking at the usefulness of webcams and the various services that are available.

Social networking sites have become very popular lately. They have become popular with many famous people such as musicians, film stars and world leaders. In this section you will be looking at the range of social networking services that are available and their uses. You will also look at the dangers that are connected with these sites.

Web cameras (webcams)

A web camera, or webcam for short, is simply a digital camera that is used to capture still images and video images (i.e. moving images). These images can then be transmitted to a computer where they can be stored in a suitable graphics format. If required, they can be published to a website.

Webcams are often included with complete computer set ups and the camera in these systems is placed on top of the screen. This simple system allows videoconferencing.

Webcams are not just restricted to the tops of computers. There are webcams everywhere. Here are some uses:

- **Distance learning** (see Topic 6).
- **Advertising** – cruise companies place them on the ship so that potential customers can see what is going on inside the ship and where the ship is at a particular time.
- **Checking on children in nurseries** – all parents worry about child abuse. When they put their children in nurseries they want to be sure that they are looked after properly. Some nurseries have webcams so that parents can see their children on the computer whilst they are at work.
- **Checking on the weather in another part of the world** – there are webcams just about everywhere. You can see what the weather is like anywhere in the world if there is a webcam there.

There are a number of disadvantages of webcams such as:

- Sometimes webcam sites show inappropriate content (e.g., pornography, torture, etc.).
- Webcams in combination with chat rooms have been used by paedophiles.
- Terrorists have used webcam services to promote terrorism.

Social networking

Social networking is a very popular use of computers connected to the Internet. Here are some of the main social networking sites and the services they offer.

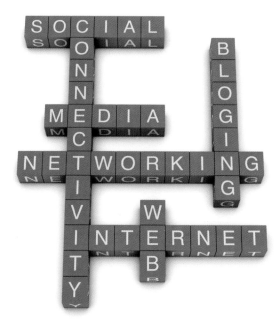

Facebook

Facebook offers a way of keeping up-to-date with your friends online. You set up a profile of yourself and you then decide what about you is displayed if someone else also on Facebook types your name. You can see small pictures of other people in their profile along with a list of the people they are friends with. You can send alerts out to all your friends about what you are up to. For example, if you decide to go away to university then everyone can be notified easily.

Facebook offers a great way of keeping in touch with people you have lost touch with.

Webcam services and social networking sites *continued*

MySpace

MySpace is a social networking site with a music connection holding the site together. Many bands and artists have chosen to have their own pages on the site along with the pages of millions of other ordinary people. MySpace has provided a way for artists to reach their audience. The site allows direct communication between famous artists and their fans. As well as musicians other celebrities have their own MySpace pages.

When you sign up for MySpace you have to design a Profile page by adding a picture, making a quote and giving some information about your favourite music. You can also add information about your hobbies, the films and books you like, who you would like to meet, and choose your top friends.

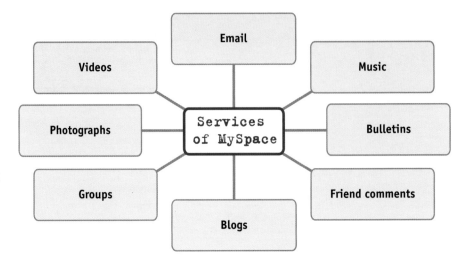

The site has a range of services such as:

- email
- bulletins
- blogs
- friend comments
- photographs
- groups
- videos
- music.

Many people put personal details up on this website and although some settings allow anyone to view them, you can set your profiles to private so you can select who sees them.

Bebo

Bebo is a popular social networking site with mainly younger users. There is a whiteboard feature where you can detail what your friends got up to the night before.

There are plans for users to be able to share and download their favourite tracks using the site.

Twitter

Twitter is the simplest of all the social networking sites. All it asks is 'what are you doing now' and you can reply using your computer or your mobile phone. Twitter then sends your reply to all your friends, so they can then repeat the process the other way around. If you are interested in the minute detail of other people's lives then Twitter is the social networking site for you.

The above explanations of some of the main social networking sites give you some of the advantages of these sites but there are some disadvantages.

"I'm updating the tragic story of Romeo and Juliet. In my version, they are destined to be apart forever because he's on Facebook and she's on MySpace."

Disadvantages of social networking sites

- Many employers and schools ban their use because some people get addicted to them and spend too much time on them.
- Paedophiles have been known to surf networking site pages for their next victim.
- Many young people share too much information on these sites and they do not realize that their teachers, potential employers, etc., can view the information.
- There is a danger of identity theft.
- You have to be on all the sites your friends use if you want to take advantage of the services they offer.

KEY WORDS

Social networking site a website that is used to communicate with friends, family and to make new friends and contacts.

Webcam a digital camera that is used to capture still images and video images (i.e. moving images).

Questions C

1. Many people have joined social networking sites.
   Explain what a social networking site is and give **two** things you might do using the site. *(4 marks)*

2. Social networking sites are not without their dangers.
   Give **two** dangers in using social networking sites. *(2 marks)*

3. Social networking sites enable new friends to be made and old friends you have lost touch with to be found again.
   Explain **two** different things you can do using social networking sites. *(2 marks)*

4. Webcams are a popular piece of hardware used with computers.
   (a) Explain what is meant by a webcam. *(2 marks)*
   (b) Describe **two** applications for a webcam connected to a computer with an Internet connection. *(2 marks)*

Extension activity

There are webcams in many places. It is interesting and fun to look at some of them and you can find many of them on the Internet. Some of the sites will allow you to control the camera by moving it as well as zooming in and out.

Use the Internet to find sites using webcams. Write a list of the web addresses of the sites that you visited and write a short sentence to describe what they are used for.

"I do all of my tweeting on Twitter now."

Music, sound and mobile phones

You will find out

▷ **About music and sound including downloading off the Internet**

▷ **About listening to radio programmes using the Internet**

▷ **About the use of mobile phones**

Most singles are purchased as downloads off the Internet but albums are usually bought as physical CDs but this will probably change.

In this section you will look at the use of ICT in the home for listening to music and radio programmes. You will also be looking at the use of mobile phones.

Downloads

Downloads are where you transfer files off a website and then store them on your computer or portable music player. For the music files to be transferred in this way, they are converted to a file format called MP3. MP3 file format involves compressing the file so that you can store more music files in the same space.

Downloads have become very popular owing to:

- the ease with which they can be obtained, e.g. 24/7

- the ability to just download tracks that you want – you do not need to buy the whole album
- you can still burn the tracks to a CD provided they are only for personal use
- the ease with which they can be loaded onto portable players such as iPods, MP3 players and mobile phones.

There are a number of problems with downloads including:

- viruses could be introduced
- many people use file sharing sites to avoid having to pay for downloaded music tracks
- people who download music or films illegally could be cut off from the Internet by their Internet service providers
- you do not have a physical CD that can be sold at a car boot sale or on e-Bay.

Listening to the radio

Many people like to listen to the radio whilst working on their computer. You can listen to the radio online using the Internet and there is a huge choice of stations.

Advantages of Internet radio

- The quality of the sound is good and there is no aerial to adjust.
- You can listen to radio stations from around the world.
- You can listen to programmes you missed.

Disadvantages of Internet radio

- You need a broadband connection.
- The service is not completely reliable.

Services obtainable through mobile phones

New services for mobile phones are being thought up all the time and who knows what they might do in the future. When they were first developed, they were the equivalent of a telephone that could be used on the move. Nowadays they offer all sorts of new services and have started to blur the difference between a computer or PDA and a mobile phone. Many mobile phones also act as portable MP3 players, enabling you to play your music on the move.

Here are some of the services available through mobile phones:

- send and receive text messages
- make phone calls
- take digital photographs
- take short video clips
- surf the Internet
- watch live TV
- send and receive email
- download and listen to music
- download and play games
- send picture messages
- play videos
- GPS (use your mobile phone as a satellite navigation system).

Advantages and disadvantages of mobile phones

Advantages

- You can be contacted in case of an emergency.
- Plans can be changed at the last minute.
- Parents like children to have a mobile phone as they feel it is safer.

KEY WORD

MP3 music file format that uses compression to reduce the file size considerably, which is why the MP3 file format is popular with portable music players such as iPods and mobile phones.

"I decided to have the surgery because I need the extra thumb for text messaging."

Disadvantages

- Many people use their phones when walking along and this has caused accidents.
- Calls can disturb other people in the cinema, theatre, cafes, etc.
- Many people still use hand-held phones when driving, which is dangerous and illegal.

"I'm still discovering cool stuff I can do with my smartphone. Today I sent a photo to my mom, bought some music, trimmed my sideburns, blended a smoothie, and neutered my cat!"

Questions D

1. Many people store and play their music using portable MP3 players rather than using CD players.
   Give **two** advantages in using an MP3 player to store and play music. *(2 marks)*

2. Besides making voice phone calls, describe **three** tasks a mobile phone can perform. *(3 marks)*

3. The use of the Internet has opened up a whole new source for music; music downloads.
   (a) Explain how the use of ICT has made it possible to load, store and transfer music files. *(4 marks)*
   (b) Storing music files in digital format has raised some issues. Explain **one** legal issue and **one** ethical issue presented by music downloads. *(2 marks)*

Extension activity

Research the features of the latest mobile phones using the Internet.

Produce a list of three most desirable mobile phones and their features.

25

END-OF-TOPIC REVIEW

Questions

 Test yourself

The following notes summarize this topic. The notes are incomplete because they have words missing.

Using the words in the list below, copy out and complete the sentences A to I, underlining the words that you have inserted. Each word may be used more than once.

digital   input   interactive   MP3

photo editing   pay-to-view   gaming

webcam   vote   download   social

A Digital TV offers many _____ features such as being able to shop from home, book holidays, place bets and vote on talent shows.

B _____ TV services are subscription-based services where you pay a monthly fee or a one-off fee for digital TV services.

C Democracy may improve with interactive digital TV as people will be able to _____ in elections without leaving their home, which is much easier than the current system.

D Many people have taken up _____ photography because they no longer need worry about taking pictures that do not turn out properly.

E Using _____ software you can edit images such as crop them to take out an unwanted part of the image or remove red-eye.

F Many people use computers in the home for _____, which include fast action games, simulations and more traditional games such as chess, Scrabble, etc.

G Many people like to see their friends when they are chatting to them over the Internet and for this they use an _____ device called a _____.

H Many people listen to music on the move and they _____ music from sites on the Internet and store the tracks on their computer and portable media player in _____ file format.

I _____ networking sites are popular with home users because they allow you to make friends with people having similar interests as well as keep in contact with all your present and past friends.

Examination style questions

1 Having your own web camera can be great fun but, like other features of the Internet, it is not without its dangers. Describe **one** danger there might be in using a web camera. *(1 mark)*

2 Discuss with reasons why it is easy to take and share digital photographs with friends. *(5 marks)*

3 Interactive digital TV offers a number of pay-to-view services. Give **two** examples of pay-to-view services you would expect to pay for. *(2 marks)*

4 The image below shows an image sensor used by a digital camera.
   (a) Briefly explain how the image sensor works. *(2 marks)*
   (b) Digital images are normally compressed before storing. Give **one** reason for this. *(1 mark)*

(c) Name **one** type of storage used in cameras for the storing of pictures. *(1 mark)*
(d) Name **one** output device used in digital photography. *(1 mark)*

5 **(a)** ICT has had a huge impact on the way children spend their leisure time. Describe **three** ways in which ICT has had an impact on the way a child spends their leisure time. *(4 marks)*
   (b) Discuss, by giving **two** examples, some of the problems that ICT has brought to the parents of young children due to their child's use of ICT. *(4 marks)*

6 Discuss the advantages and the disadvantages that the use of mobile phones has brought to society. *(6 marks)*

END-OF-TOPIC REVIEW

Exam support

Worked example

There has been a huge increase in people's use of ICT in the home, particularly in the area of entertainment. Many traditional activities such as sport and reading have been replaced by new forms of entertainment making use of ICT.

(a) Discuss, by giving **four** distinctly different examples, the benefits that ICT developments have brought to home entertainment. *(8 marks)*

(b) There are a number of disadvantages in using ICT for entertainment. Discuss by giving **two** distinctly different examples, **two** such disadvantages. *(4 marks)*

Student answer 1

(a) *One benefit is downloads where you can select which tracks you want, instead of having to buy the whole CD. This saves you money and using play-lists you can choose to listen to all your favourite tracks together.*

Another benefit is Internet shopping where for a small fee you can select all the goods that you want from the comfort of your own home and get them delivered to your house at a certain time.

Word-processing is useful at home because you can type in all your letters, school work, CVs, etc., and print them out on your home printer.

Cable TV is ideal because you can watch films by paying a small fee which means you do not have to visit a video shop any more as the film data is sent along a cable. You can also watch repeats of old series or even programmes that you wanted to watch the previous week.

(b) *You can become lazy just watching TV all day and you can end up not making friends or communicating with other people.*

There are dangers in meeting strangers from chat rooms, especially for young children who may meet without their parents' knowing. They could meet a paedophile who pretends to be a child when online.

◀ **Examiner's comment**

(a) The first two benefits are well explained and the examples given are sensible and relate to the benefit.

The third answer gives a benefit of word-processing, as a form of entertainment. This is stretching the word entertainment a bit too far, so credit is not given for this answer.

The fourth answer is correct as it describes a pay-to-view service provided by a satellite or cable TV service.

(b) Just because people watch TV does not make them lazy and this is far too general to be given any marks. The Examiner should not have to read anything into an answer in order to award it marks.

The second part of the answer is good as it clearly identifies the disadvantage and the problems it creates. *(8 marks out of 12)*

Student answer 2

(a) Many people use their home ICT equipment for digital photography. Digital photography, allows them to experiment by taking pictures, which they would not have been able to do with traditional film owing to the expense of getting them developed. They can edit these pictures, attach them to emails and send them to friends and family and print them in colour using ink-jet printers.

Some use the interactive facilities of their TV service or the Internet to gamble from their own home, using a credit card. It makes it more interesting when watching a football match to put some money on your favourite team. Using the Internet to do this is much easier than having to go to a high street betting shop.

You can use the Internet to play computer games. It is possible, for example, to play a game of chess over the Internet with your opponent in a different country. The good thing about this is that there is always someone to play with.

Mobile phones are great because you can do so much with them. For example, you can send and receive text messages, send and receive email, surf the Internet, use your phone as an MP3 player, take digital photographs and even have a telephone conversation!

(b) You have to be careful when using the Internet, as there is a tendency to slouch in your chair. This is likely to cause you back ache in the future.

Also, the repeated use of the mouse, joystick and keyboard could lead to repetitive strain injury (RSI).

Computer games can cause a problem because young children cannot seem to leave them alone so their school work suffers as a result.

Examiner's comment

(a) This is a good set of answers which are all different and are clearly explained. Full marks were given for this part of the question.

(b) The first answer was more comprehensive than the second, and therefore deserves two marks. The second answer could have been explained in more detail, so only one mark is given for this part. *(11 marks out of 12)*

Examiner's answers

(a) Any four from the following list. (One mark for the name of the item and the second mark for further amplification by describing the hardware or explaining what it has allowed the user to do.)

- MP3 player – allows people to listen to a choice of thousands of tracks on a small portable player.
- Music downloads – allows users to pick only the tracks they want rather than have to buy the entire CD.
- Digital photography – allows users to become much more proficient at taking photographs by allowing them to immediately see the results.
- Interactive TV – allows people to shop, check email, book holidays, bet, etc.
- Chat rooms – allows people to make new friends with people all around the world.
- Mobile phones – can communicate with friends in a large number of ways such as text message, voice and email.
- Betting – can place bets without leaving your home and also you do not need to pick up your winnings as they are put back on your card.
- Dating – meeting new dates is made easy by viewing the online pictures and profiles.
- Games – can play computer games on long journeys to help relieve boredom.
- Editing digital images – bad digital photographs can be improved by making use of image/photograph editing software.
- Online shopping – people are able to pick up bargains at many of the online stores that offer special discounts to online shoppers.
- Online booking – many people now choose to book flights, hotels and car hire separately as it is more flexible and often cheaper.
- Voting – you can place votes for TV shows using the Internet and this will eventually mean that you will be able to vote in local and general elections in this way.
- Improved hardware – home users are by far the biggest users of computers, so their demands are used to produce new improved hardware such as sound cards, video cards, etc.
- Speakers – the demand for high quality sound from gamers and watchers of TV has led to the design of surround sound systems.

(b) Any two from the following list. (One mark for the name of the item and the second mark for further amplification by describing the resulting problems.)

- Computer games – can be addictive and this can affect school work.
- Computer games – playing computer games is often a sedentary activity and so can lead to obesity.
- Health problems – incorrect posture can lead to back ache; repeatedly using joysticks can lead to RSI.
- Chat rooms – young children could be groomed in order to meet undesirable people.

Summary mind maps

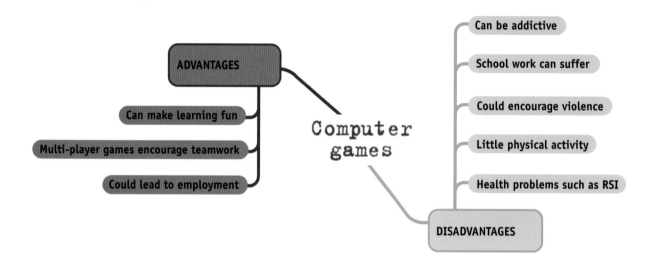

ADVANTAGES
- Can make learning fun
- Multi-player games encourage teamwork
- Could lead to employment

Computer games

DISADVANTAGES
- Can be addictive
- School work can suffer
- Could encourage violence
- Little physical activity
- Health problems such as RSI

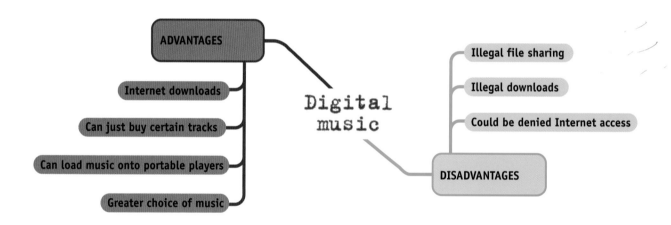

ADVANTAGES
- Internet downloads
- Can just buy certain tracks
- Can load music onto portable players
- Greater choice of music

Digital music

DISADVANTAGES
- Illegal file sharing
- Illegal downloads
- Could be denied Internet access

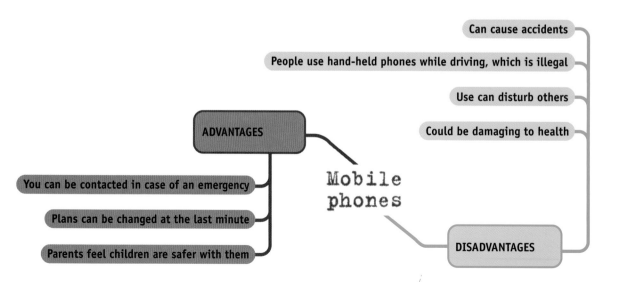

ADVANTAGES
- You can be contacted in case of an emergency
- Plans can be changed at the last minute
- Parents feel children are safer with them

Mobile phones

DISADVANTAGES
- Can cause accidents
- People use hand-held phones while driving, which is illegal
- Use can disturb others
- Could be damaging to health

Home and personal communication systems

The key concepts covered in this topic are:

- **Understand how computers can be connected to the Internet**

- **Understand wireless, Bluetooth, other emerging connection technologies and geographical information systems (GIS)**

Communication between people has never been easier. There are so many different systems you can use to communicate with each other, with each system offering a slightly different method. For example, you can connect computers and other mobile devices together using satellite, wireless, cable, etc.

In this topic you will learn about the different services offering Internet connection and the emerging technologies that will soon become commonplace – maybe as soon as you read this!

This topic will also look at the advantages and the disadvantages of these technologies.

Contents

How computers can connect to the Internet

You will find out

▷ **About satellite communication**

▷ **About wireless**

▷ **About dialup and broadband access**

▷ **About modems**

Most computers are connected to networks, which usually involves the Internet. This means that computer manufacturers include all the hardware and software you need for connection when you buy the computer. In this section you will look at ways the data can be transferred from one place to another and also at some of the devices needed to do this.

Satellite communication

Satellites are used to beam data signals from one continent to another where the terrain makes it difficult to lay cables. It is interesting to note that communication between Britain and America is via a cable laid on the ocean bed. Because of the importance of this cable, its whereabouts are kept secret to protect it from a terrorist attack.

▲ Satellites allow communication across continents.

Data signals from one continent are beamed up to the satellite in orbit and then beamed back down to a satellite dish in another continent.

Wireless

Many computers and other devices are now able to connect to the Internet or communicate with other computers in a local area network wirelessly. With wireless communication, the data travels through the air rather through cables.

▲ Wi-Fi enables connection to the Internet provided there is a network.

Wireless networks enable people to connect wirelessly to the Internet or to a network set up in a home. This means they can work anywhere they can get a radio signal for their network. Many people, especially

people who travel a lot, need to access the Internet regularly. There are many public places where the Internet can be accessed wirelessly using a laptop computer or other portable device such as mobile phone or PDA. These places where you can access the Internet using Wi-Fi are called hotspots.

KEY WORDS

Hotspot a region where the Internet can be accessed wirelessly.

Wi-Fi a trademark for products that meet certain standards for transmitting data over wireless networks.

Internet service provider (ISP) a company that provides users with an Internet connection.

Advantages of wireless communication

- You are not restricted to where you can work.
- You can work whilst on the move.
- Fewer/no trailing wires to trip over.
- It is easier to keep a working area clean if there are not as many wires in the way.
- No costs associated with sinking wires.

Disadvantages of wireless communication

- The danger of hackers reading messages.
- There are areas where you cannot get a wireless network.
- There may be a danger to your health.

▲ With wireless you are not confined to accessing networks from inside a house or office.

▲ A broadband modem.

need to share a single Internet connection. Wireless routers are very popular and allow wireless connection to the Internet by any computers in range of the router.

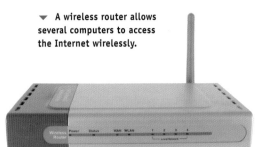

▼ A wireless router allows several computers to access the Internet wirelessly.

Modems

Modems are devices that enable a communication link to be set up between the computer and a medium such as a wire or cable that is used to carry the data. There are two types of modem.

Dialup modem

This is a slower more old-fashioned modem. When you log onto the Internet using a dialup modem it dials the number of your Internet service provider. You are then asked for your user-ID or screen name and a password. On providing this, you are connected to the Internet.

Broadband modem

Broadband modems are the latest modems and offer connection to the Internet using a broadband link. Broadband is much faster than dialup and allows you to:

- use a phone at the same time
- download files at high speed
- watch online video
- use web cameras
- listen to online radio
- watch TV programmes
- surf the Internet very quickly.

Routers

A router is a device that enables a network to be connected to the Internet. They are frequently used in homes where several computers

Questions A

1 Copy and complete the sentences by filling in the missing word in each case.
   (a) _____ is a slow connection to the Internet and connection is made by the computer dialling a number.
   (b) _____ provides high speed Internet access and no time is wasted dialling a number to make a connection. *(2 marks)*

2 An office is thinking of introducing a wireless network with a wireless connection to the Internet.
   Give **two** advantages in using a wireless network rather than a wired one. *(2 marks)*

3 A company has a wireless network installed. Give **one** reason why they might be concerned about the security of their data. *(1 mark)*

4 Describe **two** tasks that can be performed using broadband access to the Internet that would be very difficult or frustrating to do using dialup access. *(2 marks)*

Extension activities

1 Wi-Fi is a method of wireless communication for computers. Find out about Wi-Fi such as what it is, what its range is and some typical applications for its use.

Produce a short easy-to-read document in your own words on what you have found.

2 Here is a sign containing an icon.

Find out what RSS is and how it is useful.

Communication systems

You will find out

▷ **About Bluetooth**

▷ **About geographical information systems**

In this section you will look at the technologies involved in communication between devices. For example, in the past many devices needed to be connected together with a wire before communication could take place. Now communication between lots of devices can happen without wires.

▲ Bluetooth allows you to use a mobile phone when you are driving.

Bluetooth

Bluetooth is a method used to transfer data over short distances from fixed and mobile devices. For example, you could print a document using a laptop and printer even though there were no wires between them. Other applications for Bluetooth include:

- Wireless keyboards and mice avoid clutter on your desk and make the desk easier to clean.
- Wireless headsets allowing you to use a mobile phone legally when driving.
- Sharing data such as voice, music and video wirelessly with others.
- Printing a picture from your camera phone.
- Listening to music using wireless earphones.
- Bluetooth webcams – these are very small and can send a picture using Bluetooth to a computer without using wires. The snag is

that it does not produce a really good picture and the range is fairly small.
- Children's games, e.g. Wii, PlayStation and Lego Mindstorms.

Advantages of Bluetooth

- No wires are needed – you can connect several devices such as printers, cameras, mobile phones, PDAs, etc., without using a cable.
- You can synchronize devices. For example you can ensure that your music collection on your computer and your MP3 player are the same. When you add more music to your computer, it can be added to your MP3 player automatically. This keeps your music collection the same on both devices.
- It is very easy to use. In most cases no new hardware is needed and there is no new software to install.

▶ If a computer cannot use Bluetooth, you can put this device into the USB port.

Disadvantages of Bluetooth

- Can only be used over short distances – uses low power radio signals, which means you can only use it over short distances.
- Relatively small bandwidth – this limits its use. Wireless video is not as clear as the video transferred by wires.
- There are health concerns similar to the use of mobile phones.

Geographical infomation systems (GIS)

A geographical information system, or GIS for short, is an ICT system that is used to capture, manage, analyse and display geographically referenced information.

What can you use a GIS for? Using a GIS you can:

- determine how far it is from one place to another
- see a bird's eye view of your house and its surroundings
- plan the quickest route to school/ college
- view the surroundings when you go to a new place or go on holiday
- look at the surrounding area when you are thinking of buying or renting a property.

Routes and traffic

Plan a route

From

To

Get route »

Route planner classic

◀ The AA route planner allows you to get a step-by-step route for any journey.

Examples of GIS

- Satellite navigation systems – you can get navigation instructions as you drive, be directed to the nearest petrol station, locate hotels, etc.
- Google Earth.
- Multimap – useful for maps and aerial views.
- The AA – useful for finding route details from one place/postcode to another.
- The Energy Saving Trust – this site allows you to enter your postcode and it will tell you whether you could use a wind turbine to generate your own electricity.

Advantages of GIS

There are many different advantages in using geographic information systems and here are just some of them:

- They reduce fuel consumption, which is therefore greener because you do not get lost.
- You can arrive at your destination without delay, as you can be warned in advance of roadworks.
- You can save money by choosing the shortest route.
- You can choose a hotel by seeing exactly how far it is from the beach.

Disadvantages of GIS

Some of the disadvantages of GIS include:

- Satellite navigation systems can send you down very small and windy roads.
- Satellite navigation systems are sometimes difficult to use.
- Sometimes the information is out-of-date.
- Satellite navigation systems can cause accidents if people start inputting information into them whilst driving.

Activity

Use the following websites that are geographic information systems or have part of the website that is one.

For each site write a couple of sentences to explain what the GIS does.

- www.energysavingtrust.org.uk
- http://www.gis.rgs.org/whatisgis.html
- http://news.bbc.co.uk/1/hi/technology/7505774.stm

Questions B

1 Bluetooth is a method that allows devices to communicate with each other and pass data.
   (a) Give the names of **two** devices that can communicate using Bluetooth. *(2 marks)*
   (b) Explain **one** advantage in devices communicating using Bluetooth. *(1 mark)*
   (c) Explain **one** disadvantage in devices communicating using Bluetooth. *(1 mark)*

2 Many people make use of geographical information systems (GIS) whilst at home or on the move.
   Describe **two** different applications for a geographical information system. *(4 marks)*

3 Explain **two** disadvantages of using satellite navigations systems in cars. *(2 marks)*

Extension activity 1

It is useful when you are going on a journey to know how far it is, which is the best route and the likely delays. The AA site provides this information.

Using the Internet, access the following site: http://www.theaa.com/

Type in your home postcode and the postcode of a tourist attraction you would like to visit (you can search for one and get the postcode using the Internet).

Use the AA site to find a route for you.

Write a list of the main features of the site and explain why it might be useful to use this site rather than the information from an in-car satellite navigation system.

Extension activity 2

For this activity you are required to learn more about Bluetooth using the Internet.

Use the following website along with others of your choice: http://www.bluetooth.com

Produce a short magazine article, with some illustrations, which covers all aspects of Bluetooth. You will first need to explain what it is and how many of us use it without really noticing. You can also cover the applications that use Bluetooth.

You will need to collect content for your article and use appropriate design skills to make your article eye-catching and interesting.

END-OF-TOPIC REVIEW

Questions

 Test yourself

The following notes summarize this topic. The notes are incomplete because they have words missing.

Using the words in the list below, copy out and complete the sentences A to I, underlining the words that you have inserted. Each word may be used more than once.

cable	wireless	dialup	router	Bluetooth
GIS	modems	satellites	synchronize	

A _____ are used to beam data signals from one continent to another where the terrain makes it difficult to lay cables.

B With _____ communication, the data travels through the air rather than through cables.

C _____ are devices that enable a communication link to be set up between the computer and a medium such as a wire or cable that is used to carry the data.

D _____ modems make a connection with the Internet service provider by automatically dialling a number.

E _____ modems are always on, so the connection to the Internet is made almost instantly.

F The device used when several computers share a single Internet connection is called a _____.

G _____ is a method used to transfer data over short distances from fixed and mobile devices.

H A system that is used to capture, manage, analyse and display geographically referenced information is called a _____.

I Bluetooth can be used to _____ the music on your home computer and your portable music player so the tracks stored on each are the same.

Examination style questions

1 A home user has broadband access to the Internet.
   (a) Describe in detail what is meant by the Internet. *(2 marks)*
   (b) Give the names of **two** pieces of hardware (other than the computer itself) that are needed to enable connection to the Internet. *(2 marks)*
   (c) Explain what is meant by 'broadband access' and describe **two** advantages that a broadband link offers. *(3 marks)*

2 **(a)** A user who has broadband access to the Internet notices that the speed of access to the Internet appears slow. Give **two** possible reasons why this might be. *(2 marks)*

   (b) Describe **two** things that can be done using high speed broadband access to the Internet that would be difficult or impossible to do using a very slow link. *(4 marks)*

3 Internet connections may be 'broadband' or 'dialup'. Explain the differences a user would notice in using each of these connections. *(2 marks)*

4 Bluetooth is used to transfer data between devices without the need for cables and wires. Describe **two** different applications for Bluetooth. *(2 marks)*

END-OF-TOPIC REVIEW

Exam support

Worked example

Describe the differences a user would find between using dialup or broadband access to the Internet. *(6 marks)*

Student answer 1

Dialup means you have to dial a number first before you get connected.

If the number is engaged you have to try again.

Broadband uses thicker cable hence the name.

You need a telephone to use dialup but with broadband you don't need one.

You can surf the Internet faster with broadband.

▲ **Examiner's comment**

This answer is quite poorly structured. The student would have been better writing about aspects of broadband and then of dialup, which would have avoided mixing them.

The first sentence is not quite correct as the computer dials the number itself, and the second sentence is incorrect.

The part about broadband using thicker cable is not true. They should have said that it is able to support a greater throughput of data.

The part about the telephone being needed is not strictly true – it is the telephone connection that is needed, as it is to this that the computer connects with the modem sitting in between.

The final section is true and worth a mark.

This is quite a hard answer to mark because the student knows part of some of the answers.

(2 marks out of 6)

Student answer 2

Dialup needs a phone line to make the connection.

A modem is used which converts the signals into tones which pass along the line.

Dialup is slow because it takes time to connect and when you are connected it is slow.

You cannot do much as it is frustrating to use.

You need a broadband connection to surf the Internet successfully.

You cannot watch video with dialup but you can with broadband.

◀ **Examiner's comment**

It is important when answering questions that have two alternatives, such as broadband and dialup, that you make it clear which one you are talking about. For example, if you look at sentence 2 it is not clear whether they are talking about the broadband or dialup. The student was given the benefit of the doubt here. A mark was given for the points made in sentences 1, 2, 3, 5 and 6. The answer in the fourth sentence 'you cannot do much as it is frustrating to use' is far too vague. *(5 marks out of 6)*

Examiner's answers

One mark for each of the following points to a maximum of six marks.

Dialup
- Uses a modem
- Needs a telephone line
- Converts the signal into a form that can be passed along a telephone line
- Time is spent making the connection by dialling the number
- Data transfer speeds are slow
- Pages appear very slowly when browsing the Internet
- Takes much longer compared to broadband when downloading and uploading files

Broadband
- Uses a cable connection or ADSL
- Can use the telephone at the same time
- Much higher data transfer rate compared to dialup
- Can watch video/listen to radio in real time
- Can download large files such as music and video in a short time
- Can use webcam services

Summary mind maps

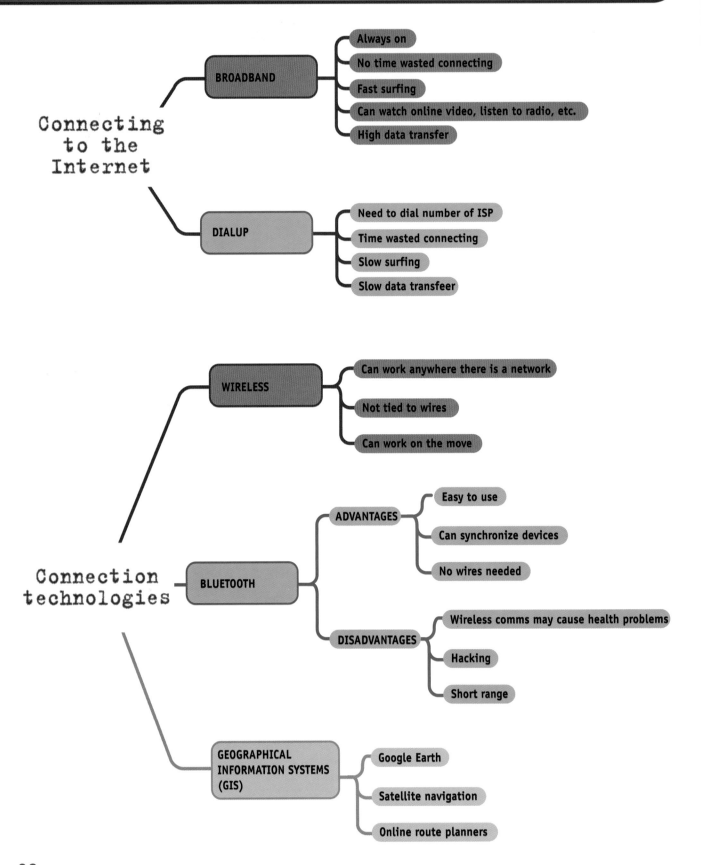

Topic 4

Home business

The key concepts covered in this topic are:

- Online shopping and searching for products on websites

- Online bookings

- Verification of data (passwords and online data entry forms)

- The advantages and disadvantages of online booking and shopping services

There are many things we need to do from home such as buy goods and services, pay bills, apply for loans, book holidays and so on. All these tasks can now be performed efficiently using the Internet and usually saving money in the process. All these tasks can be regarded as home business because they concern placing orders, keeping records, making payments, etc.

In this topic you will be looking at a range of things connected with home business that you can use your computer and Internet connection for. You will be looking at a range of tasks such as searching for products or services on websites and making online purchases. You will also look at the advantages and disadvantages of these systems.

Contents

Online shopping and searching for products on websites

▷ **About searching for products on websites**

▷ **About the advantages and disadvantages to the customers and the store**

Online shopping has grown and grown and offers many advantages to busy people who find shopping a chore. In this section you will find out about online shopping and the advantages and disadvantages it offers to both customers and the store.

Searching for products on websites

We often use online databases without really realizing they are databases. For example, when you are looking for a holiday, you are browsing an online database containing all the holidays a company has.

When you are looking for books, CDs or DVDs using an e-commerce site such as Amazon, you are using an online database.

Online stores have online databases of all the goods that they stock containing information such as:

- photographs of the goods
- details about what they are

- price
- reviews from people who have bought the product.

You can browse for goods by using a series of menus or you can enter a description of what you are looking for in a search box. Hopefully the search will successfully find the item you are looking for.

Online shopping

Online shopping means purchasing goods and services using the Internet. Most businesses have websites to show the products and services available. Lots of these websites allow customers to browse online catalogues and add goods to their virtual shopping basket/trolley just like in a real store. When they have selected the goods, they go to the checkout where they have to decide on the

payment method. They also have to enter some details such as their name and address and other contact details. The payment is authorized and the ordering process is completed. All that is left is for the customer to wait for delivery of their goods.

▲ Some of the components of an online shopping site.

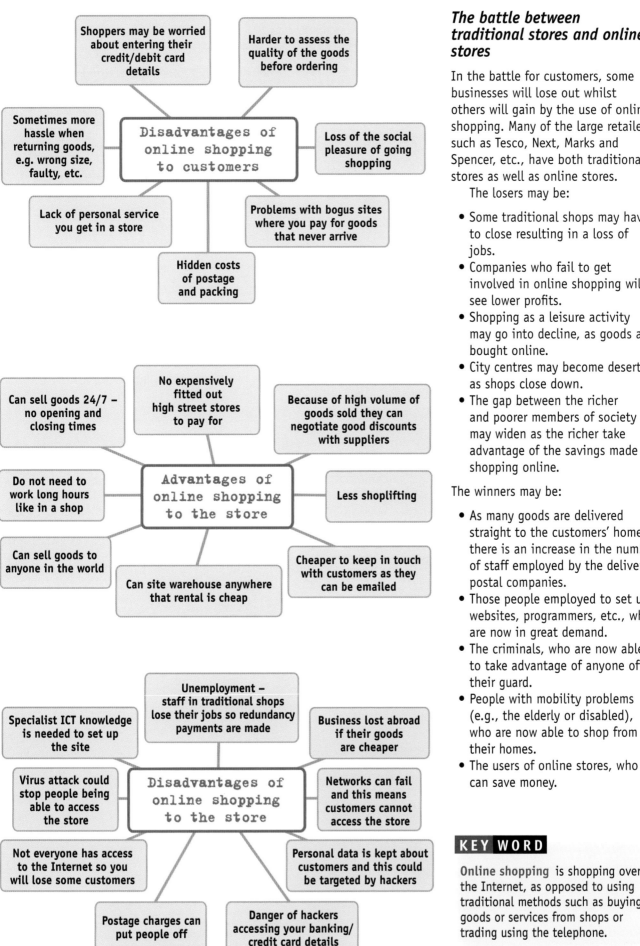

The battle between traditional stores and online stores

In the battle for customers, some businesses will lose out whilst others will gain by the use of online shopping. Many of the large retailers such as Tesco, Next, Marks and Spencer, etc., have both traditional stores as well as online stores.

The losers may be:

- Some traditional shops may have to close resulting in a loss of jobs.
- Companies who fail to get involved in online shopping will see lower profits.
- Shopping as a leisure activity may go into decline, as goods are bought online.
- City centres may become deserted as shops close down.
- The gap between the richer and poorer members of society may widen as the richer take advantage of the savings made by shopping online.

The winners may be:

- As many goods are delivered straight to the customers' homes, there is an increase in the number of staff employed by the delivery/postal companies.
- Those people employed to set up websites, programmers, etc., who are now in great demand.
- The criminals, who are now able to take advantage of anyone off their guard.
- People with mobility problems (e.g., the elderly or disabled), who are now able to shop from their homes.
- The users of online stores, who can save money.

KEY WORD

Online shopping is shopping over the Internet, as opposed to using traditional methods such as buying goods or services from shops or trading using the telephone.

Online shopping and searching for products on websites *continued*

Questions A

1 When goods are ordered over the Internet, payment has to be made.

(a) Give **one** method of payment used over the Internet. *(1 mark)*

(b) Describe why some people may not want to put their payment details into a website. *(2 marks)*

(c) Describe **one** way the online store can make sure that payment details are safe. *(2 marks)*

2 E-commerce sites are very popular for the sale of music and software.

(a) Use the list below to complete the table showing the most suitable facility needed for each task.

Email Shopping basket Encryption Links
Website Dialup Online database Modem
Broadband Fastband Virus protection PDA

Task	Facility needed
To allow lots of items to be selected for purchase	
To allow customers to enter their payment details safely	
To allow customers to browse the e-commerce site at high speed	
To allow the details of customers and their orders to be kept by the e-commerce site	
To allow customers to view all the items for sale	
To allow customers to access other websites that may be of interest	
To communicate with customers about problems with their order	

(7 marks)

(b) Music and software can be sent by post or it can be downloaded from the site.

(i) Explain what is meant by downloaded. *(1 mark)*

(ii) Give **one** advantage to the e-commerce store of downloads. *(1 mark)*

(iii) Give **one** advantage to the customer of being able to download their purchases rather than receive them by post. *(1 mark)*

3 Online shopping has changed the way that most people shop.

(a) Give **two** advantages of buying goods over the Internet. *(2 marks)*

(b) Give **two** disadvantages of buying goods over the Internet. *(2 marks)*

(c) Some organizations will benefit by the use of online shopping, whilst others will not.

(i) Give the names of **two** types of organization that would benefit by the use of online shopping.

(ii) Give the names of **two** organizations that would likely lose out by the use of online shopping. *(4 marks)*

4 Discuss in detail the advantages to shoppers in shopping online. *(6 marks)*

Extension activity

Investigating e-commerce sites

You are required to find out about e-commerce on the Internet. Use the Internet to access the following sites:

- www.play.com
- www.amazon.co.uk
- www.cd-wow.com

You will need to look closely at each site and investigate its features. Whilst you are browsing each site, you will need to answer the following questions:

1 What does the site offer?

2 Write a few short paragraphs to explain what advantages the site offers compared to making a purchase in the normal way (i.e., not using the Internet).

3 What are the main advantages to a user in using the site?

4 How does a user pay for the goods they have bought?

Now find some e-commerce sites of your own.

Write down the web addresses of the sites you have visited.

Online booking and verifcation of data

You will find out

▷ **About booking online**

▷ **About verification (passwords and online data entry forms)**

Many people prefer to book their flights and accommodation separately online rather than go along to a high street travel agent and get them to do it all for them. People who prefer the traditional package holiday where the flights, accommodation and transfers are all included, can book their holidays online. Nearly all the airlines and travel companies have online sites where you can book holidays.

In this section you will be looking at the use of ICT for making online bookings and the advantages and disadvantages it offers.

Online booking services

The introduction of low cost airlines and the ease with which hotels can be booked online has led to many people putting their own holidays together. For those who still want a package holiday, they can book direct with the travel company and make savings in the process. They can also keep going onto the sites to see if any last minute bargains crop up. If you want to book a flight or a holiday, then the first place to look is the Internet. There are many sites where you can pick the dates you wish to travel and the approximate price you want to pay, and it will search for suitable holidays.

Advantages of online booking

- You can book from the comfort of your home 24/7.
- There is more time to look for holidays than when at a travel agent.
- You can make savings when you book direct as there is no travel agent commission to pay.
- You can read reports from people who have been on the same holiday.
- You can arrange your own travel and accommodation.
- You can find out about the resort before you go.

Disadvantages of online booking

- You have to enter credit/debit card details and these may not be kept safe.
- People could hack into the site and know you were away and burgle your house.
- There is no personal service like at a high street travel agent.
- You could easily enter the wrong information and book the wrong flights.

Online check in avoids people with only hand luggage having to wait in a queue to check in.

Booking using interactive digital TV

Interactive digital TV can be used in similar ways to a home computer. Such TVs allow you to search for holidays and place bookings in the same way as you would do using a computer.

I'm looking for...

- ◉ A Holiday
- ○ Just a Flight
- ○ Just a Hotel

From

Tue 22 Sep 2009

Give or take 7 days

Duration

1 week Tue 29 Sep 2009

Preferred airport?
Any London

Choose from...
Select a Destination

Any Resort/Accommodation

Or enter a destination...

Holiday Type

☐ Family   ☐ Couples   ☐ All inclusiv

More holiday types ▾

Kids clubs, Luxury, Spa...

Accommodation Any Type
Rating Any
Number of Rooms 1

            Adults Children
Room 1   2   0

Search

▲ The search facility offered by the Thomson Holiday website.

Online booking and verification of data *continued*

Verification of data

You learnt in Topic 2 that it is important that the data being input does not have any errors introduced during the inputting. In the case of online booking or buying goods over the Internet, errors are less likely to arise than with a telephone booking. As you are doing the inputting using a keyboard, you will likely not misspell your own name or address.

With online booking and shopping the user will type the details into an online form. In order to verify the details the user will need to perform a visual check on everything they have entered. Here are some things they might check:

- Check that the credit card number entered is correct by comparing it with the number on the actual card.
- Check card expiry date.
- Check that all the fields that should have data in them do contain data.
- Check all the name and address details are correct – this is particularly important with flight tickets where the name on the passport has to match the name on the tickets.
- Check passport numbers against the numbers on the actual passports.

Verification of data is also used when you set up a user account with an online business you use regularly. The account is useful because you do not have to re-enter all your personal details such as name, address, etc.,

as the online site keeps these. You do still have to do a visual check to ensure that the details have not changed.

Some sites will even keep your card details, which means you can order without having your card details to hand.

When first setting up the account you will be asked to enter a password twice. This is so that if the two versions are not the same (because you have mistyped) the computer will query this. The online site can therefore be sure that the password you typed is the one you intended.

Questions B

1 Many people now choose to book flights, hotels and car hire separately online rather than use a high street travel agent.
   (a) Using specific examples, describe in detail how a flight is booked using an online flight booking site. *(6 marks)*
   (b) Describe **two** disadvantages in booking holidays using online sites. *(2 marks)*

2 Online sites such as holiday sites get the customers to input their own details.
   (a) Explain the advantages to the online business of the customers inputting their own details. *(2 marks)*
   (b) Explain how a customer would verify the data they have entered into an online form. *(2 marks)*

Extension activity

Access the Thomson Holiday website using the web address: www.thomson.co.uk

1 Write down a list of the various way in which you can search for a holiday using the site.

2 Browse for a holiday you would like to go on. Get a price for your holiday by following the instructions (do not worry – you can look without buying).

3 Write down a list, other than your contact details (e.g., names, address, phone number, etc.), that you must enter before the holiday can be booked.

END-OF-TOPIC REVIEW

Questions

 Test yourself

The following notes summarize this topic. The notes are incomplete because they have words missing.

Using the words in the list below, copy out and complete the sentences A to H, underlining the words that you have inserted. Each word may be used more than once.

Internet   identity   online

visual   input   debit   downloaded

music   verify   passwords

A _____ shopping means purchasing goods and services using the Internet.

B Shopping using the Internet requires payment using a credit or _____ card.

C Some people are worried that keying in personal details such as payment details could expose them to _____ theft.

D Goods such as software, films and _____ can be _____ instantly from sites, which usually means they are cheaper.

E Flights and holidays can be bought over the _____, which means savings can be made because there are no travel agent commissions to pay.

F When booking flights or purchasing goods or services, online sites require customers to _____ their own details, which means the site does not have to pay their own staff to do this.

G When customers input their own details they should always _____ the data they have input. This means doing a _____ check.

H _____ are used to identify a previous customer to an online site and when setting up, these are typed in twice to verify the data.

Questions *continued*

Examination style questions

1 Many people choose to book flights from home using their home computer and the Internet.
   (a) Other than Name, Address and Telephone numbers (home and mobile) give **three** items of data that would be essential for the booking to proceed. *(3 marks)*
   (b) Describe **two** advantages in using an online booking system. *(2 marks)*
   (c) Describe **two** disadvantages in using an online booking system. *(2 marks)*

2 Some online stores allow shoppers to download their goods once they have paid for them.
   (a) Explain the meaning of the term 'download'. *(1 mark)*
   (b) Give the names of **two** different type of product that can be downloaded. *(2 marks)*
   (c) Discuss the advantages and disadvantages of downloading goods rather than having them delivered by post or carrier. *(4 marks)*

3 A new online store is being set up.
   Using the list below, choose the most suitable facility needed for each task listed.

   Shopping cart   Broadband
   Encryption   Checkout
   Database   Customer reviews
   Search

Task	Facility needed
Go straight to a product if you know a description	
A place to put items you want to buy	
A fast Internet connection that allows you to browse quickly	
The system to ensure the security of credit/debit card details	
You can see what others say before you buy	
The place where you pay for goods	
The basis of the online catalogue of goods for sale	

   (7 marks)

4 People are able to shop using interactive digital television.
   (a) Give **one** advantage in using interactive digital TV for shopping. *(1 mark)*
   (b) Give **one** disadvantage in using interactive digital TV for shopping. *(1 mark)*

5 Many people are worried that with so many online sites, the high street will look completely different.
   Discuss the ways that online shopping changes the way we shop. *(5 marks)*

Exam support

Worked example

Many people now use online shopping for purchasing items such as food, books, CDs/DVDs and clothing. The amount of online shopping has increased considerably each year.

(a) Describe the advantages to the customers and the store of online shopping. *(6 marks)*

(b) Describe the disadvantages to the customers and the store of online shopping. *(6 marks)*

Student answer 1

(a) With online stores the goods are cheaper. You also have more choice.

Some stores can sell goods cheaper because they don't have to have shops.

Anyone can set up an online business as all you need is a website and some stock. Customers are happy because they are getting a bargain. Online stores are happy because they are making more money.

(b) Stores have to put up with people sending goods back. They also have to post the goods, which is a lot of effort. The customer finds it harder to return things that are faulty because they have to parcel the goods up and send them back by post.

▲ Examiner's comment

(a) This answer could have done with some structure. For example, it would have been a lot better if they had dealt with advantages to the customer and then to the store separately. Students that mix these up often repeat answers. The student here has mentioned that online goods are cheaper, several times.

The student's answer is repeated here and where a mark is awarded it is written in brackets.

With online stores the goods are cheaper (1). You also have more choice (1).

The stores can sell goods cheaper because they don't have to have shops.

Anyone can set up an online business as all you need is a website and some stock (1). Customers are happy because they are getting a bargain. Online stores are happy because they are making more money.

Three marks are given for this part.

(b) Like in the answer to the first section, this student would have benefited by more structure to their answer.

Here is how the marks have been allocated in this answer:

Stores have to put up with people sending goods back (1). They also have to post the goods, which is a lot of effort (1). The customer finds it harder to return things that are faulty because they have to parcel the goods up and send them back by post (1).

Three marks are given for this part.

(6 marks out of 12)

Exam support *continued*

Student answer 2

(a) Advantages to the customer:
- You have much wider choice because Internet stores hold more stock.
- The goods are usually cheaper because the costs of the business are less.
- The customer does not have to shop around to get the best price because they can use a price comparison website.
- The postage costs will often be less than the cost of travelling into town, paying for parking, etc.

Advantages to the store:
- Don't need expensive high street premises.
- Greater buying power so can negotiate large discounts with suppliers.
- Do not have to employ as many staff.
- Website offers a global market – can take orders from anywhere in the world.
- Can site the warehouse where it is cheapest.

(b) Disadvantages to the customer
- Have to be careful to use a well known site as there are many bogus ones.
- You have to pay by card, which means that there is some danger of identity theft.
- It may be harder to return goods that are faulty.

Disadvantages to the store
- Specialist knowledge is needed to set up the online store.
- There may be more returns to deal with especially with clothes when a customer has ordered the wrong size.
- Make be subject to a virus attack which could stop customers accessing the website.

▲ Examiner's comment

(a) This student has really benefited by structuring their answer. The examiner is happy as well because this answer is easy to mark.

Notice that this student has answered in complete sentences and has not simply stated 'cheaper', 'less hassle', etc.

In this part the student has made nine valid and applicable points and therefore gains the maximum marks for this part, which is 6 marks.

(b) Again this section has been well answered. Six correct answers are given so full marks here as well.

(12 marks out of 12)

Examiner's answers

(a) Advantages to the customer
(one mark each point to a maximum of three marks)

- Goods are cheaper because lower operating costs can be used to lower prices
- Greater choice as they can carry more stock
- Goods can be sent directly to someone else as a present
- If you are old or disabled you can still do your own shopping and maintain your independence
- No transport/parking costs to get to town to buy items
- Can order goods 24/7
- Can read unbiased reviews from people who have purchased the same product
- Can store a shopping list of regularly bought groceries

Advantages to the online store
(one mark each point to a maximum of three marks)

- Fewer staff needed so more profit
- No expensively fitted out high street stores to pay for
- Can site warehouse anywhere where rental is cheap
- Cheaper to keep in contact with customers as you can email them
- Do not need to work long hours
- Can sell goods 24/7 – no opening and closing times
- Because of high volume of goods sold, they can negotiate good discounts with suppliers
- Can sell goods to anyone in the world
- Less shoplifting
- Lower cost to set up the business

(b) Disadvantages to the store
(one mark each point to a maximum of three marks)

- Specialist ICT knowledge is needed to set up the site
- Virus attack could stop people being able to access the store
- Not everyone has access to the Internet so you would lose some customers
- Some customers will not buy goods over the Internet owing to identity theft fears
- Personal data about customers is kept and this could be targeted by hackers
- Staff could waste time surfing the Internet
- Problems with people using stolen cards to buy goods

Disadvantages to the customer
(one mark each point to a maximum of three marks)

- Harder to return goods as they need to be posted
- The customer may need the goods urgently
- Hard to check whether the store is genuine
- May be worried about entering credit/debit card details
- Need to have a credit/debit/PayPal account – cannot pay cash
- Cannot view the goods properly before buying
- Cannot try on clothes before buying
- Do not get the personal service that is associated with shopping in a real store

Summary mind maps

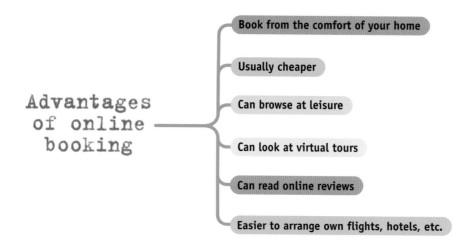

Advantages of online booking

- Book from the comfort of your home
- Usually cheaper
- Can browse at leisure
- Can look at virtual tours
- Can read online reviews
- Easier to arrange own flights, hotels, etc.

Disadvantages of online booking

- Payments by card may not be kept safe
- Hackers could know you were away and pass info. to burglars
- No personal service as with a travel agent
- Easy to enter wrong information and book wrong flight, etc.

Organizations: school, home and environment

The key concepts covered in this topic are:

- School registration systems
- Management information systems in schools
- Data logging in school activities
- Control systems (those control systems that do not use feedback)
- Weather forecasting systems

As you will already know, ICT is used extensively in schools/colleges during lessons in all subjects. Managing a school/college is no different to managing a business and ICT is used here as a tool to help manage the resources such as buildings, materials, staff and equipment. In this topic you will learn about how ICT is used in schools to perform routine administrative tasks such as registering students and supplying management information that can be used to help school/college managers make decisions.

You will also learn about aspects of ICT that are used around the school for data logging in lessons, control systems and weather forecasting systems.

Contents

School registration systems

You will find out

▷ **About school registration systems**

School registration systems are something you will be familiar with. You will know that it is important for the school to keep a record of who is on the premises and who is not. This is important in case there is a fire. They are also required by law to keep attendance records on all students. There are many different ways of recording attendance, from low tech paper registers to some high tech systems that make use of biometric measurements such as retinal scanning or fingerprinting. In this section you will learn about the methods available and the advantages and disadvantages they offer.

The old paper-based registration system

The old paper-based registration system worked as follows:

- Marks were made on a sheet of paper, called a register, containing a list of student names.
- The marks were completed by the form teacher in the morning and after lunch.
- The registers were collected and kept at a central point for reference and health and safety reasons.

- The marks were added up by the form teachers each term so that attendance statistics could be produced.

There were lots of problems with this manual system, such as:

- Registers were often left unattended, which meant students could easily alter the register.
- Mistakes in register entries meant registers were hard to understand.
- Statistics for attendance tended to only be produced each term.
- Teachers were responsible for the accuracy of the registers.
- Students could register themselves and then play truant by not attending the lessons.

The next step was the processing of the registers by computers and this meant someone had to enter all the marks from the register into the computer. The attendance marks were entered by keying in using a keyboard. Because of the problems in inputting such a large amount of data, other direct methods of input were used that removed the need to type in marks.

Computer-based methods of registration

Any ICT system used for student registration in schools or colleges should:

- capture student attendance accurately
- capture the student attendance automatically
- be very fast at recording attendance details
- as far as possible avoid the misuse of the system
- enable not only morning and afternoon attendance to be recorded but also to record attendance at each lesson

- be able to work out attendance patterns for individuals and defined groups
- be relatively inexpensive
- be able to work with other ICT systems used in the school, such as the system for recording student details.

Optical mark recognition (OMR)

Optical mark recognition works by the teacher marking a student's attendance by shading in boxes using a pencil. The forms are passed to the administration office where they are collected and batched together and processed automatically using an optical mark reader. As the forms are read automatically, it removes the problems of making mistakes when the marks are typed in using a keyboard. Once input, the attendance data is processed and reports can be generated, for example listing students where attendance is a problem.

Disadvantages of optical mark recognition

- Registration is not done in real time – if a student came in halfway through the morning this system would not record this.
- Registers need to be passed manually to the administration staff.
- Registers are easily altered by students.
- If the forms are folded or damaged, they are rejected by the reader.

Advantages of optical mark recognition

- The OMR reader is cheap.
- Reader can be used for other purposes such as reading multiple-choice answer sheets.

Smart cards

Smart cards look like credit cards and they contain a chip that can be used to hold certain information. Smart cards hold more information than cards containing only a magnetic strip.

Smart cards can be used in schools in the following ways:

- for registration of students
- for monitoring attendance at each lesson
- for the payment for meals in the school canteen
- for access to the school site, buildings and rooms to improve security
- for access to certain facilities such as the computer network, photocopier, etc.
- to record borrowing and return of school library books, digital cameras, musical instruments, etc.

In some schools, smart cards are used to purchase food in the school canteen. The cards can be topped up with money at the start of the week or daily and this reduces the time it takes for meals to be bought, as no time is spent exchanging cash.

Swipe cards

Students are given a swipe card that they use for registration purposes by swiping the card using a card reader. Swipe cards are plastic cards with a magnetic strip containing a limited amount of data on it. The swipe card is used to identify the student to the registration system and some other systems such as the library system and the school meals system. The same card can be used for access to school buildings.

Advantages of swipe cards

- The cost of the cards and the readers is low compared to other methods.
- Readers can be made that are almost vandal proof.

Disadvantages of swipe cards

- Cards are often lost or forgotten, meaning that students have to be registered using a keyboard.
- Students can be swiped in by someone else.

Biometric methods

Biometric methods provide a fast and easy way of recording student attendance. Biometric methods make use of a feature of the human body that is unique to a particular person in order to identify them.

Biometric methods include:

- fingerprint recognition
- retinal scanning.

Advantages of biometric methods

- There is nothing for a student to forget like a card.
- You have to be there to register so no-one else can do it for you and it cannot be altered by students.
- Performed in real time so the system knows exactly who has registered and when.

Disadvantages of biometric methods

- Biometric systems are expensive.
- There are privacy issues. Some people object to fingerprinting systems.
- Total reliance on the ICT system.

Questions A

1 A school is using a traditional paper-based registration system. The school uses registers to record morning and afternoon attendance details for each student.
   (a) Describe **three** advantages in using ICT systems for registration. *(3 marks)*
   (b) Describe **three** disadvantages in using ICT systems for registration. *(3 marks)*

2 **(a)** Give the name of a biometric method used for the registration of students in a school. *(1 mark)*
   (b) Describe **one** advantage the biometric method has over non-biometric methods. *(2 marks)*

Extension activity

Use the Internet to research biometric methods and their applications.

Produce a document on their advantages and disadvantages and also some of the non-school uses.

Management information systems in schools

You will find out

▷ **About management information systems in schools**

There are many different pieces of information stored by a school – the student records and the records of attendance are just two. By integrating all the systems, it is possible to extract the data needed from the system in the form of reports. A report might be a list of all those students with 100% attendance so they can be given a certificate. In this section you will be looking at management information systems in schools and how they are useful.

What is a management information system?

Management information systems (MIS) are ICT systems that supply managers and other staff with information that can help them make decisions. For example, the attendance system might produce information about those students for whom attendance is bad. The system might produce a report showing when they are absent to see if there is a pattern. The senior teachers can then take action.

Here are some other ways an MIS can be used in a school:

- To work out how many students will be in the new Year 7 and to allocate them into forms.

- To decide whether a new teacher should be employed.
- To work out the best way of allocating teachers and classrooms.
- To decide on how best to spend the training budget to keep teachers up-to-date.

Advantages

The main advantages in using school management information systems are:

- They reduce the workload for teachers in the classroom and in the school office.
- They can provide up-to-date information for parents.

Questions B

1 (a) A school uses an MIS. Give the meaning of the abbreviation MIS. *(1 mark)*

(b) Explain **one** advantage in the school using an MIS. *(1 mark)*

(c) Explain **one** disadvantage in the school using an MIS. *(1 mark)*

2 Most schools make use of a management information system (MIS).

(a) Explain what a management information system is. *(2 marks)*

(b) Give **one** suitable example of the use of a management information system in a school. *(2 marks)*

- They can support decision making for school managers.
- They can tackle truancy effectively.
- They can be used to plan timetables.

Disadvantages

The main disadvantages in using school management information systems are:

- The software is expensive to buy.
- Student data is personal, so there must be no unauthorized access.
- Software is complex, so all staff need training.

KEY WORD

Management information system (MIS) an ICT system that supplies information that helps give managers and others the information they need for them to make effective decisions.

Extension activity

There are many companies that supply school management information systems.

Your task is to find out a little more about the tasks that they can perform. Here are a couple of their websites:

- http://www.capitaes.co.uk/ sims/
- http://www.bromcom.com/

Write a list of things that these management information systems do to make the running of a school easier.

Data logging in school activities

You will find out

▷ **About data logging in school activities**

Data logging involves collecting data automatically from sensors over a certain period of time, called the logging period. Data logging can be used in science lessons for monitoring temperature, light, force, etc. In geography lessons data logging can be used to record the weather.

Data logging

Data logging is where readings are taken regularly over a period of time using sensors.

The main features of data logging are:

- The readings are taken automatically – there is no need for a human to be present. This means that it is much cheaper than employing a person to do this.
- You can set the logging period – this is the total time over which the readings will be collected.
- You can set the logging rate (also called the logging interval) – this determines how often the readings are taken. For example, in an experiment to investigate the cooling of boiling water, you might decide to set the logging rate to be every minute.

- The sensors can be put in remote locations – you can put them anywhere in the world and the data can be sent back wirelessly and even using satellites.
- The sent data can be stored and processed by a computer.
- The data can be analysed (you can do calculations such as work on the mean, mode, median, range, etc.) and graphs and charts can be drawn. The data can be processed using a spreadsheet package.

Sensors

Sensors are used to detect and measure physical quantities. Here are some examples of sensors:

- Temperature/heat sensors – can be used in school experiments such as investigating the cooling of a hot drink in different thicknesses of cardboard cup. Heat sensors can be used to control a heating system in a home or classroom.
- Light sensors – detect the brightness of light. Can be used to see how light levels affect the growth of a plant. They can be used to control lights that come on automatically when it goes dark.
- Sound sensors – measure the loudness of a sound. Can be used in noise disputes.
- Pressure sensors – barometric pressure sensors measure air pressure; other pressure sensors measure depth of liquid or something pressing on them.
- Humidity sensors – these measure the moisture in the air.
- Passive infrared sensors (PIRs) – these are the sensors used in schools and homes to detect movement. They can be used in

burglar alarms and also to turn lights on/off automatically in rooms when a person walks in/out.

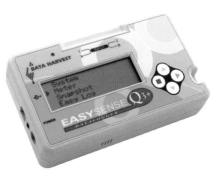

▲ This data logger contains built-in light sensor, sound sensor, temperature sensor, barometric pressure sensor and two inputs where you can attach a whole range of sensors.

KEY WORDS

Data logger a device that collects readings from one or more sensors. The time interval between each reading can be varied (called the logging rate) and the total time over which the data is logged (called the logging period) can also be varied.

Data logging the process of using an ICT system to collect data from sensors at a certain rate over a certain period of time. Remote weather stations use data logging.

Sensors devices that measure physical quantities such as temperature, pressure, humidity, etc.

Sending data to a computer

The data from a data logger can be sent to a computer. There are two ways to do this:

- Use wires to connect the data logger to the computer.
- Use wireless (usually Bluetooth).

55

Data logging in school activities *continued*

Advantages and disadvantages of data logging

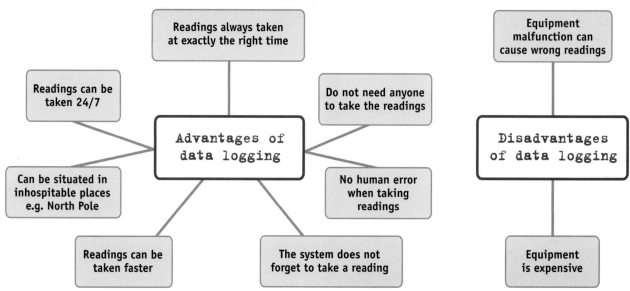

Activity

Which sensor?

A hot drink vending company wants to perform an experiment to see which cardboard cup is best at keeping hot drinks hot. They need to investigate how the temperature falls in each cup from the temperature at which the hot drinks are produced, which is about 90°C. They decide to use data logging for this.

1 Give the name of the sensor that is needed for this experiment. *(1 mark)*

2 A logging rate needs to be chosen for the data logger. Give the meaning of the term logging rate. *(2 marks)*

3 Out of the following, which logging rate should be chosen?
Per second, per minute or per hour. *(1 mark)*

4 Explain what is meant by the logging period. *(2 marks)*

5 Out of the following, which logging period should be chosen?
30 seconds, 1 hour or 24 hours. *(1 mark)*

6 Explain your choice of answer for question 5. *(1 mark)*

Questions C

1 A sensor is used in a geography lesson to investigate how the outside temperature varies over the course of 24 hours. A data logger is used to collect the data from sensors.

(a) What kind of sensor should be used with this system? *(1 mark)*

(b) Explain why the sensor you have named in (a) is needed. *(1 mark)*

(c) What is the logging period for this investigation? *(1 mark)*

(d) Explain what is meant by a logging interval and suggest a suitable logging interval for this investigation. *(2 marks)*

2 Computer control is used to control growing conditions in a greenhouse. For example, a temperature sensor will turn on a heater if the temperature inside the greenhouse gets too cold.

(a) Give the names of **two** other sensors that could be used in the greenhouse and for each one describe why it is needed. *(4 marks)*

(b) Give **two** advantages in using ICT to monitor and control the growing conditions in the greenhouse. *(2 marks)*

(c) Describe **one** disadvantage in using monitoring and control to control the growing conditions in the greenhouse. *(1 mark)*

Control systems

You will find out

▷ **About control systems (non-feedback)**

The data from sensors can be used to control a device such as a light, siren, motor, etc. The data from the sensors is sent to a computer (in most cases a very simple one) where the computer decides what control signal to issue to an output device such as a light. In this topic you will be looking at simple control systems that do not use feedback. You will learn what feedback is and how it makes a control system more useful.

The main components of a control system

The main components of a control system are:

• **Sensors** – which are the input devices that send data to the computer/processor.
• **Computer/processor** – uses a control program to decide what action to take when it receives data from the sensors. Once the decision has been made, a control signal is sent to the output device.
• **Output devices** – such as lights, heaters, motors, etc., that are controlled by the control signals.

Non-feedback control systems

If you are writing a simple program to control a robot arm by rotating it, you can issue instructions to a stepper motor. A stepper motor rotates in short steps and you can determine how many steps you need. This will determine the angle it moves through.

The motor will rotate through an angle and then stop. This is a non-feedback system because there is no way of detecting whether it has actually moved through the correct angle. If there was an obstacle in the way of the arm, it may not have been able to move the correct angle. If another instruction was issued then it will simply move from its incorrect starting point.

Simple control systems

Security light system – uses a PIR sensor to sense movement. As soon as the sensor detects movement the system turns the light on. After a period of time the system turns the light off.

▲ This security light system uses a PIR sensor to detect a person, so the security lights are turned on.

A burglar alarm – works in a similar way to the security light using PIRs as the input into the system. This time the output device is a bell or siren that sounds when the alarm is on and movement is detected.

▲ Most household electrical appliances use computer control.

▲ PIR sensors are used to detect intruders and sound an alarm siren in a burglar alarm system.

Weather forecasting systems

▷ **About weather forecasting systems**

Weather forecasting systems are used in schools and in the home to give information about the weather. In this topic you will learn about the sensors used in weather forecasting systems and how data logging is useful to weather forecasters.

Weather forecasting systems

Data is collected by sensors and then sent to the computer/base station for processing. The resulting weather information is then displayed in a variety of different ways such as:

- Using icons (small pictures of the predicted weather).
- Graphically – showing how values, such as temperature and pressure, change.
- Using text – messages about the weather are produced.
- Using numbers – values such as the maximum and minimum temperatures are displayed.

Usually the information is output on a screen.

Sensors used for the collection of weather data

Data for weather forecasting systems comes from sensors:

- Heat/temperature sensor – used to measure the temperature. As well as the current temperature, the maximum and minimum temperatures are recorded.
- Pressure sensor – used to record atmospheric pressure.
- Rain sensors – used to measure rainfall/snowfall.
- Wind speed and wind direction sensors.

▲ People use weather stations in the home – it is useful to know the outside temperature so you know what clothes to wear.

◀ Weather stations are often located in inhospitable places – this one is at the top of a mountain.

- Light sensors – used to record the hours of sunshine.
- Relative humidity – measure the amount of water vapour in the air.

Advantages and disadvantages of ICT-based weather forecasting systems

Advantages

- Data can be collected automatically.
- Data is collected at exactly the correct time.
- Mistakes are not made when taking readings.
- Weather data can be collected from remote and inhospitable locations.
- Data can be transmitted using radio/satellite communication.
- Output can be in different formats, e.g. video, audio, etc.

Disadvantages

- Equipment is expensive.
- Malfunction of equipment may lead to incorrect forecasts.

Questions E

1. A weather station in Antarctica records the temperature continuously, 24 hours per day, 365 days per year. The weather station uses data logging and the data is sent wirelessly, making use of satellites, back to the weather forecast centre in England.
   (a) Explain what is meant by data logging. *(2 marks)*
   (b) Other than temperature give **three** quantities that can be logged by a weather station. *(3 marks)*

2. Schools often use data logging in science experiments for taking readings.
   (a) Give **three** advantages in using data logging for the taking of measurements. *(3 marks)*
   (b) Give **one** disadvantage in using data logging for the taking of measurements. *(1 mark)*
   (c) Explain the difference between logging rate and logging period. *(2 marks)*

3. (a) Give **one** situation where automatic data logging equipment could be used to record data over a long period of time. *(1 mark)*
   (b) Give **one** reason why automatic data logging equipment should be used to record data over a long period of time. *(1 mark)*

Extension activity

Access the following website for the company Data Harvest: www.data-harvest.co.uk

1. Write down a list of the sensors that the company produces.

2. From your list of sensors, choose the sensor you would use for the following:

   (a) Monitoring how murky lake water is.
   (b) Monitoring the amount of moisture in the air of a greenhouse.
   (c) Measuring the aircraft noise near a busy airport.
   (d) Measuring the temperature of a classroom in a school over a day.
   (e) Measuring how quickly a cold drink warms up when taken out of the fridge.
   (f) Measuring the acidity of rainwater.
   (g) Measuring how fast your heart beats after rigorous exercise.

▲ This remote weather station sends the data from its sensors wirelessly to the computer.

Case study

Case study

Using fingerprinting in schools

Many schools are now using fingerprinting methods to help with pupil registration. One such school in South Wales has been using fingerprinting methods for a couple of years now. The system works by the pupils placing their finger on a scanner that is installed outside the classrooms. The scanner reads certain aspects of the print to identify the pupil and then records the attendance details on the computer.

The head teacher of the school has sung the praises of the system, saying how it has helped reduce truancy because pupils now know that it can be immediately identified by the system. Teachers at the school have welcomed the system because it frees them from having to do this important but time-consuming task.

If a pupil fails to register at the start of the day, a text message can be sent to the parent's mobile phone alerting them of the non-attendance of their child. This makes it virtually impossible for a pupil not to attend school without their parents knowing.

Many pupils like the system because it gives them more time to chat with friends and find out what is going on in the school with their form teacher.

Some parents and pupils were initially worried that fingerprints were being routinely taken and stored by the school and that this was personal data that could be misused. However, the company who supplied the system explained to parents that no full fingerprints are stored by the system. Instead the fingerprint is stored as a code and it is this code that is matched. They were reassured that a fingerprint cannot be re-created from this code and that it is only used by the school for identification purposes and not for some other sinister use.

Questions

1 Many schools use fingerprinting as a method for recording the presence of pupils at school.
   (a) Fingerprinting is an example of a biometric input device. Explain briefly what this sentence means. *(2 marks)*
   (b) Give **three** advantages of using fingerprinting to register attendance. *(3 marks)*
   (c) Many parents may be worried that the system stores their child's fingerprints. Write a sentence to explain how you might address this worry. *(2 marks)*

2 Describe **one** way in which the fingerprinting system helps prevent truancy in schools. *(2 marks)*

3 Give **one** example of how this fingerprinting attendance system could possibly be misused. *(2 marks)*

END-OF-TOPIC REVIEW

Questions

 Test yourself

The following notes summarize this topic. The notes are incomplete because they have words missing.

Using the words in the list below, copy out and complete the sentences A to H, underlining the words that you have inserted. Each word may be used more than once.

> data logging   period
> sensors   optical mark recognition
> management information system
> swipe   retinal   biometric

A A registration system in a school that makes use of marks made on a form to record attendance, which is then processed by a computer, is called _____ _____ _____.

B One school registration system used plastic cards containing data in a magnetic strip. The card is called a _____ card.

C A school registration system that makes use of a unique property of the human body is called a _____ method.

D A scanning system called _____ scanning uses the unique pattern on the retina (i.e., the back of the eye) to identify a student's presence.

E An ICT system that supplies information that helps give managers and others the information they need for them to make effective decisions is called a _____ _____ _____.

F Data logging involves automatically collecting data from _____.

G The time over which the whole of the data is collected is called the logging _____.

H The process of using an ICT system to collect data from sensors at a certain rate over a certain period of time is called _____ _____.

1 A home weather station consists of a base station that contains the processor and the display. Sensors are also included that are placed outside the house. Readings from the sensors are relayed back to the base station, which processes the data and produces weather information that is displayed on the screen.

(a) Give the names of **two** different types of sensor that could be used with this system. *(2 marks)*

(b) Describe **one** method by which the data can get from the remote sensors to the base unit that is situated inside the house. *(2 marks)*

(c) Once the data has been sent to the base unit it is processed and the information is output. Describe **one** way that the weather information is output from the system. *(2 marks)*

2 (a) Give the name of a household device that uses a control system. *(1 mark)*

(b) Explain how the control system controls the device you have named in part (a). *(3 marks)*

3 A school registration system uses retinal scanning to identify students present at morning and afternoon registration.

(a) Explain how retinal scanning can be used to identify whether a particular student is present. *(2 marks)*

(b) The attendance details are used by the administrative staff and senior teachers to identify those students whose attendance is a problem. Describe **two** ways in which the system will help them. *(2 marks)*

(c) Give **two** possible disadvantages of the retinal scanning system. *(2 marks)*

4 A school uses biometric methods to register its students.

(a) Explain, by giving a suitable example, what is meant by a biometric method. *(2 marks)*

(b) Explain **one** ICT method that is non-biometric that could be used to record student attendance in a school. *(2 marks)*

5 (a) Most schools use a management information system. Explain what is meant by a management information system. *(2 marks)*

(b) Describe **one** task a head teacher might perform using the school's management information system. *(2 marks)*

Exam support

Worked example

When a student is absent from school, the school attendance officer checks to make sure of the reason for the absence. When they have done this, they use the coding system here to record the type of absence:

I = Ill
D = Doctor or dentist appointment
H = Authorized holiday
A = Other authorized absence

(a) Explain the reason why a coding system is used. *(2 marks)*

(b) Explain why the attendance is recorded automatically using retinal scanning but the codes for absence have to be entered manually. *(2 marks)*

Student answer 1

(a) *It is easier to enter a code.*

(b) *When a students gets there in the morning their eyes are scanned and it knows they are there. If they are off the computer knows this because their eyes have not been scanned. So someone has to tell the system why they are off. The computer cannot find this out for itself.*

◀ **Examiner's comment**

(a) Although it is true to say that it is easier to enter a code, the student needed to say in what way it is easier. It is always best to give a specific example. So if they had said 'it is easier to enter a code because you only have to enter I for ill instead of having to type Ill', then this is a much better answer.

It is always wise to avoid general reasons such as 'easier', 'faster', 'cheaper', etc., unless you provide reasons or a suitable example.

This part gains no marks.

(b) There are three valid reasons given here and so full marks are awarded for this part.

(2 marks out of 4)

Student answer 2

(a) *Rather than type a word or several words to describe the reason, you only have to enter a single letter. This means less data needs to be entered so this speeds up the process. It is also cheaper.*

(b) *If the person is not there, the system cannot know the reason for the absence unless a human finds out from the form teacher or the parents.*

◀ **Examiner's comment**

(a) This student has clearly stated three points. Only two points are needed to gain the maximum marks.

(b) This answer is correct and clearly stated and gets full marks.

(4 marks out of 4)

Examiner's answers

(a) One mark for each point to a maximum of two marks.

- You only have to enter a letter rather than a word *(1)*.
- This makes it faster to input the details *(1)*.
- The person doing the inputting is less likely to make a mistake *(1)*.
- Because the data can be entered faster it means it is also cheaper *(1)*.

(b) One mark for each point to a maximum of two marks.

- The retinal scanning will only determine whether a person is present or not *(1)*.
- It cannot determine the reason why someone is absent *(1)*.
- This has to be determined by a person ringing up parents or by a note, etc. *(1)*.

Summary mind maps

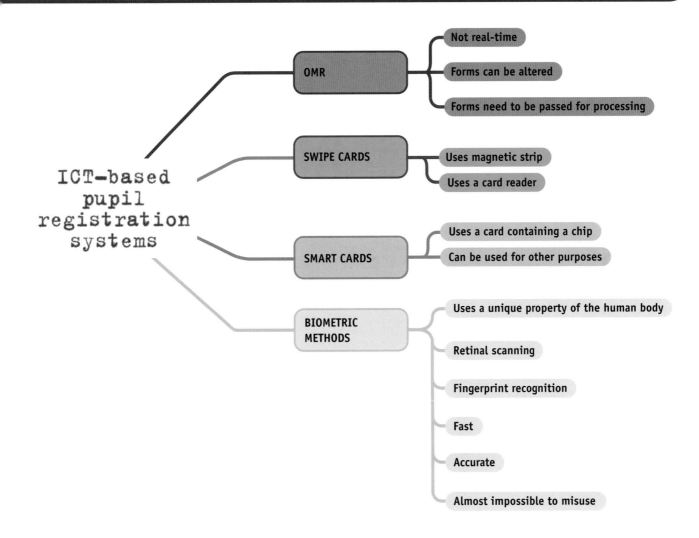

END-OF-TOPIC REVIEW

Summary mind maps *continued*

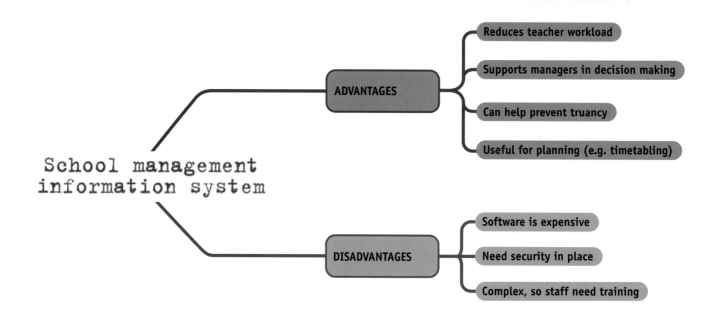

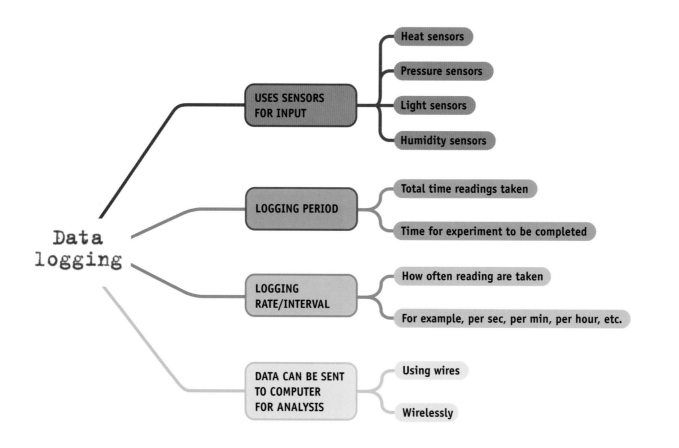

ICT and learning

The key concepts covered in this topic are:

- **Understanding the desktop environment**
- **Online and distance learning services**
- **Learning devices to support disabilities**
- **Software to support learning disabilities**

In this topic you will look at how to manage the desktop environment to enable you to work more effectively. This topic also looks at how ICT can be used to help you learn at school/college and at home. You will also look at the benefits ICT offers to those people with a variety of disabilities and how it helps them to learn despite their problems and how various devices enable them to be more independent.

Contents

Understanding the desktop environment

When you start to use a computer you often use it without making any changes to the desktop environment. However, if someone has used the computer before you and has made changes to the desktop environment, then this might prevent you working effectively. It is therefore important to know about the settings and how you can alter them for yourself. If you use a networked computer such as the ones at school, then the network will save any changes you make to the desktop environment. This means that the next time you log on using your username and password you will be presented with your own personalized desktop environment.

Changing the settings in the desktop environment

What is a desktop environment?

A desktop environment is a graphical user interface that allows a user to change certain settings of the operating system. These settings can include changes to window size, mouse settings, icon size, screen resolution, etc.

A desktop environment normally consists of:

- Icons
- Folders
- Windows
- Help
- Toolbars.

Making changes

- Adjusting window size – windows can be maximized, minimized and made any size in between.
- Mouse settings – you can change how the mouse buttons work, how the mouse pointer looks and how it works and alter the speed of the scroll wheel.
- Icon size – if you right click the mouse button when on the desktop, you can adjust the size of the icons. You can have large, medium and classic (i.e., the smallest size). By making icons bigger you can improve the use by children and people with poor eyesight.
- Screen resolution – this determines how sharp the icons, etc., appear on the screen. It also determines their size. Higher screen resolutions mean items on the screen are sharp but small. Screen resolution determines the number of pixels (i.e., dots of light) used on the screen (e.g., 1600 × 1200 pixels).

- Desktop fonts – text and other items such as icons that appear on the screen can be made bigger or smaller. This can be done by increasing or decreasing the dpi (dots per inch).
- Colour – you can change most of the colours used for the desktop. For example, you can change the colour of windows.
- Position – you can alter the position of elements on the screen such as windows and toolbars.
- Graphics – you can change the screensaver, background, customize icons and many other graphics elements.
- Contrast – contrast determines the difference between the dark and light parts of the screen. Too much contrast can cause eye strain.
- Volume – can be changed using the control panel. You can set the master volume and also change the volume for each of the programs you use.

Things you can do with files and folders (e.g., move, copy, delete, etc.)

Because of the large number of files you store on a computer, over a period of time you need to be organized in the way you maintain them.

You need to think carefully about filenames that give you some idea of their contents. Files should always be put into folders so that they can be found quickly when needed.

In order for you to use ICT successfully you need to be able to do the following on files and folders:

- move
- delete
- copy
- rename.

On-screen help

No-one can remember the steps you need to take to change settings. Instead, all you need to know is that it is possible to make the changes and then be able to access the online help. The online help gives you the instructions you need to make the changes.

▲ Always remember to use the online help to get help on how to do things such as change the screen resolution.

Features of a control panel

The control panel is part of the operating system used to change the look and settings of Windows. Here are some of the features of the control panel:

- You can alter the colour of the desktop and windows.
- You can set up hardware and software.
- The settings can be changed to cope with a variety of disabilities.
- You can change the way folders are used and displayed.
- You can change the way the computer connects to the Internet.
- You can set up user accounts.
- You can set up parental controls (useful if young children use the Internet).
- You can install or remove programs.
- You can set up security such as passwords and updates.

▲ Here is the control panel for the Windows Vista operating system.

Print settings

The print settings can be used to tell the computer which printer you want to use. It is important to note that when you use a network there are often several printers to choose from. For example, you may want a colour copy.

The print settings allow you to add or remove a printer and also set which printer will be used if you do not specify a particular one (this is called the default printer).

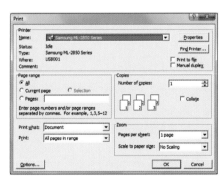

▲ Print settings can also be changed when you select File and then Print in most programs.

Password protection

Using Windows you can create a password, which means other people cannot access the computer without knowing the password. This prevents someone walking up to your computer and being able to use it or view the files and programs on it.

Shortcuts

Shortcuts enable you to do a task using the operating system quickly rather than go through a series of menus/windows, which takes time. There are keyboard shortcuts where you enter key combinations rather than go into

the control centre to change settings. The trouble is remembering the combination of keys is not easy.

Shortcuts to programs are handy if you want to access a program or file directly from the desktop by double clicking on an icon.

▲ Here is a shortcut to a program – access is by double clicking the icon on the desktop.

Activity

1 Produce a document (use the help screens in Windows to help you) that will act as a reference manual for doing each of the following:

- Adjusting the size of a window.
- Altering the position of a window.
- Adjusting mouse settings.
- Changing the size of icons displayed on the desktop.
- Altering the screen resolution.
- Changing the size of the desktop fonts.
- Changing the brightness and contrast of the screen.
- Changing the system volume.

2 Access the control panel by clicking on 'Start' and then clicking on 'Control Panel'.

   Investigate what options are available but do not alter any of the settings.

   Write a list of at least 20 things you can do using the control panel.

3 Using the online help provided by Windows, find out how to produce a shortcut to a program that you use regularly that does not have a shortcut at the moment. Create this shortcut.

Online and distance learning services

▷ **About the features, advantages and disadvantages of online tutorials**

▷ **About the features, advantages and disadvantages of online assessments**

▷ **About the features, advantages and disadvantages of virtual learning environments (VLEs)**

There are many ways in which ICT improves the learning experience for students in schools and colleges. In this topic you will be looking at the use of ICT for learning and the advantages the latest technology offers to students.

The features, advantages and disadvantages of online tutorials

Online tutorials use ICT to help you learn about a subject or topic. There are a variety of ways online tutorials can be run on a computer:

- The software can be run straight from a CD or DVD.
- It can be installed and run from a network, on its own or in conjunction with a VLE (virtual learning environment).
- The software can be run over the Internet.

The features of online tutorials include:

- Use ICT to teach a subject or topic.
- Content – to instruct students in the subject.
- Simulations – to help students understand complex situations.
- Animations – help students understand how things work.
- Drill and practice – help students consolidate the learning.
- Tests – let students know how well they have learnt the topic.
- Games – introduce fun into the learning process.
- Learning can be done at a distance (i.e., away from the school/college premises).

Advantages of online tutorials

- Students have flexibility as to where and when they want to learn.
- Materials are provided in lots of different ways (i.e., they make use of multimedia) such as text, voice, video, animations.
- You can access the material using a variety of different hardware such as laptop, PDA, mobile phone with MP3 player, iPod, etc.
- You can learn in many different environments such as in a car, while out running or walking, etc.
- They keep students using them interested and motivated by the variety of activities.
- Students can work at their own pace.
- They do not have to worry about getting things wrong – the computer will not judge them, as a teacher might.

Disadvantages of online tutorials

- The software is often complex and uses lots of animation and graphics, which makes it expensive.
- Students often need the interaction of their classmates in order to learn.
- Can present an opportunity for students to have a break rather than work on the online tutorial.
- It is hard for teachers to gauge progress using some of the packages.
- Lack of flexibility as human teachers can explain things in different ways to help you.

Online assessment

Online assessment is where you take a test or an examination online. Online assessment is often provided as part of online tutorials, so once you feel you understand a topic or subject, you can take a test or assessment on it.

Advantages of online assessment

- The results are obtained immediately.
- You can analyse what you did well on and what you did less well on so you can target your revision.
- It frees up teacher time, as there are no assessments to mark.

Disadvantages of online assessment

- Danger of hackers accessing the system and changing marks.
- Reliance on equipment that may go wrong.
- Only suitable for certain types of assessment, as it would be hard to get a computer to mark an essay.

Virtual learning environments (VLEs)

A virtual learning environment (VLE) is a software system that uses the Internet to support teaching and learning in a school, college or other educational institution.

The main features of a VLE are:

- It allows student performance to be assessed using tests and assessments that are marked automatically by the computer.
- It allows teachers to upload content – they can put their notes, presentations, videos, etc., on the VLE, so students can access them.
- Communication – it allows students to communicate with each other and also with their teachers.
- It allows students to submit their work electronically – projects, essays, assignments, etc., can be submitted to the teachers.
- It allows teachers to return marked student work.
- It allows peer assessment – this means that the students mark each other's work.
- It allows teachers to set up blogs – this allows students to discuss their work with each other and offer help to each other.
- Homework can be set and tailored more to individual ability.

Advantages and disadvantages of VLEs

Advantages

- Students can access the VLE using any computer or portable device that will connect to the Internet.
- Learning can take place at any time – the student is not restricted to learning only in lessons.
- Students can assess themselves at any time – this makes them feel more responsible for their own learning and progress.
- Individualized learning – students can do work that is more closely matched to their ability. They do not have to wait for others to catch up with them.

Disadvantages

- The software is very expensive.
- There is a danger of hackers altering reports, test marks, etc.
- Staff need a lot of training to use them.
- Entering content can be time consuming.

Questions A

1. Students can use online tutorials at home and at school to help them learn or revise certain topics.
   Describe **three** features of online tutorials. *(3 marks)*

2. Schools and colleges have to assess the progress of their students and many choose to do this using online assessment.
   (a) Explain what is meant by online assessment. *(2 marks)*
   (b) Give **one** advantage and **one** disadvantage in using online assessment. *(2 marks)*

3. (a) Give the meaning of the abbreviation VLE. *(1 mark)*
   (a) VLEs are very popular in schools and colleges.
   Write down a brief description of what a VLE is and what advantages it offers to the students who use them. *(4 marks)*
   (c) Describe **two** disadvantages in a school or college using a VLE. *(2 marks)*

Extension activity

If your school has a VLE, use it to investigate its features and produce a list of them, with a brief description for each one.

If your school does not have a VLE, find out about VLEs using the Internet and produce a list, with a brief description of their main features.

Learning devices and software to support disabilities

You will find out

▷ **About the use of specialist input devices such as Braille keyboards, microphones, touch sensitive data entry devices, etc.**

▷ **About software used to support learning disabilities**

ICT developments have helped people with disabilities gain employment and do many of the things they could not do without the use of ICT. Above all it has allowed people with disabilities to remain independent.

In this topic you will be looking at learning devices to support disabilities.

The use of specialist input devices

There is a huge range of specialist input devices that can be used by people with disabilities and help them learn.

Braille keyboards are used to enter text into a computer and are used by blind or partially sighted people.

▲ A Braille keyboard.

▲ This keyboard can be used by sighted or sight-impaired people.

Microphones

Microphones can be used to issue instructions and enter text into computer systems. They can be wired or wireless. Wireless microphones are useful because you can wander around the room whilst issuing instructions or dictating. Microphones are ideal input devices for people with certain disabilities that prevent them from using a keyboard.

▼ This wireless microphone and speaker system is ideal for inputting data into a computer and also for listening to what has been input.

Touch sensitive data entry devices

Touch sensitive data entry devices allow a person to make selections by simply touching a screen. They are used as input devices for purchasing train tickets or used as information points in tourist information offices, art galleries and museums. They can also be used to provide information on services provided by banks and building societies. Mobile phones use them as do satellite navigation systems.

The main advantage of the touch screen as an input device is that it is so simple it is capable of being used by almost anyone. It can be used by people with poor coordination skills who would find it hard to use a keyboard.

▲ Many mobile phones make use of a touch screen.

▼ Some touch screens are so small you need to use a pen/stylus rather than your finger to touch the screen.

Voice recognition software

Voice recognition software allows you to enter data by talking into a microphone. The voice recognition software can be used to:

- enter text into word-processing software
- enter text into emails
- issue commands to the operating system
- enter data into a database.

Voice recognition software works by recognizing spoken words and turning them into text that can be put into a variety of software packages. You basically speak into a microphone, which can be wired or wireless (usually making use of Bluetooth), and your speech is recognized as text or instructions.

Advantages

The advantages of voice recognition software are that it is:

- faster than typing – most people can talk faster than they can type
- accurate – provided time has been spent with the software teaching it how to recognize your voice
- cheap – it is cheaper to dictate yourself than pay someone to type, and the software and microphone are inexpensive.

Disadvantages

The disadvantages of voice recognition software are that:

- it takes a while to get used to – and can be frustrating to use at first
- it is not accurate at first – the software needs to get used to your voice/accent by you speaking and then correcting the mistakes the software makes
- there is confusion with similar sounding words, e.g. two and to
- background noise causes errors – you cannot use it in a noisy situation as the software will attempt to convert the noise as well as your speech into text or instructions.

Text to voice software

Text to voice software enables a computer to read text that has been typed in, or it can be used to give some sort of response such as the direction instructions in a satellite navigation system. The system can be used by visually impaired users to check what they have typed in using a Braille keyboard.

The output devices for a speech synthesis system are headphones or loudspeakers.

Customized desktop environments

There are many ways in which the desktop environment can be changed to suit the needs of a user who is disabled. The desktop environment can be changed in the following ways:

- You can use an on-screen keyboard and use a mouse or joystick to point and select letters from it.
- You can use an on-screen magnifier that will blow up certain areas of the screen.
- You can use what is called the narrator to read out text that appears on the screen.
- You can choose to use voice recognition to type in text or issue commands.
- You can alter the combination of colours used (this is useful for users who are colour blind).

Case study

A touch screen making use of Braille

Touch screen devices, like many mobile phones such as the Apple iPhone, are great provided you can see the screen. Imagine if you were blind, though. You would be unable to see the characters on the screen.

Braille uses raised and absent dots in order to represent a character. To represent these on a screen is difficult because screens are flat and cannot suddenly form dots.

Luckily researchers have found a solution. They have found that if they put a certain material on the touch screen, they can make a certain area such as a dot on the screen vibrate. This feels like a raised dot to someone touching the screen. The absent dots have a lower frequency of vibration, which means it is easy for someone who is blind to read the screen. This technology is set to really help blind and partially sighted people use many of the devices that at present are very difficult for them to use.

1 (a) Give the name of **one** device that makes use of a touch screen. *(1 mark)*
   (b) Give **one** advantage of using a touch screen. *(1 mark)*

2 Describe how a Braille touch screen enables blind or partially sighted people to use a touch screen. *(3 marks)*

Questions B

1 Voice recognition systems are used for entering text by dictating it rather than by using a keyboard.
   (a) Give **two** advantages of a voice recognition system to a user. *(2 marks)*
   (b) Describe **two** different ways in which a voice recognition system could be used. *(2 marks)*
   (c) Voice recognition systems are sometimes not 100% accurate. Give **two** possible reasons for this. *(2 marks)*

2 Touch screens can often be seen at tourist information offices. Give **one** advantage of using a touch screen as an input device for use by the general public. *(1 mark)*

END-OF-TOPIC REVIEW

Questions

 Test yourself

The following notes summarize this topic. The notes are incomplete because they have words missing.

Using the words in the list below, copy out and complete the sentences A to I, underlining the words that you have inserted. Each word may be used more than once.

shortcuts   folders   password   VLE   voice recognition

desktop environment   text to voice   control panel   online assessment

A A _____ _____ is a graphical user interface that allows a user to change certain settings of the operating system.

B The _____ _____ is part of the operating system used to change the look and settings of Windows.

C Files should always be put into _____ so that they can be quickly found when needed.

D _____ enable you to do a task using the operating system quickly rather than go through a series of menus/ windows, which takes time.

E Using Windows you can create a _____, which means other people cannot access the computer unless you want them to.

F _____ _____ is where you take a test or an examination online.

G A _____ is a software system that uses the Internet to support teaching and learning in a school, college or other educational institution.

H _____ _____ software works by recognizing spoken words and turning it into text that can be put into a variety of software packages.

I _____ _____ _____ software enables a computer to read out loud text that has been typed in so that a partially sighted user can check their work.

Examination style questions

1 Voice recognition systems are an ideal way for a user who is unable to use a keyboard to enter data into the computer.
  (a) Give **one** input device, other than a keyboard and mouse, that is used to input data into a computer with a voice recognition system. *(1 mark)*
  (b) Give **one** output device used by a voice recognition system. *(1 mark)*
  (c) Briefly explain how voice recognition software works. *(3 marks)*

2 Virtual learning environments are used in many schools.

  (a) Give **two** features of a virtual learning environment. *(2 marks)*
  (b) Give **two** advantages to a student in using a virtual learning environment. *(2 marks)*

3 Computer users are able to customize their desktop environments.
  (a) Explain clearly what the above statement means and give **two** examples of customization. *(3 marks)*
  (b) Give **two** examples of customization for use by students in a school who have impaired eyesight. *(2 marks)*

END-OF-TOPIC REVIEW

Exam support

Worked example

Many schools use online tutorial packages to help students learn. Schools also make use of distance learning.

(a) Give **two** advantages and **two** disadvantages in using online tutorials/distance learning. *(4 marks)*

(b) Online tutorials are sometimes used with students who have learning difficulties. Give **two** advantages and **two** disadvantages in using online tutorials with these students. Your answers must be different from those for part (a). *(4 marks)*

Student answer 1

(a) There is no teacher around to tell you off when you get something wrong.

There are ways in which you can move back to a topic you feel you did not understand.

Learning is a social thing and you do not have the chance to interact with your classmates with online learning.

There is no-one around to help you if you get stuck but if you had a proper teacher then they might be able to explain it a different way to help you understand.

(b) The online tutorial will not judge you if you make mistakes unlike a teacher who may think you are stupid.

Online tutorials cannot be used at home.

The online tutorial will make use of multimedia effects, which means that it will encourage reluctant learners to learn because it will be fun.

CAL packages are expensive because they take a long time to produce.

◀ Examiner's comments

(a) The two advantages are sensible and well expressed, so full marks for these.

Again both disadvantages are acceptable answers and are well expressed, so full marks for these.

(b) The first, third and fourth answers are justifiable reasons and they are all relevant to a student with learning difficulties.

The second answer is incorrect as many online tutorial packages can be run over a network such as the Internet.

(7 marks out of 8)

Student answer 2

(a) You can access the teaching materials from any computer, which makes it very flexible when you do the course.

You can take the course 24/7 which makes it more flexible than traditional lessons that have to be arranged according to a timetable.

(b) You can learn at your own pace and not the pace of the rest of the class.

Online tutorials often make learning a game, which is fun and keeps the students engaged in their learning.

The teacher could think you were learning on the computer when you weren't reading the information and simply guessing at the answers.

There is no competition with your classmates to see who does best so this can demotivate you.

◀ Examiner's comment

(a) These two answers are very similar as they both refer to the fact that online courses offer flexibility (e.g. time and location). Students have to be careful they do not write an answer that is just slightly different, as marks will not be given for both answers. The answers to this type of question must be distinctly different. Only one mark is given here for one advantage.

No disadvantages are given here. It seems likely that the student has forgotten to read this part of the question. It is always worth reading the question and your answer again at the end of the question to check for this.

(b) All the answers here are correct, so full marks for this part to the question.

(5 marks out of 8)

Exam support *continued*

Examiner's answers

(a) One mark each for two advantages such as:

- Students can work through the material at home or in the library.
- Useful when students cannot attend school for personal reasons (e.g. illness, etc.).
- Students become more responsible for their learning, which is useful practice for entry into higher education.
- Students can repeat the lesson if there is something they do not understand.
- Classes can be run with fewer students than normal.
- Classes can take place at any time – there need not be a set timetable.

One mark each for two disadvantages such as:

- Students need to be motivated otherwise they won't complete the tasks.
- Can be expensive.
- Lack of support and encouragement from a teacher.
- No encouragement or collaborative learning from others in the class.

(b) One mark each for two advantages such as:

- Students are able to work at their own pace.
- They do not have to worry about getting things wrong as there is no human to judge them.
- They can repeat parts many times until they fully understand them.
- The multimedia aspects of the software can be used to suit the different types of learner.
- Adds more fun to the learning process.
- Can use special input devices such as touch screens to help students who find it hard to use a keyboard and mouse.
- Learners can gauge their own progress.

One mark each for two disadvantages such as:

- Lack of teacher encouragement.
- Students may just think of it as a game and not learn anything.
- There is no collaborative learning.
- Does not teach them to interact with humans.

Summary mind maps

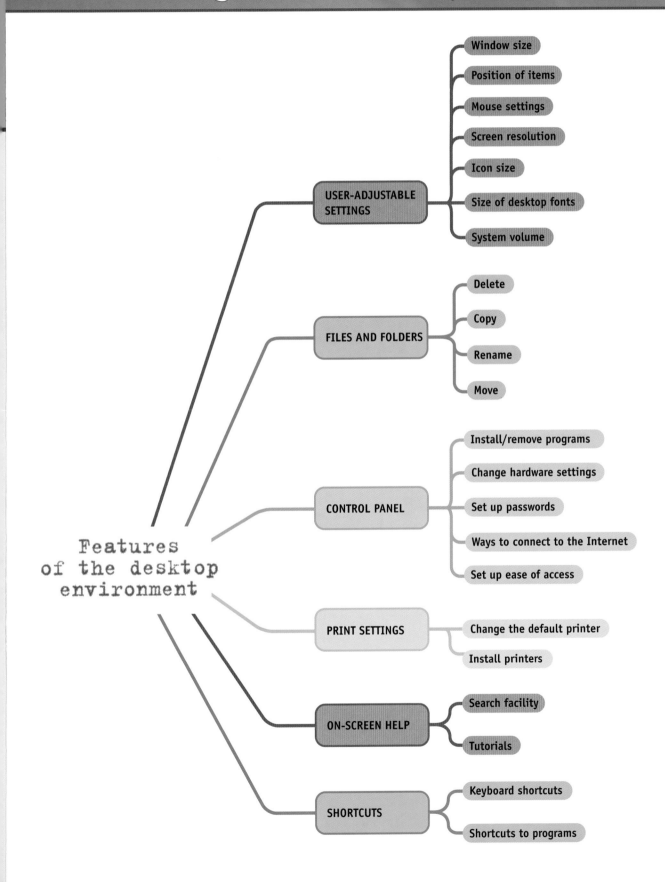

USER-ADJUSTABLE SETTINGS
- Window size
- Position of items
- Mouse settings
- Screen resolution
- Icon size
- Size of desktop fonts
- System volume

FILES AND FOLDERS
- Delete
- Copy
- Rename
- Move

CONTROL PANEL
- Install/remove programs
- Change hardware settings
- Set up passwords
- Ways to connect to the Internet
- Set up ease of access

PRINT SETTINGS
- Change the default printer
- Install printers

ON-SCREEN HELP
- Search facility
- Tutorials

SHORTCUTS
- Keyboard shortcuts
- Shortcuts to programs

Features of the desktop environment

Sources of information, and purpose and appropriate use of applications software

When you complete a task using ICT, such as producing an essay, writing a letter, producing a brochure, etc., you need information sources. These sources of information are often in digital format, such as files on disk, material on the Internet, etc., so you can use them immediately. In this topic you will learn about the various sources of information.

You will also be looking at applications software and how it can be used to further process information to complete a task such as produce a letter, a poster, etc.

Sources of information

Organizations need information in order to function and this information can come from a variety of different sources such as:

- files on disks
- files on removable media such as pen drives/flash drives/memory sticks
- CD-ROMs or DVDs
- databases
- the Internet.

Files on disks – many computers have pre-installed software that is ready to use when you buy the computer. For example, you may have an Office suite of software on your computer and you may use the library of clip art and images when you create a document using word-processing or desktop publishing software.

Files on removable media – many people work on many different computers, so they need a way of storing and transferring files. Often work is stored on removable media because it is easy to transfer files to other computers. Sometimes a group of people are working on the same project and they need to show others what they have done.

CD-ROMs or DVDs – these are most often used for the transfer of video and music files but they can hold large databases. For example, there is a CD-ROM produced by the Royal Mail that contains the address details that go with all the postcodes in the country. This means that an organization can type in the postcode and the full

address will appear, which saves them a lot of typing time.

There are other examples of searchable databases such as encyclopaedias and medical dictionaries that are available on CD-ROM.

Databases – these are stores of data that you can buy or set up yourself and access in a variety of different ways. Schools keep large stores of data about their present and past students that can be searched using search conditions to find specific information such as students in a form, students whose attendance is poor, details of students who get free school meals and so on.

The Internet – this is the biggest store of information and the most popular source of data, as you can access it using so many different devices such as computers, PDAs, mobile phones, etc. Software called search engines are used to find information by putting in search criteria.

The Internet can be used for finding sounds, music, clip art, photographic images, animations, text and so on.

Applications software

Applications software is software that is capable of doing a specific job. A job is called an application. When you buy applications software, you need to make sure of the following:

- That it will work with the hardware that you are using.
- That it will work with the operating system that you are using.

Some software, called general purpose software, can be used in any type of business. General purpose software includes:

- word-processing
- spreadsheet
- database
- desktop publishing
- presentation.

Some software, called specialist software packages, is developed for a particular application. For example, there is software that helps in the running of a school. It helps keep details of staff, students, timetables, etc. It would only be of use in a school. Other examples include software to run libraries, software for garages, etc.

▲ Examples of applications software.

Applications software is written in a programming language by a person called a programmer. The programmer designs and then puts together the step-by-step instructions that tell the computer what to do. The whole set of instructions to do a task is called the program code.

KEY WORDS

Applications software software designed to do a particular job.

Operating system the software that controls the hardware and also runs the programs.

Program the set of step-by-step instructions that tell the computer hardware what to do.

Software the programs used by computers.

◀ Applications software can be bought physically (on CDs or DVDs) and needs to be installed.

DOWNLOAD

▲ Applications software can be downloaded off the Internet and then installed.

Activity

Find out the names of the individual packages in the integrated applications package called Microsoft Office.

For each of the packages named, write a short paragraph explaining the purpose of the package.

Questions A

1 In order to do a useful job a computer needs software.
- **(a)** Explain what is meant by software. *(2 marks)*
- **(b)** Computers need two different types of software in order to function. Give the names of these **two** types of software. *(2 marks)*

2 When using applications software you need to use sources of information.
- **(a)** Explain what is meant by applications software. *(2 marks)*
- **(b)** Describe **three** sources of information that can be further processed using applications software. *(3 marks)*

3 Copy and complete the sentences by filling in the missing word in each case.
- **(a)** The _____ is the biggest store of information in the world and the information is easily found by making use of software called search engines.
- **(b)** _____ are stores of data that you can buy or set up yourself and access in a variety of different ways. *(2 marks)*

Extension activity

There are many specialist applications software packages. Basically if there is a type of job or business then there will be applications software to help with it.

Use the Internet to find out job-related applications packages and write a short sentence about each one.

END-OF-TOPIC REVIEW

Questions

 Test yourself

The following notes summarize this topic. The notes are incomplete because they have words missing.

Using the words in the list below, copy out and complete the sentences A to G, underlining the words that you have inserted. Each word may be used more than once.

> program   database   applications software   files
>
> Internet   operating system   DVDs   word-processing   payroll

A The largest source of information that can be used by applications software for further processing is the _____.

B Other sources of information include _____ on disk and CD-ROMs and _____.

C Structured data that can be searched by performing queries is called a _____ and is a useful source of information.

D The step-by-step instructions that tell a computer what to do are called a computer _____.

E Software that controls the hardware directly is called _____ _____ software.

F Software which does not control the hardware directly and performs a particular job or task is called _____ _____.

G Applications software includes general purpose software such as _____ software and specialist software such as _____.

Examination style questions

1 The owner of a dog boarding kennels wants to use a computer system to carry out the following tasks:

   Task 1   Produce a price list to give to the customers.
   Task 2   Send special offer advertisements to all customers.
   Task 3   Store the upkeep costs such as feed and vet's bills.
   Task 4   Keep a record of bookings for all the dogs.

   Here are some pieces of applications software. Choose the best piece of software to complete each task.
   • spreadsheet   • desktop publishing
   • word-processing   • database.
   (4 marks)

2 Choose the **three** tasks from the list below that are carried out by applications software. *(3 marks)*

   Underlining text in a word-processing program.
   Controlling output devices such as printers.
   Deciding where to store data on a disk drive.
   Adding up columns of numbers.
   Adjusting the size of an image taken using a digital camera.

3 When we use applications software such as word-processing software, we need sources of information to use to complete a task.
   Outline **three** sources of information and for each source describe what the source of information would likely contain. *(6 marks)*

Exam support

Worked example

(a) There are two types of software: applications software and operating system software.

Name **two** different types of applications software. *(2 marks)*

(b) Give **two** tasks for each of the types of software you have named in part (a) for which they are particularly suited. *(2 marks)*

(c) Windows Vista is an operating system. Give the names of **two** different operating systems. *(2 marks)*

Student answer 1

(a) Word and Excel.

(b) You can add up columns of numbers.

You can produce documents such as letters and edit and then print them.

(c) Unix and MacOS.

▲ Examiner's comment

(a) Word and Excel are brand names and not types of software. Do not use brand names for types of software. The student should have used the names word-processing and spreadsheet software. Unfortunately they get no marks for this part of the answer.

(b) It is not clear in their answer which piece of software they are referring to.

It would have been better to have written the answer like this:

- Spreadsheet: You can add up columns of numbers.
- Word-processing: You can produce documents such as letters, and edit and print them.

Remember that the examiner should not have to be a mind reader and try to guess what you intended, so you need to be clear what you are referring to in your answers.

One mark is awarded for this part.

(c) Both of these answers are correct, so full marks for this part. *(3 marks out of 6)*

Student answer 2

(a) Payroll software and desktop publishing software.

(b) Payroll software for working out worker pay at the end of the month.

CAD software for designing a car engine for a Formula 1 racing car.

(c) Linux and Mac OS.

▲ Examiner's comment

(a) Both these are applications software so two marks here.

(b) The first answer is correct but the second answer does not refer to what was written for the second piece of software in part (a). This student has forgotten that their answer must refer to the software named, which is a shame. A check through the answer against the question might have revealed this error, which could have been corrected.

Only one of the two marks can be given here.

(c) Both these are correct names of operating systems, so two marks for this part.

(5 marks out of 6)

Exam support *continued*

Examiner's answers

(a) One mark each for two pieces of applications software such as:

- Payroll
- Database
- Word-processing
- Spreadsheet
- Graphics
- Photo/image editing
- Web authoring
- Desktop publishing

(b) One mark for a description of a task performed by the software. It must be clear which of the two pieces of software each task refers to.

e.g. desktop publishing – designing a catalogue of goods for publication, which includes text and graphics.

(c) One mark for each correct operating system to a maximum of two marks.

Examples include:

- Unix
- DOS/Disk Operating System
- MAC OS
- Apple
- Leopard
- Windows XP
- Windows Vista
- Windows 7
- Sun
- Snow Leopard

Summary mind maps

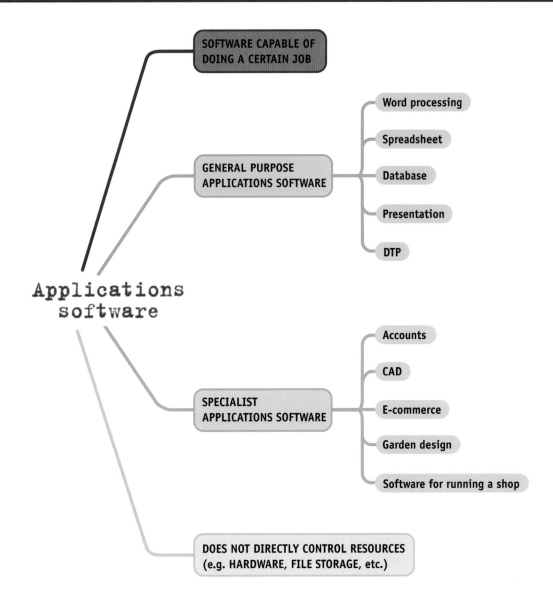

SOFTWARE CAPABLE OF
DOING A CERTAIN JOB

GENERAL PURPOSE
APPLICATIONS SOFTWARE

- Word processing
- Spreadsheet
- Database
- Presentation
- DTP

Applications
software

SPECIALIST
APPLICATIONS SOFTWARE

- Accounts
- CAD
- E-commerce
- Garden design
- Software for running a shop

DOES NOT DIRECTLY CONTROL RESOURCES
(e.g. HARDWARE, FILE STORAGE, etc.)

Summary mind maps *continued*

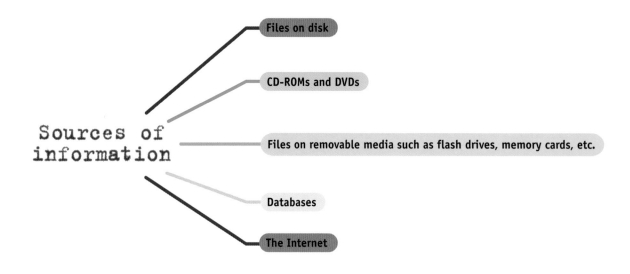

Sources of information
- Files on disk
- CD-ROMs and DVDs
- Files on removable media such as flash drives, memory cards, etc.
- Databases
- The Internet

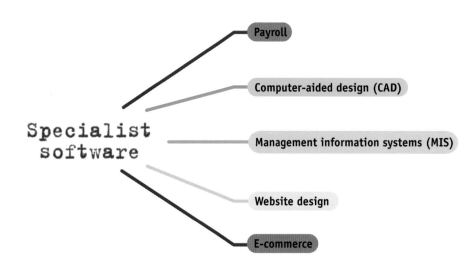

Specialist software
- Payroll
- Computer-aided design (CAD)
- Management information systems (MIS)
- Website design
- E-commerce

Information handling software

The key concepts covered in this topic are:

- Updating, deleting, sorting and searching
- The appropriate use of operators
- Data types
- Fields, records and files
- Searching for information
- Outputting information in report format
- Calculated fields
- Validation checks such as lists, range checks, format checks and input masks
- The benefits of using information handling
- Security issues

Information handling software is any software that is able to store the data in a structure that allows the processing of that data to produce meaningful information.

You normally think of information handling software as being database software but it is possible to hold stores of information and be able to manipulate it using other software such as spreadsheet software.

Contents

Updating, deleting, sorting and searching

In order to ensure the integrity (i.e., the accuracy) of data in a data handling system it is necessary to take steps to update and delete data on a regular basis. If this is not done, then the amount of data stored quickly rises, increasing the amount of storage needed. It also makes it harder to search for specific data and to sort or copy the data. The amount of incorrect data increases and users can no longer trust the data being held.

Information handling software includes facilities to sort data into certain orders. It also offers ways of searching for specific data.

Updating

Updating means bringing data up-to-date because of changes that may have occurred since the data was originally input. There are many situations that result in the data needing to be changed and here are just a few of them:

- A woman changing her surname when she gets married.
- A person changing their credit card (i.e., different credit card company, different credit card number, different start and expiry dates).
- A person changing their address.
- A person changing their car.
- A person paying a bill.

Deleting

Deleting means removing some of the data from a data handling system. For example, a person may no longer want to receive mail from a certain company, so they will need to be removed from their mailing database.

Here are some other situations where data needs to be deleted:

- Where personal information is wrong and a data subject has asked for it to be deleted.
- When a person dies.
- When a customer has not placed an order for a certain period of time.

It is important to delete data for the following reasons:

- You can waste money sending mail shots and other correspondence to people who have moved.
- It is a requirement under the Data Protection Act that personal information that is incorrect should be either corrected or deleted.

Sorting

Data can be sorted into ascending or descending order and it can be sorted on one or more fields.

Ascending order: in the case of numbers the smallest number is first and the largest number is last. In the case of text the letter A is first and the letter Z is last.

Descending order: in the case of numbers the largest number is first and the smallest number is last. In the case of text the letter Z is first and the letter A is last.

Reasons for sorting data include:

- If lists are printed, then it is easier to find a particular person if they are ordered according to surname.
- You can identify who your best customers are by the amount they have spent in a year. To do this you can sort them according to the total amount they have spent.

Searching

In order to narrow down information we can restrict it by asking only for data satisfying certain criteria. For example, in a list of all the pupils in a school, we might only want a list of boys. This is classed as searching using a single criterion. The single search criterion could be as follows: Sex = Boys

Searches can also be performed using multiple criteria. This means that data is being searched for using more than one criterion. For example, we could search for all the boys in a school born before a certain date. The search criteria might be set up something like this:

Sex = Boys AND Date of Birth < 01/09/99

The appropriate use of operators

Operators are used when creating search criteria. Here is a table of the main operators and what they do:

Operator	Meaning	Example of use
=	Equals	Surname = 'Jones' lists all the details for people having the surname Jones
<>	Is not equal to	Code <> 3 would list all the details for those codes other than with Code 3
>	Greater than	Qty > 20 lists the details where the field Qty is over 20
<	Less than	Age < 18 lists the details where the age is less than 18
>=	Greater than or equal to	Price >= 20 lists those details where the price is 20 or more
<=	Less than or equal to	Date <= 01/12/10 means the date must be on or before 01/12/10
AND	Where the data is only listed where both conditions are true	Surname = 'Jones' AND Age <16 Gives details when the surname is Jones and the age is less than 16
OR	Where the data is only listed where either or both conditions are true	Surname = 'Jones' OR Age <16 Gives details when the surname is Jones or the age is less than 16 or both
LIKE	Where a perfect match is not needed – perfect and close matches are listed	Like Surname = Jon will list those surnames starting with the letters Jon

Data types

Information handling systems have to cope with different types of data and these are summarized here:

Data type	Description
Text	Used for storing names, words and numbers that are not used in calculations (telephone numbers, code numbers, credit card numbers, etc.).
Number	Used for storing numbers that can be used in calculations.
Date	Used for storing dates.
Time	Used for storing times.
Currency	Used for storing monetary values to two decimal places.
AutoNumber	These are numbers allocated by the computer. It is useful when you want to give each record a unique number (student number, bank account number, etc.).
Boolean	This is used when there are only one of two choices that can be entered for a field (Yes/No, Male/Female, etc.).
Lists	Useful where there are a limited number of choices a user can choose from. The user is presented with a list to choose from. (For example, enter the year 7, 8, 9, 10 or 11.)
Picture	Databases often have a picture. It could be of a person, a product, etc. There are also information handling systems that help you organize a large collection of digital images.
Sound	Information handling systems are used to organize music or sounds. You can create playlists and organize the music you like into categories.
Video	Information handling systems can store and organize video collections. These can range from home video selections to huge collections such as YouTube.

The structure of data in information handling systems

You will find out

▷ **About fields, records and files**

▷ **About searching for information using tools such as key words and search engines**

Information handling software is used to put data into a certain structure. Once the data is put into this structure it can be manipulated and output in lots of different ways.

In this section you will learn about the structure and the concept of a key field.

Fields, records and files

An organized store of data on a computer is called a database.

Choosing the software to create a database structure

There are two types of software you could use to produce a database:

• spreadsheet software
• database software.

You can build a simple database by organizing the data in rows and columns in a table. In the database shown below the columns represent each of the fields and the rows are the records.

Note:

RECORDS are always ROWS
FIELDS are always COLUMNS

Fields, records and files: what do they all mean?

There are some database terms you will need to familiarize yourselves with. These are:

Data: These are facts about a specific person, place or thing.

Information: Information is data that has been processed into a form that is useful to the user.

Field: A field is an item of data. In other words it is a fact. A Surname would be an example of a field.

Record: The detail relating to a single thing or person is called a record. A record consists of fields.

File: A collection of related records is called a file. The group of records for all the pupils in the school is called the pupil file. Often a simple file holding a single database is called a table.

Table: In databases a table is used to store data with each row in the table being a record and the whole table being a file. When only one table is used, it is a very simple database and it is called a flat-file database.

For more complex databases created using specialist database software, lots of tables can be used and such a database is called a relational database.

Key fields

A key field is a field in an information handling system that is unique to a particular record. For example, in a file of all the children

Each column represents a field of the database

Sex	Year	Favourite sport
M	7	Football
M	7	Golf
F	8	Hockey
F	7	Football
M	7	Tennis
F	8	Tennis

Each row is a record of the database

▲ The structure of a database.

in a school a record would be the details about a particular pupil. The key field would be Pupil Number, which would be a number set up so that each pupil is allocated a different number when they join the school. No two pupils would have the same number. Surname would not be unique and so is unsuitable for a key field. It is possible to have more than one key field in a record.

Searching for information

There are a number of ways that information can be searched for. Here are some of them.

Search engines

Search engines are used to find information on the Internet but they can also be used to search for information on an organization's intranet (a type of internal network that uses the same technology as the Internet).

Key word searches

All information stores provide ways of searching for information using key word searches. When information is sought, the person searching for the information may not know such things as the key field and they have to use several key words.

Questions B

1 A luxury car rental firm keeps the details of the cars it rents out in a table. The structure and contents of this table are shown below.

Reg-number	Make	Model	Year
DB51 AML	Aston Martin	DB7	2009
CAB 360M	Ferrari	360 Modena	2008
P 762 GT X34 FER	Ferrari	355 Spider	2000
MAS 12	Maserati	3200 GTA	2001
FG09 FRT	Porsche	911 Turbo	2009
M3 MMM	BMW	M3 Conv	2010
T433 YTH	Jaguar	XK8	2009

(a) Give the names of **two** fields shown in the above table. *(2 marks)*

(b) Give the name of the field that should be chosen as the key field. *(1 mark)*

(c) Explain why the field you have chosen for your answer to part (b) should be chosen as the key field. *(1 mark)*

(d) The highlighted details are an example of which one of these? *(1 mark)*

    a record   a table

    a field   a file.

(e) How many records are there in the above table? *(1 mark)*

2 Here is a sample of the data that is to be stored in an employee database. The data items shown are the employee's surname, initial, street, postcode and telephone number.

    Adams, V, 123 The High Street, L23 6DE, 0151-264-1112

    Dolan, N, 64 North Way, L9 8SS, 0151-267-0011

    Doyle, B, 12 Crosby Road, L23 2DF, 0151-264-1212

    Carrol, A, 15 Barkfield Drive, L23 7YH, 0151-261-0899

    Conway, T, 6 Windle Hey, L23 6ER, 0151-289-0899

    Harvey, J, 4 Empress Road, L22 7ED, 0151-340-9090

    Harvey, J, 4 Empress Road, L22 7ED, 0151-340-9090

(a) A table is to be set up with four fields. Give names for the four fields that would be suitable for the above set of data items. *(4 marks)*

(b) The person who is designing the database looks at the sample of data above and notices that there are two people with the same surnames and address who live at the same address.

(i) Explain why the surname would be an unsuitable key field. *(1 mark)*

(ii) It is decided that each employee should be given a unique number. What would be a suitable field name for this field? *(1 mark)*

(iii) Rather than have to keep remembering the last number used, it is decided that it would be better if this number were given automatically by the computer. What type of field should be given to this field from this list: Text, Numeric, AutoNumber or Boolean? *(1 mark)*

Reports, calculated fields and validation techniques

You will find out

▷ **About the outputting of data in report formats**

▷ **About how simple calculated fields are produced**

▷ **About the purpose and suitable application of validation techniques such as lists, range checks, format checks and input masks for common fields**

The whole point of storing data in information handling systems is so that it can be manipulated and extracted flexibly. Information that is printed out from these systems is called a report. Using reports allows users to be very specific about the information that needs to be on the report and the way it is laid out. Calculations can be performed on fields, so it is possible, for example, to multiply two numbers in different fields together. Reports are only of use if the data used to produce them does not contain any errors, so the validation of data when it is entered at the input stage is very important.

Outputting information in report format

Reports are used to present the output from an information handling system. Reports are used to present the data in such a way that it is more suited to printing.

Here are some points about reports:

- Reports should have a relevant title.
- The report should contain a date. Information changes, so the person looking at the information needs to know that it is the latest version.
- Only data or information that is important should be included.
- The details of the report should be clearly laid out.
- The report should present the information in the clearest way possible (in some cases this will be using a graph or chart).
- The pages of the report should be suitably numbered (NB you can use headers and footers).

How simple calculated fields are produced

Calculated fields are those fields whose contents are worked out from data in other fields using calculations that the information handling software performs.

New fields can be created containing the results of calculations and these are called 'calculated fields'. For example, you might want to multiply the price of an individual article by a quantity to give the total price. To do this a new 'total' field would be created to contain the results of a calculation involving the other two fields.

Validation checks

Validation was covered in Topic 1. If you are unsure about it you should look back at it. When data is being entered into a structure it is important that certain types of error are spotted by the data handling software. The user can then be alerted to check and possibly re-enter the data.

When the structure of a store of data is being designed, a series of validation rules can be devised to govern what can and cannot be entered into each field. It is impossible to trap every type of error; if someone's address is 4 Bankfield Drive and the user incorrectly types in 40 Bankfield Drive, then no simple validation check would detect this.

Here are the main types of validation check you need to know about:

- **Data type check** – data handling software automatically checks to make sure the data being entered into a field is of the type allowed by the data type for that field, so, for example, text cannot be entered into a field that has a numeric data type. This type of check is called a data type check.
- **Range checks** – are performed on numbers to make sure that they are within a specified range. Range checks will only pick up absurd values. For example, if you typed in the number of children in a household as '50' rather than '5' then a range check will spot the error; if you typed in '7' then the range check would not pick up the error.
- **Presence checks** – check to ensure that data is always entered

into certain fields. For example, every pupil must have a pupil number, since it is allocated to them automatically when they join the school. Some fields, such as email address, can be left blank, since not everyone has one. Checks such as this are called presence checks. Presence checks make sure that data has been entered into a field.

- **Format checks –** check that the data being entered conforms to a certain arrangement. For example, all product codes for goods stored by a system might start with a letter followed by four numbers. A format check would check that the first character is a letter and the next four characters are all numbers. Any other combinations would be rejected.

Lists

If there are a small number of options that a user can type in for a field you can set these up in the form of a list. The user is presented with a list of possible data and they simply click on one of them to choose it. For example, sizes could be presented as a list such as S, M, L and XL. Lists restrict the user to allowable data. Of course the data can still be incorrect as the user could click on the wrong item in the list.

Input masks

In some fields, data might all have the same format, so to simplify data entry an input mask can be used. The input mask supplies the invariable characters in a field so that the user need only enter the data that differs from one field to another. This is best illustrated by taking an example of entering telephone numbers. If all the telephone numbers to be entered have the same format (0151) 876 2341, for example, we can use the input mask to supply the brackets and spaces between blocks of numbers.

As well as saving some input time, input masks help to ensure that the data entered adheres to a format.

If an order number field contains customer numbers that each start with a single letter of the alphabet followed by four numbers, this can be specified in the input mask.

Microsoft Access uses the following mask characters. Note the difference between 'may be entered' and 'must be entered'.

Let us now look at constructing some input masks using these characters. For a telephone number such as (0151) 876 2341 we could use the following input mask: (0000) 000 0000

But if we want dashes between the groups of numbers we should instead use this mask: (0000)-000-0000

Mask character	Can be used in the input mask to mean
0	A digit must be entered here
9	A digit may be entered here
#	A positive (+) or negative (–) sign may be entered here
L	A letter must be entered here
?	A letter may be entered here
A	A letter or a digit must be entered here
a	A letter or a number may be entered here
&	Any character or space must be entered here
C	Any character or space may be entered here
<	All characters to the right are converted to lower case
>	All characters to the right are converted to upper case
. , : ; – /	Decimal point, thousands, date and time separators
!	Mask fills from right to left (useful if the optional characters are on the right-hand side of the mask)
\	Character to the right is interpreted as an ordinary character and not part of the mask

KEY WORD

Validation check a check performed by the information handling software to make sure that the data is allowable.

Questions C

1 **(a)** Explain what is meant by a validation check. *(2 marks)*
(b) Give the names of **two** different validation checks that may be performed on data. *(2 marks)*

2 Information is often extracted using information handling software in report format.
(a) Explain what is meant by a report. *(2 marks)*
(b) Other than the results (i.e., the information itself) give **two** things that would be included on a report. *(2 marks)*

Extension activity

Investigate how validation checks can be produced in specialist database software or spreadsheet software.

The benefits of using information handling, and security issues

▷ **About the benefits of using information handling**

▷ **About security issues**

Information handling software has many advantages over the manual storage of data. In this section you will look at the advantages, which include faster access to data, the variety of different output formats for the information and improved data integrity. Another big benefit is the fact that information in information handling systems is better secured than information kept in manual systems.

The benefits of using information handling

Information handling packages offer many advantages which include:

- Faster access to data
- A variety of output formats
- Improved data integrity.

Faster access to data

There are a number of ways information handling software can provide faster access to data:

- Search engines can be used to quickly access information on the Internet.
- Key word searches can be performed.
- Search criteria can be used to extract specific information from huge databases.
- Information searches can be performed even if only part of the search details are known. For example, a car could be searched for if only part of the registration number is known and a few other details such as a white Honda.

Variety of output formats

Information contained in manual systems can only be output on paper, but with information handling systems the information can be output in a variety of different formats such as:

- on screen
- as hard copy (i.e., printed on paper)
- as a copy on a disk or other removable media

- as sound (very useful if someone who is blind needs to use the system).

Data integrity

Data integrity means the correctness of the data. As soon as some of the data contained in the database is discovered to be inaccurate, the users start to lose faith in all the data in the database.

To make sure data integrity is maintained you can:

- Ensure that errors are not introduced when data is input into the system, by using verification techniques – these include visual check (proof reading) and double entry of data.
- Use validation checks – these will ensure that only data which passes the validation checks is entered.
- Ensure that the data is updated regularly.
- Ensure that data no longer needed is deleted.

Security issues

Data held in information handling systems is more secure than data held manually mainly because it is easily copied and transferred off-site. It is also more secure because of restricted access.

Password protection

Access to files is restricted using usernames and passwords. The username allocates the user with certain access rights to data and the password ensures that the person using the system is who they say they are. Passwords protect against unauthorized access.

A password is a series of characters (usually letters, numbers and other characters on the keyboard) that are set up by the user and known only to them. They have to enter these each time they log-in to the network.

Password protocols

Password protocols are steps that need to be taken regarding passwords such as:

- Ensuring that users change their passwords on a regular basis.
- Training so that users understand that they should keep their passwords private and not disclose them to others.
- Telling users not to write their passwords down.
- Explaining to users the need to use passwords that are not easily guessed.

Access rights to data

Access rights are given to staff by the network manager. These rights allow certain staff to access only certain files. For example, a member of staff who deals with customer orders can have access to those files such as the customer file needed to perform their job. This member of staff would not be given access rights to the personnel or payroll files.

In addition to this, access rights determine what you can do with the data in the files you have access to. For example:

- Read only access – you can only look at the data and not alter it.
- Read/write – you can view and alter data.
- Create – you can create new records.
- Delete – you can delete records.

Backup procedures

Information handling systems store huge amounts of information and this must be protected against loss. Backup copies of the data must be kept and procedures must be put in place to ensure that data can be easily recovered from the backups.

Backup procedures are needed to:

- specify who is responsible for the taking of the backups
- specify how often the backups are taken (every hour, every day, etc.)
- state what media is used for the storing of backups
- specify where the backup copies are kept (e.g., fireproof safe, kept off-site, transferred using the Internet)
- specify how any data can be recovered from the backups
- ensure that staff are trained in the recovery of data from backups.

▲ Backup procedures must specify the media used – in this case a CD.

Questions D

1 A pupil information handling system is used to hold pupil details in a school. Some of this information is personal and needs to be protected and this is done by using passwords. Staff who use the system are given access rights.
   (a) Explain what is meant by a password. *(1 mark)*
   (b) Password protocols ensure that there is no unauthorized access to the personal data held. Describe **two** things that can be done concerning passwords that will help ensure that there is no unauthorized access to data. *(2 marks)*
   (c) Explain what is meant by 'access rights'. *(2 marks)*

2 One advantage in using information handling software is the improvement in data integrity.
   (a) Explain what is meant by 'data integrity'. *(1 mark)*
   (b) Describe **one** way data integrity is improved by the use of data handling software. *(2 marks)*

Extension activity

Produce a poster entitled 'password protocols' that will alert users about the need to take certain actions and procedures when using passwords.

END-OF-TOPIC REVIEW

Questions

 Test yourself

The following notes summarize this topic. The notes are incomplete because they have words missing.

Using the words in the list below, copy out and complete the sentences A to I, underlining the words that you have inserted. Each word may be used more than once.

sorted   record   criteria

validation   updating

searching   file   operators

field   key   fields

A _____ means bringing data up-to-date owing to changes that may have occurred since the data was originally input.

B Data can be _____ into ascending or descending order.

C _____ picks out data matching one or more _____.

D Equals, greater than, less than are all examples of _____ that can be used when performing searches.

E A _____ _____ is a field in an information handling system that is unique to a particular record.

F The detail relating to a single thing or person is called a _____.

G A record consists of many _____.

H A collection of records is called a _____.

I A check performed by the information handling software to make sure that the data is allowable is called a _____ check.

96

Examination style questions

1 Most schools now use databases to store details about each pupil. The table shows some of the fieldnames and data types stored in one pupil database.

Fieldname	Data type
UniquePupilNumber	Number
Firstname	
Surname	Text
FirstLineAddress	Text
SecondLineAddress	Text
Postcode	
LandlineNo	Text
DateOfBirth	Date
FreeSchoolMeals(Y/N)	

(a) Give the most appropriate data types for the fields:
  Firstname
  Postcode
  FreeSchoolMeals(Y/N) *(1 mark)*

(b) Give the names of **three** other fields that are likely to be used in this database. *(3 marks)*

(c) Explain which field is used as the key field in the database and why such a field is necessary. *(2 marks)*

(d) It is important that the data contained in this database is accurate. Describe how **two** different errors could occur when data is entered into this database. *(2 marks)*

(e) Explain how the errors you have mentioned in part (d) could be detected or prevented. *(2 marks)*

2 Explain **one** difference between the database terms 'search' and 'sort'. *(2 marks)*

3 Security is improved with an information handling system compared with a manual system. Give **one** example of how security is improved. *(2 marks)*

4 A store keeps details about their customers and their orders in an information handling system. Part of the data in this system is shown below:

Customer number	Name	Item code	Size	Cost	Delivery
2314	J. Hughes	464	Small	£290	N
9819	D. Wong	255	Large	£767	Y
1311	C. Khled	747	Small	£239	N
8276	K. Lee	299	Small	£200	Y
9223	F. Smith	108	Large	£823	Y

(a) Give the names of **two** key fields used in the above table. *(2 marks)*

(b) There is one 'Boolean' field in this database. Give the name of it. *(1 mark)*

(c) Give the names of **two** other fields that could be sensibly used in this table other than customer name, customer address and customer telephone number. *(2 marks)*

(d) Give the name of a suitable validation check that could be used for the Size field and describe how it can reduce errors. *(2 marks)*

(e) The store offers free delivery on all items with a cost greater than £200.
How many of the customers shown would qualify for the free delivery? *(1 mark)*

(f) A member of staff in the warehouse wants to find out details of all small goods that are to be delivered. Complete the tables below to show how she can obtain this information from the system. *(2 marks)*

Fieldname	Operator	Search criteria

AND

Fieldname	Operator	Search criteria

Exam support

Worked example

A school keeps details of all its students on a computer. Part of the data is shown below. The data is structured in fields, records and files.

Student_Number	Surname	Forename	Date of birth	Form
1211	Lee	Jaccck	12/11/99	11T
1225	Hughes	Amy	34/08/09	11G

(a) Explain the terms:

(i) Field   (ii)   Record (iii)   File   *(3 marks)*

(b) The data contained in the above structure contains two mistakes. One of these mistakes could have been discovered by a verification process and the other mistake by a validation process.

Complete a table as below by explaining what the mistake is and whether verification or validation could have detected the mistake and describe a method that could be used to prevent the error. *(6 marks)*

Description of mistake	Discovered by verification or validation?	Description of method that could have been used to prevent the mistake

---

Student answer 1

(a) **(i)** *The information about a thing or person.*   **(iii)** *The whole lot of information about a thing or person.*

    (ii) *A row in the table.*

(b)

Description of mistake	Discovered by verification or validation?	Description of method that could have been used to prevent the mistake
Wrong date of birth 34/08/09 is impossible as the days in August only go up to 31	Validation	Range check on the days in the date to ensure it is equal to or less than 31
Forename has wrong name entered – Jaccck should be spelt Jack	Verification	Use a spellchecker to make sure that the name is spelt correctly

---

▲ **Examiner's comment**

(a) **(i)** The student has defined a record here instead of a field. No marks.

    (ii) This answer is a bit brief but worth one mark. A more complete answer would be to say that it is the details about a person, thing or transaction. An example would be the detail about one student which is a row in the table.

    (iii) This statement is a bit vague so no mark is given. If they had given an example such as a collection of all the records about students in the school, then this would have been clearer.

(b) The first row of answers are all correct. The last answer about a range check is OK but if you allocate a data type of Date to a field then you cannot enter an impossible date.

The second row contains a typing error and it is not appropriate to use spellcheckers with the names of people. The first two answers are correct for a mark each but the last answer gains no marks. *(6 marks out of 9)*

Student answer 2

(a) (i) A field is an item of data or a fact about a student. Date of birth is an example of a field.

(ii) A record is a collection of fields about a person or thing. Here it is information about a particular student.

(iii) A file is a complete collection of records and would be the complete records of every student in the school.

(b)

Description of mistake	Discovered by verification or validation?	Description of method that could have been used to prevent the mistake
Incorrect date of birth 34/08/09 This is an impossible date	Validation	Use Date format for the field. Once this is set, the computer will not allow an incorrect date to be entered
Typing error Jaccck should be spelt Jack.	Verification	Use a visual check Check by reading the entered data on the screen and correct any mistakes

▲ **Examiner's comment**

(a) (i) This is a good answers and notice the way the student has referred to the data in the table as an example. One mark for this.

(ii) Another good answer gains another mark.

(iii) Again another mark.

(b) The answers to all the parts to this answer are clear and the student has used and understood the terminology. Full marks are given for this part.

(9 marks out of 9)

Examiner's answers

(a) (i) One mark for a definition such as:

A field is an item of data such as surname, date of birth, etc.

(ii) One mark for a definition such as:

A record is a collection of fields about a person or thing.

A line in the table about one particular student is a record.

(iii) One mark for a definition such as:

A file is a collection of records that forms the complete set of information about a thing or person.

The details of all the records of all the students in a school is a file.

(b) One mark for each correct answer in the table to a maximum of six marks.

Description of mistake	Discovered by verification or validation?	Description of method that could have been used to prevent the mistake
Invalid date/wrong number of days for the month/cannot have more than 31 days in a month	Validation	Use Date format/set data type to Date Use a range check/restrict day to 31 or less
Typing error/transcription error Jaccck should be Jack	Verification	Use a visual check/proof read/get person who is the data subject to check their record

Summary mind map

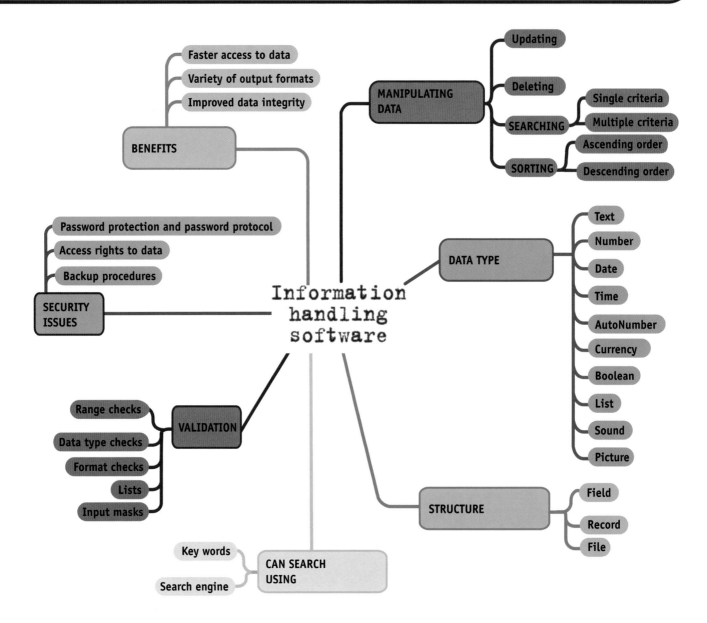

Email

The key concepts covered in this topic are:

- **The facilities offered by email**
- **The advantages and disadvantages of using email**
- **The measures taken to prevent misuse of email services**

Email has become as familiar to most people as receiving their normal post through the letter box. It is a service we all use and like mobile phones it would be difficult to do without. Much of the material in this topic will be familiar to you, as you will likely use email on a day-to-day basis. There will be some things that will be new to you.

Contents

The facilities offered by email

You will find out

▷ **About how to create a standard outgoing signature and message**

▷ **About how to send the email to one other email address**

▷ **About how to send a group email**

▷ **About the use of cc and bcc**

▷ **About the use of file attachments**

▷ **About how to forward email to another email address**

▷ **About how to create and manage an address book**

▷ **About how to organize and name email groups and folders**

An email is an electronic message sent from one communication device (computer, telephone, mobile phone, or PDA) to another.

All web browser software has email facilities.

Creating a standard outgoing signature and message

Email signatures allow you to add a personal touch to your email by adding some or all of the following:

- name
- screen name
- address
- phone number
- job title
- a brief message
- favourite quote.

Signatures can be added after you have composed your email by clicking on the signature button. You then get a window where you can enter the details for your signature. The email program will remember this for next time so you only have to enter it the once. You can have lots of signatures depending on who you are sending the email to and each signature can be given a name.

There are many email facilities but those shown here are the main time-saving ones.

Search: Search allows you to find an email using keywords in the title or you can search for all the emails from or to a certain email address.

Reply: This allows you to read an email and then write the reply without having to enter the recipient's email address. As the recipient is sent both the original email and your reply they can save time because they know what your email is about.

Activity

Looking for online quotes

Some people put interesting quotes in their email signature.

Use the following to find a suitable quote for use in the next activity: http://www.wisdomquotes.com/

Forward: If you are sent an email that you think others should see, you can forward it to them. An email, for example sent to you by your boss, could be forwarded to everyone who works with you in a team.

Address book: In the address book are the names and email addresses of all the people to whom you are likely to send email. Instead of having to type in the address when writing an email, you just click on the email address or addresses in the address book.

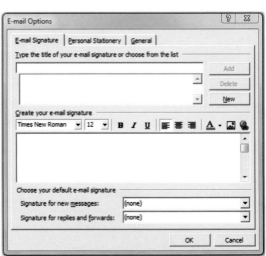

▲ When you set up a signature, a window appears where you type in the information for your signature.

Creating a signature

For this activity you have to find out how email signatures work for the email software you use. If you get stuck remember that you will be able to get online help about this.

Send the email containing the signature to yourself (i.e., the sent to address will be your own email address).

Creating and sending an email to a group

For this activity you are required to produce a distribution list so that the same email can be sent to a group of people. You will need to find out how to do this yourself.

Send the same email to four of your friends and check that they all received it.

▲ The screenshot shows an address book. Rather than type in the email address of the recipients and maybe make mistakes, you can simply click on their address. Notice the facility to create groups.

You can get the email software to automatically add people to your address book if they have sent you or you have sent them email.

Groups

Groups are lists of people and their email addresses. They are used when an email needs to be distributed to people in a particular group. For example, if you were working as part of a team and needed to send each member the same email, then you would set up a group. Every time you needed to send the members of the group email, you could then just send the one email to the group thus saving time.

▲ Using the advanced features of email, you can create groups.

Using cc (carbon copy) and bcc (blind carbon copy)

cc means carbon copy and it is used when you want to send an email to one person but you also want others to see the email you are sending. To do this you enter the email address of the main person you are sending it to and in the box marked cc you enter all the email addresses, separated by commas, of all the people you wish to receive a copy.

bcc means blind carbon copy and this is where you want to send an email to one person and others but you do not want the others to see each other's email addresses.

For example, a form teacher may send an email to a student about their bullying and send copies of the same email to the students and parents of the children who had been bullied. It makes sense not to allow the person doing the bullying to see the email addresses of all the people sent copies.

File attachments

You can attach files to emails. For example, you could attach a file containing a photograph of yourself obtained from a digital camera, a piece of clip art, a picture that you have scanned in, a long document, etc. Basically, if you can store it as a file, then you can attach it to email.

You can attach more than one file to email, so if you had six photographs to send, then you could attach them and send them.

Before you attach a file you must first prepare an email message to send, explaining the purpose of your email and also giving some information about the files that you are sending (what their purpose is, what file format they are in, etc.). Once the email message has been completed, you click on the file attachment button and select the file you want to send. A box will appear to allow you to select the drive, folder and eventually the file that you want to send.

The facilities offered by email *continued*

If you want to send more than one file, you can select a group of files and attach them. Usually, if there are lots of files to send, the files will be compressed to reduce the time taken to send them.

Create and manage an address book

An address book is part of an email package and it is here you can enter all your contacts' details such as names, addresses, telephone numbers and email addresses. Setting this up takes a little time but once it is set up it is easy to send emails because you only have to click on the name and the email address is automatically entered.

You can also set the address up so that everyone who sends you an email has their address automatically added to your address book.

Organize and name email groups and folders

Rather than keep all the emails together it is better to be organized and set up folders. The way this is done depends on the email package you are using. When sending emails you can organize them in a similar way. For example, you could keep your personal emails in a separate folder to school/college-related work.

It is important to remember to back up emails, as people tend to forget to do this.

KEY WORD

File attachment a file that is attached to an email.

To...	email adress of the person to which you want to send the original email
Cc...	email address 1, email address 2, email address 2
Subject:	Re: School bullying

▲ The cc section contains the email addresses of all the people to be sent a copy of the original email.

Questions A

1 Most schools email as a method of communication between staff and students.
   (a) Define what is meant by email. *(2 marks)*
   (b) Teachers often use carbon copy (cc) emails. Explain what is meant by a carbon copy email and give **one** example of how a teacher might use the facility. *(3 marks)*
   (c) Teachers also make use of a facility of email called groups. Explain the purpose of this facility and give **one** example of how a teacher might use groups. *(3 marks)*

2 There are a number of facilities that help a user of email. Give **one** way in which each of the following can help a user of email:
   (a) Address book. *(1 mark)*
   (b) Groups. *(1 mark)*
   (c) File attachments. *(1 mark)*

Extension activity

Practise the use of some of the techniques covered in this chapter. As all email software is slightly different, they all include the facilities covered here.

You should check that you can create an address book and set up groups.

Also try attaching files so that you can send them to yourself at your home email address. This is a good way of backing up your work.

The advantages and disadvantages of email and preventing misuse

You will find out

▷ **About the advantages and disadvantages of using email**

▷ **About the measures taken to prevent the misuse of email services**

There is no doubt that emails have made most people's lives easier, for example enabling us to receive confirmations about products and services we have bought online.

In this section you will be looking at the advantages that email offers and also some of the disadvantages. As always there are people around who misuse the email service and you have to be aware of the various misuses and how to protect against them.

The advantages and disadvantages of email

There are many advantages and disadvantages in using email and here are some of the main ones.

Advantages

- Virtually instantaneous – mail is sent immediately and a reply can be received as soon as the recipient checks their email box.
- No need for the formality of a letter. Email is meant to be quick and to the point. You do not need to worry about the odd typing or spelling mistake.
- You can easily attach a copy of the sender's message with your reply so they do not have to search for the original message.
- If you discount the cost of hardware and software that the user will probably already have, then an email is virtually free to send.
- Emails can be accessed using a large number of devices from mobile phones to television.
- Emails are more environmentally friendly since less energy is used in delivering the mail from source to destination.

Copyright 2005 by Randy Glasbergen.
www.glasbergen.com

Disadvantages

- Not everyone has a computer, so ordinary post is still used.
- It may make users more casual about their approach to business and they may not realize that anything they say is as legally binding as if they had written it in a more formal document such as a letter or a contract.
- Junk mail is a problem, although there are software solutions that filter junk mail out from your important mail.
- There are worries about the security aspects.
- The system relies on people checking their email boxes regularly.
- Emails and particularly those containing file attachments can contain viruses.
- Email is not secure and emails can be intercepted and read.

"I sent you an e-mail and forwarded a copy to your PDA, cell phone, and home computer. I also faxed a copy to your office assistant and laptop. Then I snail-mailed hard copies to you on paper, floppy, and CD. But in case you don't receive it, I'll just tell you what it said..."

The advantages and disadvantages of email and preventing misuse *continued*

The measures that need to be taken to prevent the misuse of email services

There are a number of misuses of email services and precautions need to be taken in order to prevent damage from these misuses. These precautions include:

- Email monitoring – this can be done by the state to detect and prosecute terrorists and criminals. It can also be performed by software that automatically detects abusive emails or those containing inappropriate language. Monitoring can help prevent cyberbullying.
- Email parental control – parents can set whether their children can send or receive all email or just to or from selected people.
- Email encryption – encrypting email messages means they can only be read by the intended recipient.
- Spam (unsolicited/unasked for email) – use software called a spam filter that will remove spam automatically.
- Virus attack – attachments to emails should not be opened unless you know who they are from or they are from a trusted source. The latest virus scanning software should be used to ensure any viruses that enter are discovered and removed.

▼ Parental controls prevent young children sending and receiving inappropriate email.

▲ Spam filters trap spam email but sometimes emails you want can end up there.

▲ Emails can be monitored by the network manager.

Cyberbullying

Sending lots of personal email in firm's time

Inappropriate language (e.g., swearing)

Examples of email abuse

Inappropriate attachments (e.g., offensive jokes, pornography, etc.)

Sending spam

Attaching files containing viruses

Questions B

1 **(a)** Other than the speed at which emails can be sent and received, describe **two** advantages in using email. *(2 marks)*

(b) Other than the fact that emails are not secure, describe **two** disadvantages in using email. *(2 marks)*

2 Email systems can be subject to misuse.
Describe **two** misuses of email services and explain what can be done in order to prevent each misuse. *(4 marks)*

Extension activity

Imagine you are the owner of a firm that employs a number of people. All of your employees need to use email as part of their job.

There have been a number of incidents where the email system has been abused and you want to make sure that it does not happen again.

Write a list of rules that your employees must follow when using the email facilities.

Questions

 Test yourself

The following notes summarize this topic. The notes are incomplete because they have words missing.

Using the words in the list below, copy out and complete the sentences A to J, underlining the words that you have inserted. Each word may be used more than once.

address	bcc	forward	spam	cc

encrypted	attachment	monitoring	signature

A In order to send an email you need the other person's email _____.

B You can add an email _____ at the end of an email that can include your name, phone number, your job and even a fun quotation.

C The names and email addresses of all the people to whom you are likely to send email are stored in an email _____ book.

D If you are sent an email that you think others should see, you can _____ it to them.

E When you want to send the one email to a person and then send copies to other people you can use _____.

F If you want to send copies of an email to others but you do not want them to see all the other recipients' email addresses then you can use _____.

G A file that is attached to an email is called a file _____.

H If it is important that the email is not intercepted and read by hackers then the email should be _____.

I Email _____ is sometimes performed by the state to detect and prosecute terrorists and criminals.

J It is possible to use special software to filter out emails that are unasked for, which are popularly called _____.

Examination style questions

1 A teacher at a school likes students to word-process their homework and submit it to her by email.
   (a) Define what is meant by email. *(2 marks)*
   (b) Give **one** advantage in a student sending their homework to their teacher by email. *(1 mark)*
   (c) In order to send the homework to the teacher the student uses a file attachment.
       Explain what is meant by a file attachment. *(1 mark)*
   (d) When the file attached to the email is large, the email says that the file is being compressed. Give **one** reason why the email package compresses the file before sending. *(1 mark)*

2 A health centre has lots of people working there such as doctors, nurses, midwives, physiotherapists, etc., who work together as a team. They need to pass messages to each other. As the staff work different hours and in different parts of the building, communicating with each other can be difficult.
   (a) Explain **three** advantages of the staff contacting each other by email rather than by phone. *(6 marks)*
   (b) Describe **two** facilities provided by email software that will make it a lot easier to work as a team. *(4 marks)*

END-OF-TOPIC REVIEW

Exam support

Worked example

A software developer is working as part of a team of ten developers who are developing new software for an online loans company. The team members work in different parts of the country.

The developers need to keep in touch with each other and need to pass work (mainly programs, screen designs, etc.) to each other.

(a) Explain **three** advantages of the developers contacting each other by email rather than by post. *(6 marks)*

(b) Describe **two** facilities provided by email software that will make it a lot easier to work as a team. *(4 marks)*

Student answer 1

(a) Cheaper
Faster
Better

(b) Being able to send the email to more than one person.

Being able to attach a file to an email.

Student answer 2

(a) Sending emails speeds things up. An email can be sent and replied to in seconds, whereas a letter sent and replied to takes several days.

It is cheaper, as there is no cost for paper, printing, envelopes and stamps.

It is faster to send an email and get a reply.

(b) It is possible to create groups and send the same email to all the members of the group rather than send each email separately.

They can attach other files to the email such as programs and screen design and this avoids them having to save them onto removable media such as CD.

▲ **Examiner's comment**

(a) The word 'explain' means that a one word answer is not enough. There are 6 marks allocated here. One mark will be allocated to the clear explanation of the advantage with the other mark for the brief explanation of how it relates to working in teams.

Avoid general words like 'better'. You need to be specific. General words such as faster, cheaper, better gain no marks. *(0 marks out of 6)*

(b) 'Being able to send the email to more than one person' is a facility of email software but there needs to be a fuller explanation as to how this facility will make things easier when working as a team.

It is important to tailor answers to the information given in the question.

Again 'Being able to attach a file to an email' is a facility provided by email software. There needs to be further elaboration on why this is an advantage. *(2 marks out of 4)*

▲ **Examiner's comment**

(a) The first two answers are good answers and would get full marks.

The third answer is almost a repeat of the first answer. It is always important to check your answer is not similar to an answer already given. *(4 marks out of 6)*

(b) Both answers are good and gain full marks. *(4 marks out of 4)*

Examiner's answers

(a) Any three advantages (2 marks each) such as:

- Email is cheaper than a letter. No stamp, envelope or paper is needed. There is also a time saving so this makes email cheaper. Even if the email is sent across the world, it will not cost any more than a local email.
- Quick to write. They are informal, meaning that people do not spend time on the layout and the odd spelling mistake is acceptable.
- Ideal if there is a time difference. The reader can check email when they are ready.
- Inexpensive and easy to send the same email message to lots of different people.
- You can attach a copy of the sender's email with your reply, so this saves them having to search for the original message.
- You do not have to go out to a post box, so it saves time.
- You do not have to waste time shopping for stamps, envelopes and paper.
- Fast. It takes seconds to send and receive email. If the person at the other end checks their email regularly, then a reply can be sent very quickly.

(b) Two facilities (2 marks each) such as:

- Groups/distribution lists – allowing you to send the same email to a group of people without having to select individual email addresses.
- File attachments – being able to attach files to an email so others can download the work onto their own computers and can comment on it.

EXAM TIPS

If you are asked to 'explain' something then giving a one or two word example is not sufficient. You must include a sentence.

If you are asked to 'give' an answer, then a one or two word answer is ok.

The word 'describe' means that you must give your answer in sentences. Be guided by the mark scheme as to how much you need to write. If there are two marks then the minimum you need is two clearly different points. It is important to note that you are never penalized for writing too much, although you may waste some time.

Be careful about being too creative in your English. You are always limited by the number of lines given for your answer on the paper. Most students get to the end of the number of lines and stop. You need to work out your answer and try to convey it with the minimum number of words. This gives you plenty of room for making more points.

Summary mind maps

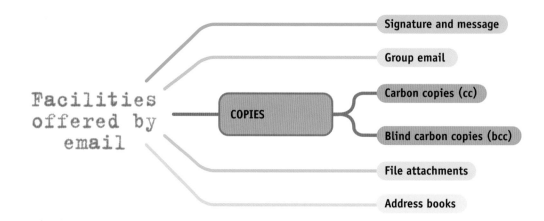

Facilities offered by email
- **COPIES**
  - Signature and message
  - Group email
  - Carbon copies (cc)
  - Blind carbon copies (bcc)
  - File attachments
  - Address books

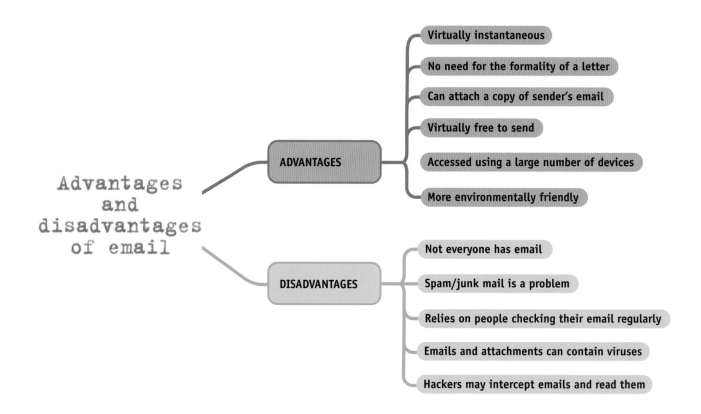

Advantages and disadvantages of email
- **ADVANTAGES**
  - Virtually instantaneous
  - No need for the formality of a letter
  - Can attach a copy of sender's email
  - Virtually free to send
  - Accessed using a large number of devices
  - More environmentally friendly
- **DISADVANTAGES**
  - Not everyone has email
  - Spam/junk mail is a problem
  - Relies on people checking their email regularly
  - Emails and attachments can contain viruses
  - Hackers may intercept emails and read them

Topic 10
Spreadsheet software

The key concepts covered in this topic are:

- **Labels, data and formulas**
- **Formulas and functions**
- **Absolute and relative cell referencing**
- **Formatting techniques**
- **Cell merging**
- **The benefits of using spreadsheets**

You will have used spreadsheet software before as part of your Key Stage 3 studies. Spreadsheets are ideal if you are dealing with numerical data or need to produce graphs and charts.

In this topic you will be building on your knowledge of spreadsheets.

Contents

Spreadsheet basics

You will find out

▷ **About labels, data and formulas**

▷ **About formulas and functions**

▷ **About absolute and relative cell referencing**

You will already be familiar with many features and functions of spreadsheet software. This section seeks to revise some of the basics of spreadsheets but also to let you know what other features are available in spreadsheet software and how they are used.

You will, of course, have to develop spreadsheets and build up your practical skills in using some of the techniques and knowledge covered in this topic.

Labels, data and formulas

Just as a reminder, here are the basics of spreadsheets.

The concept of rows, columns, cells and cell references

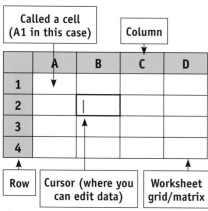

▲ Rows, columns, cells and cell references.

Labels

Labels are used for titles, headings, names, and for identifying *columns* of data. You should never have values on a spreadsheet without labels, as a user will be left wondering what they represent.

Data

Data are the values (text or numbers) that you enter into the spreadsheet. It is the data that will be used for calculations or for producing graphs and charts.

Formulas

Formulas are used to perform calculations on the cell contents.

In order to distinguish between text and formulas a symbol, =, needs to be typed in first, like this =B3+B4.

Here are some calculations and what they do. Notice that you can use upper or lower case letters (i.e. capital or small letters).

=C3+C4 (adds the numbers in cells C3 and C4 together)
=A1*B4 (multiplies the numbers in cells A1 and B4 together)
=3*G4 (multiplies the number in cell G4 by 3)
=sum(b3:b10) (adds up all the cells from b3 to b10 inclusive)
=C4/D1 (divides the number in cell C4 by the number in cell D1)
=30/100*A2 (finds 30% of the number in cell A2)

Formulas and functions

A function is a specialized calculation that the spreadsheet software has memorized. There are many of these functions, some of which are very specialized.

A function must start with an equals sign (=) and it must have a range of cells to which it applies in brackets after it.

Average:
For example, to find the average of the numbers in a range of cells from A3 to A10 you would use: =AVERAGE(A3:A10)

Maximum: =MAX(D3:J3) displays the largest number in all the cells from D3 to J3 inclusive.

Minimum: =MIN(D3:J3) displays the smallest number in all the cells from D3 to J3 inclusive.

Mode: =MODE(A3:A15) displays the mode (i.e., the most frequent number) in the cells from A3 to A15 inclusive.

Median: =MEDIAN(B2:W2) displays the median of the cells from cells B2 to W2 inclusive.

Sum: =SUM(E3:P3) displays the total of all the cells from cells E3 to P3 inclusive.

COUNT: Suppose we want to count the number of numeric entries in the range C3 to C30.

We can use =COUNT(C3:C30). Any blank lines or text entries in the range will not be counted.

COUNTA: To count a number of items or names of people we need to be able to count text entries. To do this we can use =COUNTA(C3:C30).

You need to make sure that headings are not included in the range so that they are not counted as well. Again blank lines are not counted.

IF: The IF function is called a logical function because it makes the decision to do one of two things based on the value it is testing. The IF function is very useful because you can use it to test a condition and then choose between two actions based on whether the condition is true or false.

The IF function makes use of something called relational

operators. You may have come across these in your mathematics lessons but it is worth going through what they mean.

Relational operators
(=, <, >, <>, <=, >=)

Symbol	Meaning	Examples
=	equals	5 + 5 = 10
>	greater than	5*3 > 2*3
<	less than	-6 < -1 or 100 < 200
<>	not equal to	"Red" <> "White" or 20/4 <> 6*4
<=	less than or equal to	"Adam" <= "Eve"
>=	greater than or equal to	400 >= 200

▲ Relational operators.

Here are some examples of the use of a single IF function:

=IF(B3>=50,"Pass","Fail")

This function tests to see if the number in cell B3 is greater than or equal to 50. If the answer is true, Pass is displayed and if the answer is false, Fail is displayed.

=IF(A2>=500,A2*0.5,A2)

This tests to see if the number in cell A2 is greater than or equal to 500. If true, the number in cell A2 will be multiplied by 0.5 and the answer displayed (i.e. 250 will be displayed). If false, the number in cell A2 will be displayed.

Absolute and relative cell referencing

There are two ways in which you can make a reference to another cell and it is important to know the difference if you want to copy or move cells. An absolute reference always refers to the same cell. The other type of reference, called a relative reference, refers to a cell that is a certain number of rows and columns away. When the current cell is copied or moved to a new position, the cell to which the reference is made will also change position.

To understand the difference we will look at two examples. The first example shows relative referencing with cell B4 containing a relative reference to cell A1. This reference tells the spreadsheet that the cell to which it refers is 3 cells up and one cell to the left of cell B4. If cell B4 is copied to another position, say E5, then the reference will still be to the same number of cells up and to the left, so the reference will now be to cell D2.

	A	B	C	D	E
1		←			
2					←
3					
4		=A1			
5					
6					

▲ Relative cell referencing.

With absolute cell referencing, if cell B4 contains a reference to cell A1, then if the contents of B4 are copied to a new position, then the reference will not be adjusted and it will still refer to cell A1.

In most cases we will want to use relative cell references and the spreadsheet will assume that ordinary cell references are relative cell references. Sometimes we want to refer to the same cell, even when the formula referring to the cell is copied to a new position. We therefore need to make sure that the formula contains an absolute cell reference. To do this, a dollar sign is placed in front of the column and row number.

Cell B6 is a relative cell reference. To change it to an absolute cell reference we would add the dollar signs like this: B6.

	A	B	C	D	E
1		←			
2					
3					
4		=A1			
5					
6					

▲ Absolute cell referencing.

Questions A

1 Cells can contain labels, data or formulas.
   (a) Explain what is meant by labels. *(1 mark)*
   (b) Explain what is meant by data. *(1 mark)*
   (c) Explain what is meant by a formula. *(1 mark)*

2 There are **two** different types of cell reference. Give the names of both of them. *(2 marks)*

3 Give the names of **two** functions that can be used in a spreadsheet. *(2 marks)*

Formatting techniques and the benefits of using spreadsheets

▷ **About a range of formatting techniques such as borders, formatting cells to currency, etc.**

▷ **About the benefits in using spreadsheet software**

You can make a document you produce using word-processing software easy to read by formatting it. For example, you can use different font styles for headings and subheadings and you can alter the font size so that the more important text is larger. You can change the colours and can use bold, italics, etc. In a similar way you can format the data and labels in a spreadsheet to improve its readability and appearance.

In this section you will learn about the different types of formatting that you can use with a spreadsheet.

You will also learn about the benefits in using spreadsheet software.

Formatting cells to match data types

There are many different types of data and some of these are shown in the following table:

Type of data	Example of data
Date	12/12/10
Integer (a whole number)	34
Decimal number	3.14
Percentage	4%
Currency	£3.45
Text	Jenny Hayter

If the general number format is used (which it will be unless you tell the software otherwise) the numbers will be shown with up to eleven digits (including all the numbers up to and after the decimal point). A cell that has a formula typed in will show the results of the formula rather than the formula itself.

Cells need to be able to hold the data you want to put into them. The spreadsheet will interpret the data you put into the cell. What is displayed in a cell depends on the cell format.

Although each cell is set to the general number format, it can change automatically depending on the data you type in. If you type in a pound sign followed by a number, the spreadsheet will assume that you are dealing with currency and will format the cell to currency automatically. It will only show the currency to two decimal places, so if you typed in £1.349, '£1.35' would be shown.

For large numbers you often use a comma to make them easier to read (e.g. 3,000,000). As soon as such a number is entered with the commas, the spreadsheet will apply the number format with the thousands separator and use a maximum of two decimal places.

If a number is entered ending in a % sign (e.g. 4%), then the spreadsheet will set the cell automatically to the percent format with two decimal places.

Cell presentation formats

Data can be presented in cells in a variety of different ways. We will look at these in this section.

Aligning cells

When you enter data into a cell, the spreadsheet automatically aligns (i.e. positions) the cells according to the following:

- Numbers are aligned to the right.
- Text is aligned to the left.

Do not put any spaces in front of numbers in order to align them as this will make it impossible for the spreadsheet to use the numbers in calculations.

If you want to align the data differently, you can use the special buttons for alignment on the formatting toolbar. Using this method, you can align them to the left, right or centre.

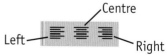

▲ **Text alignment buttons.**

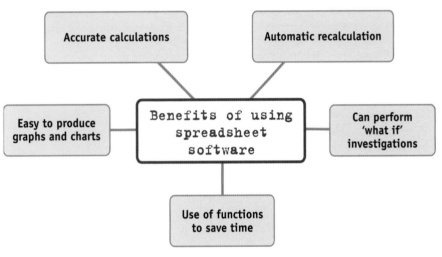

Arial | 10 | **B** *I* <u>U</u> ≡ ≡ ≡ ⊞ | 💲 % , ⁺⁰⁰ ⁺⁰⁰ | 律 律 | ⊞ ▾ ◇ ▾ **A** ▾

▲ Formatting toolbar.

Formatting text to make it stand out

Text can be made to stand out by formatting it in a number of ways:

Font type – changes the shapes of letters and numbers.

- Font size – used to make headings, subheadings, etc., stand out.
- Bold, Italics, Underline – used to draw attention to text.

Borders and rotating text

Using borders you can: put a border around cells or groups of cells, shade in certain cells or groups of cells.

Rotating text is useful when you want a narrow column but the column heading is wide.

Adding colour

Colour may be added to:

- text
- borders
- background colours for cells.

Cell merging

Sometimes a label may be too big to fit into a single cell and when this happens it can be made to overflow into the other cells. This is called cell merging.

The benefits of using spreadsheet software

There are lots of benefits in using spreadsheet software such as:

- You can perform 'what if' investigations – you can make changes to the spreadsheet values to see what happens. For example, you may set up a spreadsheet to manage your money. You could see the effect on your finances of getting a part-time job paying £80 per week.

- Automatic recalculation – when an item of data changes, all those cells that are connected to the changed cell by a formula will also change.
- Accurate calculation – provided the formulas are all correct, the calculations on the numbers will always be correct.

- It is easy to produce graphs and charts – once the data has been entered, it is very easy for the spreadsheet to produce graphs and charts based on it.

Accurate calculations

Automatic recalculation

Easy to produce graphs and charts

Benefits of using spreadsheet software

Can perform 'what if' investigations

Use of functions to save time

▲ The benefits of using spreadsheet software.

Questions B

1 Here are some statements concerning the reasons for putting formulas into spreadsheets.
Put a tick next to those reasons that are correct. *(1 mark)*

Reason	Tick if reason is correct
If a cell changes, then all those cells that depend on the cell will change	
A more accurate answer is produced than with a calculator	
It improves the appearance of the spreadsheet	
The formulas in the spreadsheet need to be kept secret	

2 Describe **two** different ways a cell can be formatted to make it stand out. *(2 marks)*

END-OF-TOPIC REVIEW

Questions

 Test yourself

The following notes summarize this topic. The notes are incomplete because they have words missing.

Using the words in the list below, copy out and complete the sentences A to J, underlining the words that you have inserted. Each word may be used more than once.

predictions   data   specialist

formulas   labels   absolute

relative   recalculation

A _____ are the text and numbers that are entered into the spreadsheet.

B _____ are used for titles, headings, names and for identifying columns of data.

C _____ are used for performing calculations on the contents of cells.

D Functions are _____ calculations.

E There are two ways in which a cell in a formula can be referenced; relative cell referencing and _____ cell referencing.

F Unless you tell it otherwise, a formula in a spreadsheet will always use _____ cell referencing.

G A reference to a cell in a formula where, when the formula is copied to a new address, the cell address does not change, is called _____ referencing.

H When a cell is used in a formula and the formula is copied to a new address and the cell address changes to take account of the formula's new position this is called _____ referencing.

I One advantage of a spreadsheet is that you can change information/data in a spreadsheet model to make and test _____.

J When a value in a spreadsheet changes, then all those cells which depend on that and are linked with a formula will also change. This is called auto _____.

Examination style questions

1 Explain the meaning of the following mathematical operators that are used in spreadsheets. *(4 marks)*

/

+

*

–

2 The diagram shows a simple spreadsheet that a student uses to help budget her money.
  (a) Write down the contents of cell A4. *(1 mark)*
  (b) Write down the contents of cell B7. *(1 mark)*
  (c) Put a tick in the boxes next to those formulas that would correctly work out the total of her expenditure when placed in cell B8. *(2 marks)*

Formula	Tick if formula gives correct total
=B2+B3+B4+B5+B6+B7+B8	
+A2+A3+A4+A5+A6+A7	
=sum(B2:B7)	
=sum(A2:A7)	
=B2+B3+B4+B5+B6+B7	

	A	B	C
1			
2	Rent	£32.50	
3	Food	£13.00	
4	Electricity	£2.50	
5	Phone	£1.50	
6	Gas	£4.00	
7	Entertainment	£15.00	
8	Total		
9			

3 A teacher has produced the following spreadsheet that records the marks in four examinations and works out the total mark.

	A	B	C	D	E	F	G
1	Forename	Surname	Exam 1	Exam 2	Exam 3	Exam 4	Total
2	Amy	Huges	56	34	67	78	235
3	Jack	Danniels	56	58	45	56	215
4	John	Harris	77	89	77	89	332
5	Asif	Khan	57	79	75	78	289
6	Ian	Handley	33	75	85	88	281
7	Daisy	Doyle	74	45	88	90	297
8	Jane	Adams	90	89	55	87	321
9	Danielle	Prescott	87	90	77	77	331
10	Harry	Sumner	99	100	88	90	377
11	Jane	Hughes	45	56	65	66	232
12	Adam	Jackson	55	50	45	54	204
13							
14							
15	Average mark for all pupils						

(a) Which of the following formulas would correctly give the total in cell G2? *(1 mark)*
  A   =SUM(C2:C12)
  B   =C2+D2+E2+F2+G2
  C   =SUM(C2:F2)
  D   =SUM(C2*F2)

(b) Give a suitable formula to put into cell D15 to calculate the average of the numbers in column G. *(1 mark)*

(c) Which cell formatting feature has been used in column A? *(1 mark)*

(d) The text 'Average mark for all pupils' has cell formatting applied to it. Give the name of the cell formatting used. *(1 mark)*

(e) Give **two** advantages of using spreadsheet software rather than working out the totals using pen, paper and a calculator. *(2 marks)*

Exam support

Worked example

Yasmin has started work after leaving university and has to live away from home. She has recorded her wages and costs in a spreadsheet and this is shown here.

	A	B	C	D	E	F	G	H	I	J
1	Month	Wages	Electricity	Gas	Phone	Rent	Clothes	Food	Total costs	Money left over
2	Jan	£1,500	£60	£55	£62	£210	£40	£600	£1,027	£473
3	Feb	£1,520	£60	£55	£65	£210	£40	£600	£1,030	£490
4	Mar	£1,550	£60	£55	£64	£210	£40	£600	£1,029	£521
5	Apr	£1,550	£60	£55	£50	£210	£40	£600	£1,015	£535
6	May	£1,680	£60	£55	£47	£210	£40	£600	£1,012	£668
7	Jun	£1,690	£60	£55	£47	£210	£40	£600	£1,012	£678
8	Jul	£1,730	£60	£55	£53	£210	£40	£600	£1,018	£712
9	Aug	£1,742	£60	£55	£54	£210	£40	£600	£1,019	£723
10	Sep	£1,800	£60	£55	£62	£210	£40	£600	£1,027	£773
11	Oct	£1,800	£60	£55	£44	£210	£40	£600	£1,009	£791
12	Nov	£1,800	£60	£55	£39	£210	£40	£600	£1,004	£796
13	Dec	£1,745	£60	£55	£53	£210	£40	£600	£1,018	£727
14										

(a) Which one of the following formulas could be used to work out the **Total costs** in cell **I2?** *(1 mark)*

A =SUM(I2:I13)
B =I2+I3+I4+I6+I7+I8
C =SUM(B2:H2)
D =B2+C2+D2+E2+F2+H2+I2

(b) Give a suitable formula that could be entered into cell J2 to work out the money Yasmin has over at the end of the month. *(1 mark)*

(c) The cells apart from cells in column A and row 1 have been formatted.

Which of the following types of cell formatting have been used for these cells? *(1 mark)*

A Euros
B Calculation
C Currency
D Right align

(d) Labels are important in spreadsheets. Give the cell reference of a cell containing a label. *(1 mark)*

(e) Give two advantages of Yasmin using a spreadsheet such as this to help her budget her money. *(2 marks)*

Student answer 1

(a) D

(b) B2–I2

(c) C

(d) A1

(e) It is quicker

It is more efficient

◀ **Examiner's comment**

(a) When adding up cells you do not include the cell where the answer is to be put so this answer is wrong.

(b) The student has forgotten to put the equals sign in front of this formula (i.e. =B2-I2). This small point has cost this student a mark here.

(c) This is correct so one mark here.

(d) A label is any cell that describes data on the spreadsheet so this is correct and gains one mark.

(e) This is a typical answer given by a weak student. The student needs to say in what way is it quicker and in what way is it more efficient. No marks for either of these answers.

(2 marks out of 6)

Student answer 2

(a) C=SUM(B2:H2)

(b) =B2–I2

(c) C Currency

(d) Row 1

(e) Provided the calculations have been set up correctly and tested, the formulas will always produce a correct calculation.

When one of the numbers in the spreadsheet is changed, the cells that depend on the changed cell will recalculate automatically.

◀ **Examiner's comment**

(a) This is correct so one mark here.

(b) This is correct so one mark here.

(c) This is correct so one mark here.

(d) All the cells in row 1 do contain labels but the question asks for a cell reference so this is an incorrect answer so no marks.

(e) These are both very good answers and worth a mark each.

(5 marks out of 6)

Examiner's answers

(a) One mark for the letter, formula or both (i.e. C = SUM(B2:H2))

(b) One mark for a correct formula which must include the equals sign

(i.e. =B2–I2)

(c) One mark for C Currency

(d) One mark for any cell reference in row 1 or column A. It must be a cell reference and not a column letter or row number.

(e) One mark for each of two advantages of a spreadsheet such as:

- If set up correctly, the formulas will always produce a correct calculation.
- Automatic recalculation when numbers are changed in the spreadsheet.
- Once the spreadsheet has been set up it can be reused for different years by putting in different data.
- The data can easily be represented pictorially by getting the spreadsheet to produce graphs and charts.
- You can change the information in the spreadsheet in order to make and test 'what if' scenarios.

Summary mind map

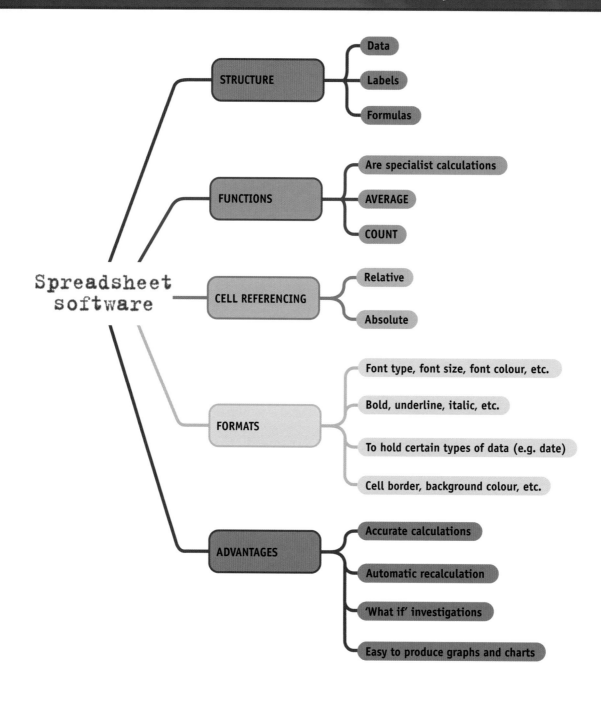

Topic 11

DTP software

The key concepts covered in this topic are:

- The purpose and use of a spellchecker, online thesaurus and mail merge
- Automatic routines such as: style sheets, headers and footers, pagination and automatic table of contents production
- Justification (e.g., left, centre, fully justify)
- Changes in font type, font style and font size
- Importing different file formats (e.g., clip art, csv, txt, rtf, etc.)
- Tabulation
- Tables
- Borders
- Single and double line spacing
- Manipulation of graphics such as resizing, cropping, rotating and mirror imaging
- AutoShapes
- Watermarks

The distinction between word-processing and desktop publishing is blurred because there are many desktop publishing features in word-processing software. Bringing lots of different files together to form a document is the main feature of a specialist desktop publishing package. In this topic we will cover features that are either features of word-processing software or desktop publishing software.

Contents

Spellchecker, online thesaurus, mail merge and automatic routines

When using ICT for the production of documents there are a number of special features that help take the drudgery away. For example, performing a mail merge can save a huge amount of time when sending slightly different letters to lots of people.

In this section you will be looking at some of the automatic routines in DTP that save time. These routines enables things to be included on each page in a document. They can also be used to make changes to headings or subheadings only the once and the changes are automatically made on all the pages in the document.

Spellcheckers

Nearly all word-processors contain a dictionary against which all the words in a document may be compared to check their spelling. Most allow you to add words to the dictionary, which is particularly useful if you use special terms such as are used in law or medicine. It is important to note that spellchecking a document will not get rid of all the errors. For instance, if you intended to type 'the' and typed 'he' instead, then the spellchecker will not detect this since 'he' as a word is spelt correctly. After using a spellchecker it is still necessary to visually check or proof read a document.

Thesaurus

A thesaurus is useful for ensuring that you use a variety of words in a sentence. This allows you to highlight a word in a document and the computer lists alternative words with similar meanings (called synonyms).

Mail merge

A mail merge involves combining a list of, say, names and addresses, with a standard letter, so that a series of similar letters is produced, each addressed to a different person. The list is created either by using the word-processor or by importing data from a database of names and addresses. The letter is typed using the word-processor, with blanks where the data from the list will be inserted.

The steps involved in mail merging are outlined below:

- Create a letter to be sent to different people.
- Create a name and address list for the recipients of the letter.
- Insert the variable fields into the letter.
- Merge the names and address details with the letter to produce the personalized letters.

<<Forename>> <<Surname>>
<<Street>>
<<Town>>
<<Postcode>>

Dear <<Forename>>

As you know you will soon be taking your end of year examinations. For those of you in year 11, these will be your GCSE exams. We will be holding a revision club on Mondays and Wednesdays from 4 p.m. to 6 p.m. A variety

▲ **Part of a letter, showing the variable fields.**

▼ **The letter with the variable information added.**

Kerry Jones
3 Grove Street
Liverpool
L7 6TT

Dear Kerry

As you know you will soon be taking your end of year examinations. For those of you in year 11, these will be your GCSE exams. We will be holding a revision club on Mondays and Wednesdays from 4 p.m. to 6 p.m. A variety of staff will be on hand to help you with your revision questions. You should take advantage of this as it is completely free.

There will be a meeting on Wednesday 3rd May at 4 p.m. in the hall for any of you interested in taking up the offer.

Happy revision and good luck.

Automatic routines

Style sheets

It is important to make a document consistent through all its pages. Style sheets are used to help make the text, headings and subheadings consistent throughout all the pages in a document. It means that a heading or subheading is changed once in the style sheet and all the headings or subheadings throughout the document will be changed automatically.

Templates

Rather than create a design from scratch, you can use a design that has already been created. These designs are called templates. Some templates allow you to alter them slightly. The template will often guide you though a series of choices that will tailor-make the design.

Some programs include their own set of designer templates for a variety of documents.

Templates determine the structure of the document. They set things like:

- font types: the style of the letters and numbers used
- page layout: margins, justification (how the sentences are lined up), indents, line spacing (i.e., the spacing between lines of text), page numbering, etc.
- special formatting: bold, italics, etc.

Headers and footers

Headers and footers are used to hold information that appears at the top of the page in the case of a header, and at the bottom of each page of the document in the case of a footer. Headers are placed in the top margin whilst footers are placed in the bottom. You can choose whether the text included in the header or footer is included on every page or just some of the pages.

Here are some types of information that are commonly put into headers and footers:

- page numbers
- today's date

- the title of the document
- a company logo (it can be a graphic image)
- the author's name
- the filename name of the file that is used to hold the document.

Pagination

Pagination is concerned with the appearance of the text on the page and it determines when a page finishes and a new page starts. You could of course leave it to the computer to sort all this out but there are problems in doing this. For example, you may find that a heading appears at the bottom of a page where the reader is least likely to look. It would be even worse if the heading appeared at the bottom of the page on its own with the text to which it refers over the page. It is therefore important during the proof reading process to look out for this and correct it. You can make the computer start a new page by inserting what is called a page break.

Pagination is also concerned with the way the pages are numbered. Pages in documents should always be numbered, as people need to refer to the content of the page by its number.

Automatic table of contents production

Contents are a list at the front of a document outlining the headings and the subheadings of material in a document. If you take a look at the Contents at the front of this book you will see the topic numbers and main headings. Each topic also has its own Contents list with the headings for the material under each spread.

You can identify headings to put into the contents manually or you can specify that all the headings and subheadings are automatically used to create the contents list.

KEY WORDS

Style sheet a document which sets out fonts and font sizes for headings and subheadings, etc., in a document. Changes to a heading need only be made in the style sheet and all the changes to headings in the document will be made automatically.

Templates electronic files that hold standardized document layouts.

Footer text placed at the bottom of a document.

Header text placed at the top of a document.

Questions A

1. (a) Explain the use of a spellchecker. *(2 marks)*
   (b) Explain why despite the use of a spellchecker a document will still need to be proof read or visually checked. *(1 mark)*

2. Explain how the use of the feature called mail merge enables lots of personalized letters to be produced quickly. *(3 marks)*

3. Describe, by giving an example, how an online thesaurus could be used by the writer of a novel. *(2 marks)*

Extension activity

Find out how to perform a simple mail merge using word-processing software.

Use the mail merge to send a personalized letter to ten of your friends.

DTP techniques

You will find out

▷ **About justification (alignment) (e.g., left, right, centre, fully justify)**

▷ **About changes in font type, font style and font size**

▷ **About importing different file formats (e.g., clip art, csv, txt, rtf, etc.)**

▷ **About tabulation**

▷ **About tables**

▷ **About borders**

▷ **About single and double line spacing**

▷ **About manipulation of graphics such as resizing, cropping, rotating and mirror imaging**

▷ **About AutoShapes**

▷ **About watermarks**

In this topic you will lean about the various DTP techniques for laying out pages, formatting text and so on including borders and line spacing. You will also cover using AutoShapes and watermarks.

Also in this section you will look at manipulating graphic images by resizing, cropping, rotating and so on.

Justifying (aligning) text

Justifying text means aligning (lining up) the text in some way. The main buttons for justifying text are shown below.

Align left (also called left justified)

This lines the text up with the left margin but leaves the right-hand side ragged. This alignment is the most common and is the one used by a word-processor unless we tell it to use another.

Align right (also called right justified)

This lines the text up with the right margin but leaves the left-hand margin ragged.

Centre

This lines text up with the centre of the page.

Fully justified (also called justified)

This lines text up with both the right and left margins.

Font type and font size

Changing the font type (e.g., Arial, Times New Roman, etc.) alters the appearance of the characters. Font types are given names and you can change the font by selecting the text and then clicking on the correct part of the formatting toolbar shown

below. Notice also that there is a section for altering the font size (i.e., how big the characters appear).

Click here to alter the font size.

Click here to alter the font type (each font is given a name. In this case the font is called Times New Roman).

Font styles

Font styles include bold (text in heavy type), italic (text slanting to the right) and underlining. These can be used to highlight certain words or text in order to draw particular attention to them.

Importing different file formats

Sometimes data you want to use in a document has been created in a different package. You could of course simply print the document out and then key the material into the DTP software. This takes time and effort. It is usually possible to import the data into the software you intend to use to process the data. If the data is not saved in the same format, you may find that some of the formatting is lost and you may have to spend time correcting this.

Comma separated value/ variable files (CSV files)

When data is to be used by lots of different packages it is best stored as a file format called a comma separated value/variable file, or CSV for short.

The reason for using a CSV file is that it can be loaded into most other software packages including DTP software. This means that you could read the file using the spreadsheet software Excel or use the database software called Access or put into a DTP package such as Publisher. Packages that are not part of Microsoft Office could be used to read the file. This flexibility means the file can be used by a lot more people.

Once the file has been opened by the software you want to use, you can save in it the normal file format used by the software.

      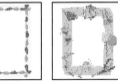

▲ **Examples of page borders.**

Jones,19/12/99,Leeds Utd,Britney Spears
Huges,01/08/99,Liverpool,Keane
Ahmed,09/08/97,Chelsea,Delta Goodrem
Lee,24/06/99,Manchester Utd,U2
Jackson,06/08/96,Everton,Doves

▲ **This is an example of a csv file.**

Tabulation

Tabulation means to arrange information in tabular form by condensing it and listing it.

Tables

Tables are ideal for organizing facts and figures and they are easily created. You only have to specify the number of columns and rows in the table. There are also lots of pre-stored styles of tables to choose from.

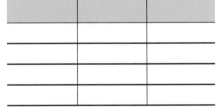

▲ **Once you have decided on the style of the table all you need to do is specify the number of rows and columns.**

Borders

A border can be used to add more emphasis to a word, section of text, paragraph or table. A border can be just a line or you can have a picture border such as a row of Christmas trees around the edge of a page. If you look at the selection of clip art, then it usually includes a good selection of picture borders.

Single and double line spacing

Line spacing, as the name suggests, refers to the spacing between each line in document.

Single line spacing – this is just normal line spacing. The computer will apply single line spacing to a document unless you tell it otherwise.

Double line spacing – a single blank line is left between each line of text. For example, when work needs to be marked, space needs to be left so that the marker can leave their comments. Sometimes a document is produced and other people need to look at it and make corrections or insert comments, so double spacing is used.

Manipulation of graphics

Once a graphic has been obtained, it may need adjusting in some way. Graphics software is available that allows you to alter (i.e., manipulate) images. Here are some of the ways that an image can be manipulated:

- It can be resized (i.e., made bigger or smaller).
- It can be rotated through a certain angle.
- It can be mirror imaged (i.e., like reflecting the image in a mirror).
- Part of the image can be cropped (this is just like cutting the part you want out of the picture).

DTP techniques *continued*

AutoShapes

AutoShapes are shapes that are already stored by the software. You can select the shapes from the various menus and edit them (e.g., resize, rotate, reflect, coloured and combined to make more complex shapes). The AutoShapes can be seen on the drawing toolbar and include the following:

- lines
- connectors
- basic shapes (e.g., squares, rectangles, triangles, etc.)
- block arrows
- flowchart symbols
- stars and banners.

You can turn any of the boxes used into text boxes, which means you can enter text inside the box. If you then apply a change to the box such as rotate, the text inside the box will also rotate.

Watermarks

You can use an image such as a photograph or graphic as a background to a document. The image has to be adjusted so that it is very light because there needs to be contrast between the image and the text. A very light image used as a background is called a watermark.

A life on the ocean wave

- See the world
- Get paid for travelling
- Meet a great bunch of people
- Free board and food
- Free uniform

▲ Adding a watermark can add interest but it does affect the readability of the text on the document, so use it with care.

Questions B

1 John is doing a project about space and to brighten up the page he has imported some clip art into it.
  - **(a)** What is meant by 'clip art'? *(1 mark)*
  - **(b)** Explain briefly what 'imported' means in the above sentence. *(1 mark)*
  - **(c)** Describe **two** places where clip art can be found. *(2 marks)*

2 Graphics often need to be manipulated before they can be used in a document.

  - **(a)** Give **two** ways in which a graphic can be manipulated. *(2 marks)*
  - **(b)** Graphics can be used as watermarks. Explain what is meant by a watermark. *(2 marks)*

3 Define each of the following terms about fonts.
  - **(a)** Font type *(1 mark)*
  - **(b)** Font size *(1 mark)*
  - **(c)** Font style *(1 mark)*

Extension activity

Produce a poster for a Halloween party making use of any software of your choice.

You are free to choose the text but you must ensure your poster makes use of the following:

- A watermark (remember to make the image very feint by adjusting the brightness).
- Use of appropriate font types, font sizes and font styles.
- Use of appropriate clip art.

END-OF-TOPIC REVIEW

Questions

 Test yourself

The following notes summarize this topic. The notes are incomplete because they have words missing.

Using the words in the list below, copy out and complete the sentences A to I, underlining the words that you have inserted. Each word may be used more than once.

thesaurus	AutoShapes	watermark	spellchecker	table
documents	borders	resizing	mail merge	double line

A DTP software is software that is used for the production of _____ that contain text, images, tables, etc.

B DTP software includes many features that help ensure the accuracy and reliability of text such as the use of an online _____.

C Another feature that is useful is _____ _____, which allows you to send personalized letters to lots of different people.

D Rather than list lots of numbers and facts, it is better to organize them by putting them into a _____.

E _____ can be put around the edge of a page or text box to make the document look more attractive.

F _____ _____ spacing can be used when the document is to been seen by people who may wish to add their comments to the document.

G When graphics are placed in a DTP document they are often manipulated by _____ so that they are able to fit into the size available.

H Pre-stored shapes that can be manipulated by the DTP software are called _____.

I A feint image which is used as the background to a document is called a _____.

Examination style questions

1 A school secretary needs to send a personalized letter to the parents of all Year 11 students. As there are 180 students in Year 11 she decides to use a mail merge.
 (a) Explain what is meant by a personalized letter. *(1 mark)*
 (b) Explain what is meant by a mail merge. *(3 marks)*
 (c) Give **one** advantage in using a mail merge for the production of these letters. *(1 mark)*

2 Here are some of the features of DTP used for the production of documents:
 Mail merge
 Online thesaurus
 Spellchecker.

 (a) Give the name of the feature in the list that can be used to find a word with a similar meaning to the word the user has typed in or highlighted in a document. *(1 mark)*
 (b) Give the name of the feature that compares words typed in with a pre-stored dictionary of words. *(1 mark)*
 (c) Give the name of the feature that can be used to produce personalized letters to lots of different people easily. *(1 mark)*

3 You are producing a school magazine using DTP. Compare the different methods you could use to obtain pictures for inclusion in the magazine. *(6 marks)*

Exam support

Worked example

Here is a first draft of a poster used to advertise a Halloween party at a school.

Mount Hill School
Years 10 and 11
Halloween party
Friday 30th Oct 09
Starts 7:30 pm
Music Hall
Tickets £2.50

Some features of DTP have been used to improve the appearance of this poster.

(a) Describe **three** features of DTP software that have been used to improve the appearance of this poster. *(3 marks)*

(b) Give **one** other feature of DTP that they could use to improve the design. *(1 mark)*

(c) The person who produced the poster spellchecks it before printing.

State what is meant by spellchecking. *(2 marks)*

Student answer 1

(a) Graphics

Text

Centre.

(b) Use a different font type such as Gothic.

(c) The computer does this automatically. It spellchecks all the spelling.

◄ Examiner's comment

(a) The ability to import clip art/graphics would have been an acceptable answer to this but the answer given is not worth a mark.

Text is not a feature and it would have been too brief an answer anyway so no marks are given here.

Centre is a feature but there is no description of how it is used. Students must look at the question carefully: to any question that asks a user to 'give', a one-word answer is OK, but where they are asked to 'describe', a one-word answer is not sufficient.

(b) This is a correct answer. The student has clearly stated font type rather than font on its own. One mark is given here.

(c) This a typical answer from a weak student. Students must remember not to simply write down an answer which anyone could guess from the word 'spellchecking'. There needs to be detail about how the spellchecking is done. No marks are given for this answer.

(1 mark out of 6)

Student answer 2

(a) All the text used has been centred to make it look more interesting.

The font size has been increased for some of the text to make it stand out.

Clip art images have been imported to improve the appearance.

(b) Use a border to go around the edge of the page. This can be obtained from clip art libraries.

(c) Checks all the words in a document against words that are in a stored dictionary to make sure they are spelt correctly. If they are not they can be corrected automatically or underlined in red so that the user can decide what to do.

◀ **Examiner's comment**

(a) These are all very good answers. The student has clearly identified the features and described how they are used. Three marks out of three for this answer.

(b) This is a good feature to include on a poster so one mark here.

(c) This is a very good answer and the student has clearly identified that the software uses a dictionary against which the words are compared. There are two marks here, so there must be two points made. The student has made two valid points in their two sentences so full marks are given for this answer.

(6 marks out of 6)

Examiner's answers

(a) One mark (up to a maximum of three marks) for each feature, which must have been used on the poster such as:

- Increase in font size to make more important text in the poster stand out.
- Centring of all the text so that it draws attention and looks like a poster.
- Use of coloured text to make the important text stand out the most.
- Importing clip art to add interest to the page.
- Use of bold to make the name of the school prominent.

(b) One mark for one feature similar to:

- Use different fonts.
- Use a page border.
- Use a watermark.
- Use a background colour.

(c) One mark for each point to a maximum of two marks.

- Checks the spelling of each word in a document.
- Against a pre-stored dictionary.
- Automatically changes the spelling as a user types.
- Highlights misspelt words for user action.
- Suggests correct spelling of words.

Summary mind map

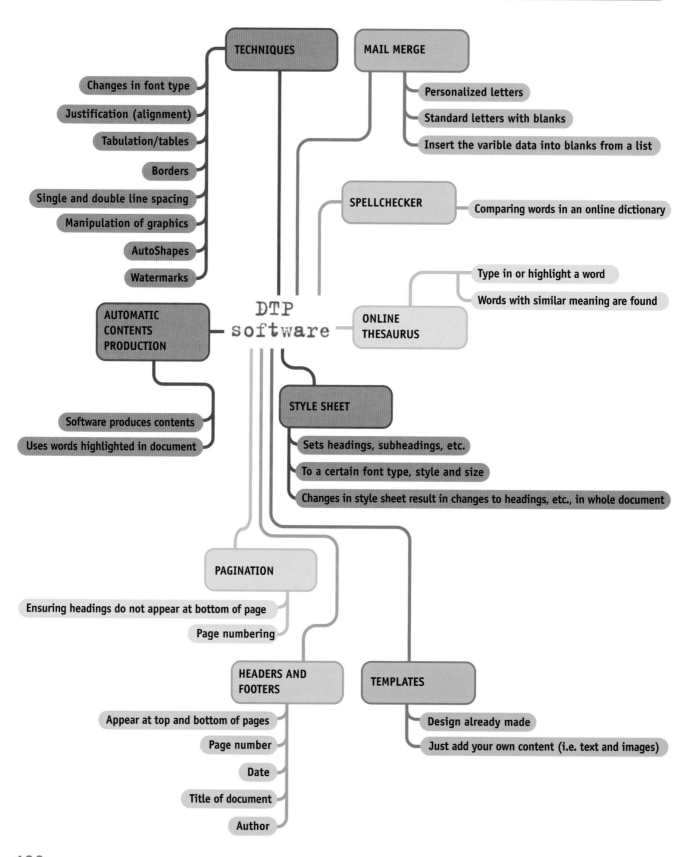

TECHNIQUES

MAIL MERGE

Changes in font type

Justification (alignment)

Tabulation/tables

Borders

Single and double line spacing

Manipulation of graphics

AutoShapes

Watermarks

Personalized letters

Standard letters with blanks

Insert the varible data into blanks from a list

SPELLCHECKER

Comparing words in an online dictionary

Type in or highlight a word

Words with similar meaning are found

AUTOMATIC CONTENTS PRODUCTION

DTP software

ONLINE THESAURUS

Software produces contents

Uses words highlighted in document

STYLE SHEET

Sets headings, subheadings, etc.

To a certain font type, style and size

Changes in style sheet result in changes to headings, etc., in whole document

PAGINATION

Ensuring headings do not appear at bottom of page

Page numbering

HEADERS AND FOOTERS

TEMPLATES

Appear at top and bottom of pages

Page number

Date

Title of document

Author

Design already made

Just add your own content (i.e. text and images)

Web and presentation software

The key concepts covered in this topic are:

- Animations
- Links
- Transitions
- Consideration of target audience
- Appropriate use of standard navigation techniques
- Disability considerations (sound, font style, font size, pop-up comments over images)

Designing good webpages and presentation slides is not simply about using the software correctly. You need to develop good practice when creating these so that all the pages or slides are professional looking. They also need to keep your audience interested.

In this topic you will be learning about the appropriate use of good practice in designing webpages and slide presentations.

Contents

Good practice in designing webpages and slide presentations

You will find out

▷ **About animations**

▷ **About links**

▷ **About transitions**

▷ **About considerations of target audience**

You will have used lots of websites and also seen and maybe used presentations other people have produced. You will have realized that there are good ones and bad ones.

In this section you will be looking at the things you can do to ensure that the webpages and presentations you produce are fun to use, appropriately aimed at the audience, contain interactive links enabling the user to decide what to do next and are easy to navigate. You will also learn about the need to consider that your users may have certain disabilities and that there are things that you can do to help them.

Animations

Animations can range from a simple moving logo or banner to a full length cartoon. You can get simple animations in much the same way as you can get clip art off the Internet. Some of these are copyright free and you can include them in your slides and webpages. You can produce your own animations using programs such as Flash and how this is done is covered in Topic 17.

Links

Links provide a way for the user to move from one webpage or slide to another. The use of links means that a user viewing a series of webpages or slides does not have to view them in a set order. The user decides the order they want to view the material by clicking on the links. As well as providing links to webpages and slides, the links can also enable users to view files that have been

▲ Cartoons are examples of more complex animation.

created using software such as word-processing software.

One way of providing a link is for the user to click on an image. You can also link to different webpages or slides depending on what the user has typed in. For example, you could have a multiple-choice question on a slide whose correct answer is, say, C. If the user types in A, B or D then the link will take the user to a slide telling them that they got the answer wrong and why they got the answer wrong. If they type in the correct answer, C, then the link takes them to a slide telling them that they have got the answer correct.

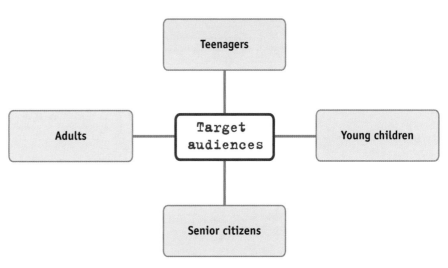

It is common to classify a target audience according to their age.

Links enable a user to take different paths through the material.

Transitions

The movement from one webpage to another is called a transition. It is possible to fade one webpage out and then make the next one slowly appear. This can add interest to the website but the trouble is that most users just want to see the webpage quickly and transitions tend to delay this.

Target audience

The target audience are the people your document is aimed at.

Finding out about your target audience

Once you have identified who your audience is, you still need to find out more about them. You must ask yourself questions such as:

- **What are their needs?**
  Your audience will look at your document for a reason. Think about what this reason is and what the audience will need from your document. For example, if you have designed a poster advertising a school/college night out, think about what information they will need. Satisfying your audience's needs is an important part in creating any document.

- **How much do they know already?**
  It is essential to assess how much your audience knows about the subject of your document. If they have a good knowledge of the subject, you will not have to start at the beginning.

- **What is the knowledge of the reader about the subject?**
  If you were writing an article on a subject such as the Data Protection Act 1998 for computer users, then it would need to be different from the same article aimed at lawyers, who are able to untangle the intricacies of the law.

- **What level of literacy do they have?**
  Not everyone is good at English. Any document aimed at the whole of the adult population will need to be written simply. Generally, to make a document as readable as possible, you would need to make sure that:
  - only well-known words are used
  - the sentence length is kept short
  - as few punctuation marks as possible are used.

- **How much specialist vocabulary can they handle?**
  Most subjects have a series of words that tend to be used only within that subject. The subject is said to have a specialist vocabulary. For example, medical staff, doctors, nurses, etc., have special medical terms for illnesses. You need to make sure that if you are using any specialist words to people not knowledgeable in the area, then you will need to explain them carefully.

- **How interested are they likely to be in the subject?**
  Some topics or subjects are more interesting than others. Also different people find different things interesting. If the information you have to present is uninteresting to the audience then you will need to try to make it as interesting as you can.

Good practice in designing webpages and slide presentations *continued*

Thinking about the target audience

The target audience are the people your document is aimed at. You need to make sure that the design of the document is appropriate for the people who will be reading it. For example, a poster advertising a school disco for 14–16 year olds would need a different design compared to a poster advertising a drink driving campaign. If you are talking about ICT to others who also know about ICT then you can use technical terms without explaining them. They should know what they mean.

Who is your target audience?

The information you have will need to be presented. Before you present the information you need to think about who the intended audience for the information is. The data needs to be presented in a manner that the audience can use and understand. The way you would present the information to an adult audience would be totally different from the way you would present the same information to a young audience.

Presenting the same information to different audiences

It is possible to present the same item of information in different ways. For example, you could have a poster giving the key information and then a leaflet giving more details.

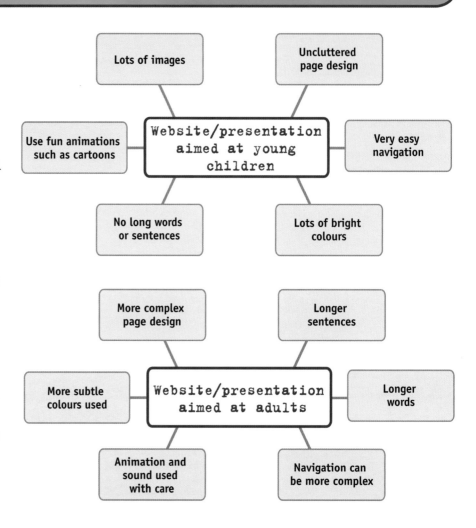

Questions A

1 'Webpages and presentations should be aimed at a target audience.'
Explain what this statement means. *(3 marks)*

2 Give **three** things a website aimed at an adult audience should have. *(3 marks)*

Extension activity

Use the Internet to find two websites in each of the following categories:

- Websites aimed at very young children.
- Websites aimed at an adult audience.

- Websites aimed at people with specialist knowledge about the subject.

Write a few sentences about each one explaining how they meet the needs of their target audience.

Standard navigation techniques, disability considerations and data compression

You will find out

> **About the appropriate use of standard navigation techniques**

> **About disability considerations**

> **About the advantages and disadvantages of data compression**

Users find websites and presentations easy to use if they adopt navigation methods that they are familiar with and have used before. This is why, once you have used one website, it is easy for you to use other websites. You can use them without the need for instructions. In this section you will be looking at what standard navigation techniques are.

As websites and presentations need to be used by everyone, it is important that the designers of these products think about some of the disabilities that their users may have. They then need to think how they can make their products usable by these people. Here you will be looking

Appropriate use of standard navigation techniques

Computers have to be used by everyone, so it makes sense to create software that offers a standard way to move around (called navigate) to enable the user to obtain the information they need. Having standard navigation techniques means that users do not have to learn how to navigate each time they use a different system.

For example, you will have used the forward and back buttons when navigating webpages. All browsers have these buttons, so if you have to use a browser or other software you are not familiar with, you already know what these buttons will do.

at those things you can do to ensure that products you create can be used by people with certain disabilities.

Data compression is a technique used to reduce the file size. In this section you will be looking at the advantages and disadvantages of data compression.

Here are some standard navigation techniques:

- Use of forward and back to move to the next or previous webpage/slide.
- Use of the home button to enable users to return to the home page.
- Use of menus to provide simple ways for the user to make selections.
- Use of hyperlinks to link to other pages/slides.
- Bookmarks/favourites to enable users to go back to a webpage/website they like.

More details on navigation are included in Topics 13 and 14.

Disability considerations

When designing websites and presentations you must be aware that users with a range of disabilities will be using the products you produce.

You will need to consider people who are visually impaired (i.e., blind or partially sighted) by:

- having a facility to speak words on the screen
- having a facility to zoom in so that the page is magnified
- increasing the font size
- choosing those font types that are easy to read
- using plenty of contrast between the text and the background
- allowing the user to change the colour scheme.

Standard navigation techniques, disability considerations and data compression *continued*

You will need to consider people who have a hearing impairment (i.e., completely or partially deaf) by:

- using visual warnings rather than sound warnings
- using typed versions of any speech used
- using subtitles for any video used.

Data compression techniques

If images are to be used on a website or a presentation, they can take time to load, so it is best to use compressed images. Compressing files makes the file size smaller, which makes it quicker to load by the software and also to copy onto other media. If the presentation is to be provided as a download on a website, it will be quicker to upload (i.e., save onto the server) and to download by users.

Bitmap image
1280 × 960 pixels

File size:
3150 KB (3.5 MB)

Compression

JPEG image
1280 × 960 pixels

File size:
292 KB

▲ How compression reduces the file size.

Audio files such as files containing speech or music are extremely large and these are normally saved in MP3 format, which compresses the file and makes the file more manageable. Movie/video files are even bigger than audio files and so need to be compressed.

▲ Portable music players use compressed files.

Advantages of data compression techniques

The advantages of data compression techniques include:

- More files can be stored on the storage medium (e.g., DVD, memory card, hard disk, pen drive, etc.).
- It is much faster to upload to put it on a webpage.
- It is much faster for others to download it from a webpage.
- It is faster to load when viewed with any software used to view or edit it.
- It is faster to transfer as an email attachment.

Disadvantages of data compression techniques

The disadvantages of data compression techniques include:

- Images are not as high quality as images without compression.
- Sound quality is not as high with compression such as that used with MP3 files, although not many people would notice the difference.
- Compression means it is much faster to transfer movie files and this causes problems with people illegally copying movies.

Questions B

1 Image files are often compressed before they are stored on a computer.
   (a) Explain what is meant by the term compression. *(1 mark)*
   (b) Give **one** advantage in compressing a digital photograph file. *(1 mark)*
   (c) Give **one** disadvantage in compressing a digital photograph file. *(1 mark)*

2 Disabled people often use websites.
   (a) Describe **one** thing the website designer can do to help a user who is partially sighted. *(1 mark)*
   (b) Describe **one** thing the website designer can do to help a user who is deaf. *(1 mark)*

Extension activity

Use the Internet to find out which file formats use compression for each of the following:

- **Images**
- **Music**
- **Video/movies.**

Questions

 Test yourself

The following notes summarize this topic. The notes are incomplete because they have words missing.

Using the words in the list below, copy out and complete the sentences A to G, underlining the words that you have inserted. Each word may be used more than once.

standard	sizes	displayed	designing
animations	types	audience	transition

A Moving text and images on a website are called _____.

B The way one slide changes into another in a presentation is called the slide _____.

C Target _____ are the people who will be mainly viewing a presentation or website.

D Forward and Back buttons on websites and presentations are examples of _____ navigation techniques.

E In order for partially sighted users to be able to use websites and presentations you need to be careful when _____ them.

F Large font _____ and clear font _____ should be used to aid readability.

G Users with a hearing impairment should be catered for by allowing any spoken material to also be _____ on the screen for them to read.

Examination style questions

1 A website is designed to help young children with their reading.
   (a) Explain what is meant by a target audience and state who the target audience is for this website. *(2 marks)*
   (b) Give **three** things you will need to consider when designing this website for the target audience. *(3 marks)*

2 Good websites and presentations use standard navigation techniques.
   (a) Give **three** examples of standard navigation techniques used on a website. *(3 marks)*
   (b) Some websites include animation. Describe what is meant by animation and give an example of animation you have seen on a website. *(2 marks)*

END-OF-TOPIC REVIEW

Exam support

Worked example

A presentation is to be used by visitors to a castle. The idea is that users will be able to find out about the history of the castle and what it was like to live in a castle in that era.

Explain how each of the following could be used in the design of this presentation.

(a) Animations *(2 marks)*

(b) Links *(2 marks)*

(c) Slide transitions *(2 marks)*

Student answer 1

(a) Use moving things. Makes it better.

(b) You can move from one slide to another.

  The user can click on a hotspot.

(c) The material on the slide can shoot in from the side of the slide. It makes it exciting for the user.

◀ **Examiner's comment**

(a) This is a vague and poor answer and no marks are awarded.

(b) Both of these are valid answers and two marks are awarded.

(c) Material such as bullet points shooting onto the slide is not really an example of slide transition as the slide is already on the screen. One mark (just) is given for the second answer.

  (3 marks out of 6)

Student answer 2

(a) Use moving images showing what is in each room.

  Have a heading showing the names of the castle which moves from left to right.

(b) Allow the user to decide what they want to see next by allowing them to click on links that take them to other pages.

  Links could be used to allow the user to visit each of the rooms virtually and look around.

(c) These are pictures around the edge of a slide.

  You can sometimes find these included with clip art.

◀ **Examiner's comment**

(a) These are both suitable examples so two marks are awarded.

(b) These two very good answers explaining how links might be used are awarded two marks.

(c) What the student has described here are borders. Slide transitions are the way one slide is removed and the next slide appears. No marks for this answer.

  (4 marks out of 6)

Examiner's answers

(a) One mark for each point (NB must be a sensible use of animation) to a maximum of two marks.

- Have a cartoon showing what life was like.
- Use animation to show how certain parts of the castle were used.
- Etc.

(b) One mark for each point to a maximum of two marks.

- Link to an aerial view such as Google Earth.
- Link to other pages in the presentation.
- Link to the Internet so that they can access further information.
- Etc.

(c) One mark for each point to a maximum of two marks.

- Have one slide fading as another slide appears.
- Have one slide shooting in from the side.
- Etc.

EXAM TIPS

Make sure you refer to the scenario, if there is one

When a scenario is given, this sets a context for the answer you should give. For example, in this question you would need to tailor your answer to a presentation used to help people learn about the castle and what it was like to live in one.

One mistake that many students make is that they totally ignore the scenario and give a general answer. Usually when they do this, students fail to get all the marks as they have not exactly done what the question has asked.

Do not get confused between slide transitions and animations

It is easy to get confused here.

Slide transitions are the way one slide disappears and one slide appears.

Animations are the movements of the content on the screen. This can be the way the content is added to the screen. For example, an image of a knight on a horse could be added to the slide by it moving in from the side of the slide.

Be specific

Most people know what the word animation means. As a student of ICT you need to make your answer specific to a presentation used to inform visitors to a castle. If you start mentioning about what an animation is, then you will not get any marks as this is not a question about the definition nor is it a question about the various ways that animations can be produced.

Summary mind map

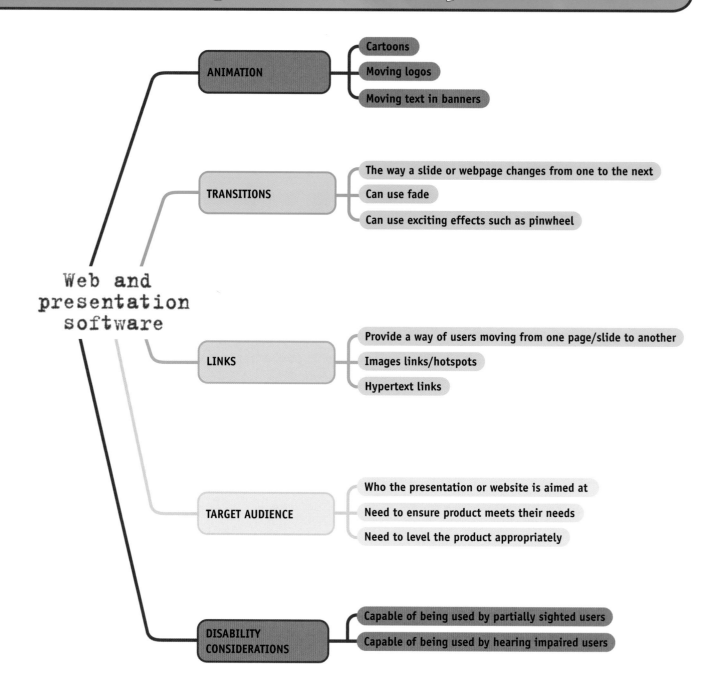

ANIMATION
- Cartoons
- Moving logos
- Moving text in banners

TRANSITIONS
- The way a slide or webpage changes from one to the next
- Can use fade
- Can use exciting effects such as pinwheel

Web and presentation software

LINKS
- Provide a way of users moving from one page/slide to another
- Images links/hotspots
- Hypertext links

TARGET AUDIENCE
- Who the presentation or website is aimed at
- Need to ensure product meets their needs
- Need to level the product appropriately

DISABILITY CONSIDERATIONS
- Capable of being used by partially sighted users
- Capable of being used by hearing impaired users

Topic 13
Web software

The key concepts covered in this topic are:

- **Understanding browser software**

- **Analysing existing webpages**

- **Searching for and searching on webpages**

- **Comparisons on house style, audience, size and technique used**

- **Use of interactive features (e.g., online forms, email, games, quizzes and questionnaires)**

- **Tools and techniques for creating websites**

- **The issues in hosting websites and factors affecting uploading times**

- **The advantages and disadvantages of webpages and their features**

- **RGB colours, decimal and hexadecimal code used for colour**

Web software includes the software that is needed to view webpages on the Internet and also the software used to create the webpages. As part of your GCSE course you will need to experience and understand both of these types of Web software.

Web browser software is the software used to find and access webpages and you will need to understand its operation. In this topic you will also be looking at the features of webpages and websites and the tools and techniques for their creation.

Contents

Understanding browser software, searches and interactive features

You will find out

▷ **About web browser software**

▷ **About making comparisons of websites**

▷ **About interactive features**

In this section you will be looking at web browser software and how is it used to search for and view webpages on the Internet. You will also learn about some of the interactive features of websites.

▲ Many URLs start this way.

Web browser software

Web browser software is a program that allows access to webpages stored on the Internet. A web browser allows the user to find information on websites and webpages quickly and it does this by making use of:

- URLs
- key word searches
- links
- menus.

URL

URL stands for Uniform Resource Locator, which is a complicated way of saying a website address. One of the ways of accessing a website is to type the URL (i.e. website address) into a web browser.

Key word searches

If you want information about a certain topic but do not have the URLs of any websites, then you can simply type some key words into the search box on the web browser.

Links

Links are sometimes called hyperlinks and by clicking on them the user moves to another place on the same webpage, a different webpage on the same site or a webpage on a completely different site. You can also link to files such as a presentation file.

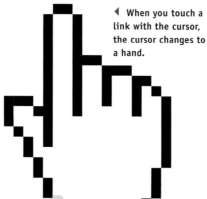
◀ When you touch a link with the cursor, the cursor changes to a hand.

Menus

Menus offer the user a series of selections that they make by clicking on one of them. The menus can use text or you can use images, usually with some explanation on them.

Analysing existing webpages

You will by now have used hundreds of different webpages and so will be knowledgeable about their features. Many of the features are common to all webpages and it is only the content (text, images, etc.) which is different.

There are activities in this topic that will give you practice at analysing webpages.

Search for and search on webpages

Searching for information is performed using a search engine such as Google or Yahoo. The search results are displayed on the basis of relevance or who has paid the most money to get in the top results.

Clicking on a search result takes you to a website and may take you straight to the information you want or you may go to the home page of the website. It may then be necessary to perform a search of the content of the website. This is done by entering key words into a search box.

▲ A key word search on a website.

Making comparisons of websites

You will have used lots of webpages and found some good and some bad. It is important to be able to spot things that frustrate and annoy you and things you find good. By looking at other websites you can make sure that your own is good. When creating your own website make sure you consider the following carefully:

House style – websites need to convey an image that reflects the organization. It needs to fit in with other material produced by the organization such as brochures, business cards, adverts, etc.

Audience – you always need to know who your main audience will be and tailor the content, look and navigation to suit them.

Size – you need to consider the number of pages. Remember that websites often start small but begin to grow rapidly as they become popular.

Techniques used – there is a huge difference between a website for a large company produced by professional website designers and a personal website produced by someone with few design and technical skills.

Interactive features

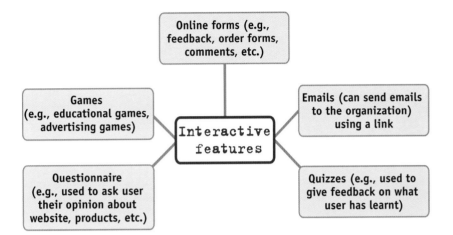

Questions A

1 There are millions of websites on the Internet.
   (a) Describe **two** ways in which a user can find a specific piece of information using the Internet. *(2 marks)*
   (b) Give the names of **two** interactive features that can be used on a website. *(2 marks)*

2 **(a)** Give the meaning of the abbreviation HTML. *(1 mark)*
   (b) Websites can be created using HTML. Give a different way of creating a website. *(1 mark)*

Extension activity

Choose two completely different websites (i.e., created for different purposes and aimed at difference audiences).

Write down the URL (i.e., the website address) for each of your chosen websites.

Investigate each website by following links, searching for information, looking at the size of the website.

Then, compare and contrast the two websites, looking at each of the following:
• house style
• audience
• size
• techniques used.

You should write a few sentences about each item in the bulleted list for each of the two sites.

Tools and techniques for creating websites

You will find out

▷ **About master pages/ templates**

▷ **About the home page**

▷ **About site navigation**

▷ **About the golden triangle**

▷ **About graphical hyperlinks/ hotspots/rollover buttons and polygon links**

▷ **About bookmarks and anchors**

▷ **About leader boards**

▷ **About banners**

▷ **About web icons**

▷ **About hosting websites**

▷ **About RGB colours**

In order to be able to create your own website it is necessary to understand the facilities that most websites offer. You can then find out how to create these facilities using the tools and techniques of your web design software.

Master pages/templates

Master pages/templates provide a quick way of creating webpages. They supply the structure for the website and the navigation that is used to move around the site. They act as a framework for the website and all the developer has to do is fill in their own content. They are ideal for people who need to develop websites quickly and have no design or website development skills.

Home page

The home page is the main webpage of a website for a person, business or organization. It is the page most users will arrive at and is therefore the starting page of a website. It is important that the most important information is located on this page along with the ways a user can navigate to the other pages in the website.

Site navigation

Good navigation means how easy it is to move around a website. Navigation enables users to get to the information they want as quickly as possible using the minimum number of selections or mouse clicks. A user of a website should not be left wondering what to click next.

Navigation can be:

- Linear – where the user will take the same path through the pages.
- Menu structure – where the user can choose what to look at.
- Tree structure – where the user can take different paths through the documents based on their interests.

Golden triangle

When users search for information using a search engine they are presented with a list of results. Experiments conducted to see where users looked on a results page showed that they tended to concentrate on a triangular area of the screen called the golden triangle.

This means it is really important, if you are producing a website that you want to be viewed by a lot of people, that your website appears in the golden triangle when it is searched for.

Hyperlinks

Hyperlinks allow you to jump from one part of website to another or even to a completely different website. Links are fundamental to the Internet but they can be used with any multimedia product such as presentations, as you will see in the next topic.

There are two types of hyperlink:
- Hypertext links – these are text that you can click on to activate the link and take you to somewhere else.
- Graphical links – these are graphical images that you click on to activate the link. You can tell whether an image is a hyperlink because when you move the cursor over the graphic, and the graphic is a hyperlink, the cursor changes to a hand shape.

Hotspots

Hotspots are an image or piece of text used as a link on a webpage. When you click on the image or text, you are taken to another part of the same page, a different page or a different site, or it may open a new file or a new window.

Rollover buttons/images

A rollover button/image is a button/image that changes its appearance when a cursor is moved over it.

Polygon links

These are links that are formed using various shapes.

Back and forward

▲ Back and forward allow a user to move to the previous webpage or the next webpage. Most websites offer this simple form of navigation.

Overviews and sitemaps are forms of navigation. They allow a user to see exactly what is included on the site and to move around the site without having to use the normal navigation on the webpages.

Sitemaps can be a graphical map or text-based. A text-based sitemap is sometimes called a table of contents (TOC).

▲ A sitemap for a website.

Bookmarks (also called favourites)

When you surf the Internet, you quickly move from one webpage to another. You often find interesting webpages that you would like to revisit in the future. To keep a record of the webpage you can use a bookmark. The bookmark records the web address with a title in a list that you can display at any time.

All you need to do to go back to the webpage is to click on the name of the site in the list that is displayed.

Anchor links

If a webpage is long, you can use an anchor link that allows a user to jump to the section of content they are interested in. This saves a user having to read all the content they are not interested in to get to the part they want.

Navigation bars

Web browsers contain a toolbar, called a navigation bar, containing buttons that you use to move around the site and perform certain actions.

▲ The navigation button for the ISP AOL.

These buttons would typically include:

- **Back** – go back to the previous page.
- **Forward** – jump forward to the next page.
- **Refresh** (also called Reload) – refresh the contents of the page.
- **Home** – return to the page that you use as your home page (i.e., your starting point) or the page that your ISP uses as their home page.
- **Stop** – stop trying to load the page.
- **Key word search** – to search a site using one or more key words.

Leader boards and banners

A web banner is a rectangular area on a website that displays advertisements and also acts as a link to the advertiser's site. Banners come in all sizes but one popular-sized banner is called a leader board and it is 728 pixels long by 90 pixels wide.

▲ Web icons.

Web icons

Web icons are small pictures on websites that enable users to do certain things when they click on them. There are lots of different web icons but it is always best if it is obvious what the icon does from its picture. This can be quite difficult as the set of icons in the diagram above shows.

HTML (HyperText Markup Language)

HTML is short for HyperText Markup Language and is the special code that is used for making webpages. HTML consists of special markers called tags that tell the computer what to do with the text that is entered. It could tell the computer to present the text in a certain way. For example, the tags could tell the computer that the text being entered is intended to be a heading or to make a certain block of text bold.

HTML is a text file, just like Word, except that it contains the special markers called tags. Tags basically tell the computer how to display the text or format the page.

Tools and techniques for creating websites *continued*

```
<!DOCTYPE html PUBLIC "-//W3C//DTD XHTML 1.0 Transitional//EN"
    "http://www.w3.org/TR/xhtml1/DTD/xhtml1-transitional.dtd">
<html xmlns="http://www.w3.org/1999/xhtml" lang="en" xml:lang="en">
<head>
    <meta http-equiv="Content-Type" content="text/html; charset=utf-8" />
    <meta http-equiv="cache-control" content="no-cache" />
    <meta http-equiv="pragma" content="no-cache" />
    <meta http-equiv="expires" content="Sun, 1 Jan 2005 00:00:00 GMT" />
    <meta name="Description" content="Folens are one of the leading publishers of Primary
and Secondary educational texts, classroom resources and software for both students and teaching
professionals, publishing primary school curriculum materials and secondary school resources" />
    <meta name="Keywords" content="Folens, educational publishers, Education, books,
academic, Primary, Secondary, belair, curriculum online, school, art, citizenship, Design & technology,
elc, english, GCSE, geography, health, social, history, ict, Key stage, languages, literacy, maths,
numeracy, PE, religious, Science, special" />
    <title>Folens &mdash; New Secondary Resources</title>
    <style type="text/css">@import "/includes/folens.css";</style>
    <link rel="stylesheet" type="text/css" href="/includes/folens_print.css" media="print" />
    <script type="text/javascript" src="/includes/folens.js"></script>
```

▲ **Here is a section of HTML code.**

Important note

HTML is not a programming language as such. It just tells the computer how to display text and pictures in webpages.

RGB

There is a need to have a standard colour system so that different people using different computer systems can produce the same colour on the screen.

Coloured pixels are produced by mixing different amounts of the colours red, green and blue, and this particular colour system is called RGB.

Mixing light is not the same as mixing pigments such as ink or paint. You can get white light when you mix red, blue and green light, you would not get white if you mix the same colour paints.

The amounts of red, green and blue are expressed as numbers, which range from 0 to 255. The numbers are usually represented as hexadecimal numbers (don't worry about what these exactly mean). Hexadecimal numbers are very easy to convert into binary which the computer can understand.

Here are some colours made by mixing different amounts of Red, Green and Blue.

Red	Green	Blue	
255	255	255	= White
255	0	0	= Red
0	0	0	= Black

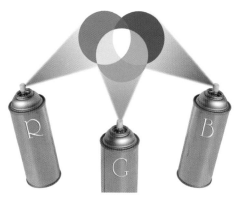

Hosting of websites and uploading times

Hosting of websites

A web server is a computer that contains the information that users of the Internet can access using their web browser. A web server needs to be permanently connected to the Internet so that all users are able to access the information. Web servers for Internet service providers (ISPs) contain many websites. If you develop your own website, then the site will usually be stored on the web server of the ISP that you use.

Uploading times

The uploading time is the time it takes to take a website that has been produced on a computer and then transfer it over a network (usually the Internet) to a web server.

▼ **Mixing red, green and blue light gives white light.**

Uploading time will depend on the following:

- The resolution of any images used on the website.
- Whether or not the webpage contains animations or movies.
- The number of webpages on the website.
- The complexity of the design.
- The amount of content on the webpages.

Advantages and disadvantages of webpages and webpage features

Advantages

- Makes the information available to a huge number of people.
- Enables anyone who has access to the Internet to be able to access the information.
- Uses multimedia features to make the site interesting to users.

HyperText Markup Language (HTML) used to create documents on the World Wide Web. You use it to specify the structure and layout of a web document.

Tags special markers used in HTML to tell the computer what to do with the text. A tag is needed at the start and end of the block of text to which the tag applies.

Hotspot an image or piece of text used as a link. When you click on the image or text, you are taken to another part of the same page, a different page or a different site, or it may open a new file or a new window.

Hyperlink a feature of a website that allows a user to jump to another webpage, to jump to part of the same webpage or to send an email message.

Image map an image that contains more than one hotspot.

Rollover button/image a button/image that changes its appearance when a cursor is moved over it.

URL Uniform Resource Locator, a web address.

Disadvantages

- Some features such as Flash movies can take time to load and this can put off users from using the site.
- People who do not have access to the Internet are at a huge disadvantage.
- Some of the features such as links to movies may not be accessible to those users who do not have a fast broadband connection.

Questions B

1 One quick way of developing webpages is to use a template. Explain what a template is and how one can be used to create a website. *(3 marks)*

2 A homepage contains a number of hotspots and a banner.
   (a) Explain what is meant by a hotspot. *(1 mark)*
   (b) Explain what is meant by a banner. *(1 mark)*

Extension activity

Viewing HTML code

In this activity you will look at how you can view the HTML code (i.e., the set of instructions) used to produce a website.

1 Log on to the Internet and access any website you like.

2 Rather than look at the content of this site we are going to look at the HTML code used to produce the website.
   To do this, position the cursor anywhere on the webpage.
   Right click the mouse button.
   The following window appears:

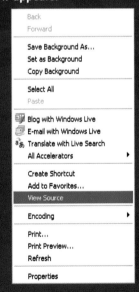

3 Select View Source by clicking on it.

4 You will now be able to see the HTML code for the webpage you have just viewed.

END-OF-TOPIC REVIEW

Questions

 Test yourself

The following notes summarize this topic. The notes are incomplete because they have words missing.

Using the words in the list below, copy out and complete the sentences A to F, underlining the words that you have inserted. Each word may be used more than once.

URL   anchor   website   web servers

    address   web browser   hyperlinks

A _____ stands for Uniform Resource Locator, which is a complicated way of saying a web _____.

B _____ allow you to jump from one part of website to another or even to a completely different website.

C If a webpage is long, you can use an _____ link that allows a user to jump to the section of content they are interested in.

D Most companies and organizations have a _____ where outsiders can access details about the company or organization.

E A program that allows access to the Internet is called a _____ _____.

F Some computers are permanently connected to the Internet and you can connect to the Internet via them. These computers are called _____ _____.

Examination style questions

1 There are two types of web software. Give the names of them and describe briefly how they are used. (4 marks)

2 Links are used in websites to move from one part of a webpage to another or from one website to another.

(a) Explain how a graphical hyperlink is used on a website. (1 mark)

(b) Explain the purpose of an anchor link. (1 mark)

(c) Explain how a rollover button works. (1 mark)

END-OF-TOPIC REVIEW

Exam support

Worked example

In order that a website can be accessed and used by others, it needs to be hosted.

(a) Describe **one** way in which a website can be hosted. *(2 marks)*

(b) Websites need to be uploaded on the host computer. Explain what this means. *(2 marks)*

(c) In the context of a website give **two** things that would affect the uploading time. *(2 marks)*

Student answer 1

(a) You can store it on your own computer and others will be able to access it.

(b) It means putting the website on the computer so others can access it.

(c) How large the website is. A website with hundreds of webpages will take a lot longer to upload than a website with just a few webpages.

How much multimedia there is, as movies and some animation can make the file for the website very large.

◄ Examiner's comment

(a) This answer is too vague to be awarded even one mark. After all, anything produced on a computer is likely to be stored on a computer. The student needed to mention a web server or the fact that the computer would need to be permanently connected to the Internet.

(b) Only one mark is awarded here. Two points are needed to gain two marks.

(c) Both of these will affect the uploading time so two marks are awarded here.

(3 marks out of 6)

Student answer 2

(a) The company who is your ISP can host it on their computer as they have a computer that is connected to the Internet all the time.

(b) It means storing the website on a computer that is connected to the Internet all the time. This means users can access it 24/7.

(c) How much material there is in the website.

◄ Examiner's comment

(a) Two valid points are made in this sentence so two marks are awarded for this answer.

(b) This is also correct and two points are made which means another two marks.

(c) This is one factor. From the previous answers given this looks a good student and they look as though they could easily have given another correct answer. Maybe they did not read the question and realize that two things are needed here.

(5 marks out of 6)

Examiner's answers

(a) One mark for a method and one mark for further detail or an example.

Website can be hosted by the Internet service provider (ISP) (1) who will store the website on a computer that is permanently connected to the Internet (1).

Website can be hosted on a web server (1) which is owned by the organization who has produced the website (1).

(b) One mark for two points such as:

Taking the website that has been developed (1) and saving it on a computer that is permanently connected to the Internet (1).

(c) One mark for two of the following:

- The speed of the Internet connection.
- The number of pages/size of the website.
- The file size of the website.
- The number of large files such as movies and animation.

Summary mind map

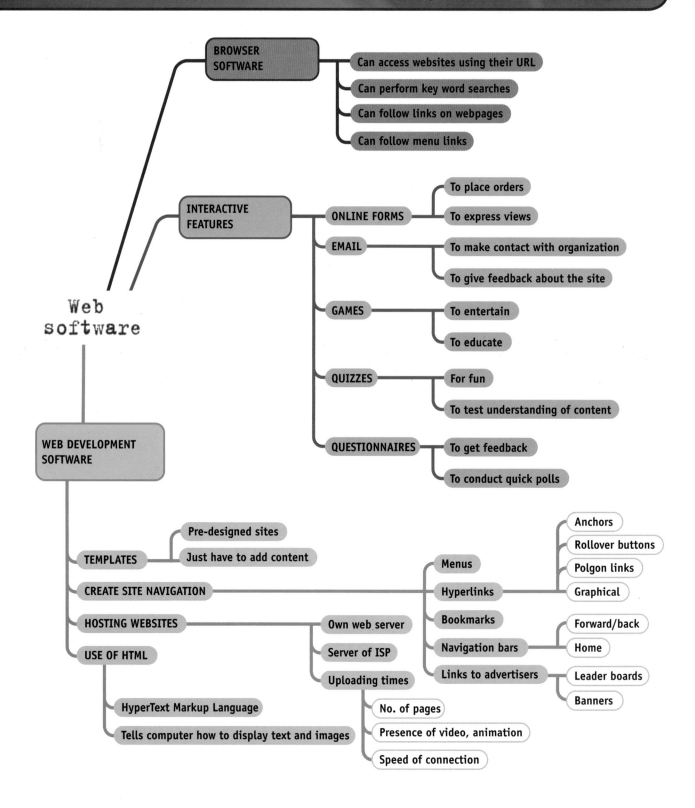

BROWSER SOFTWARE
- Can access websites using their URL
- Can perform key word searches
- Can follow links on webpages
- Can follow menu links

INTERACTIVE FEATURES
- ONLINE FORMS
  - To place orders
  - To express views
- EMAIL
  - To make contact with organization
  - To give feedback about the site
- GAMES
  - To entertain
  - To educate
- QUIZZES
  - For fun
  - To test understanding of content
- QUESTIONNAIRES
  - To get feedback
  - To conduct quick polls

Web software

WEB DEVELOPMENT SOFTWARE
- TEMPLATES
  - Pre-designed sites
  - Just have to add content
- CREATE SITE NAVIGATION
  - Menus
  - Hyperlinks
    - Anchors
    - Rollover buttons
    - Polgon links
    - Graphical
  - Bookmarks
  - Navigation bars
    - Forward/back
    - Home
  - Links to advertisers
    - Leader boards
    - Banners
- HOSTING WEBSITES
  - Own web server
  - Server of ISP
  - Uploading times
    - No. of pages
    - Presence of video, animation
    - Speed of connection
- USE OF HTML
  - HyperText Markup Language
  - Tells computer how to display text and images

Presentation software

The key concepts covered in this chapter are:

- **Design templates**
- **Animation**
- **Transitions and timings**
- **Video and sound**
- **Navigation, bookmarks, hyperlinks and hotspots**
- **Printing formats**
- **Advantages and disadvantages of presentation software**

In this topic you will learn about presentation software. You will already have used presentation software but you probably only used some of the capabilities of the software. As well as for making presentations to a group you can also use presentation software to create multimedia products that people can use on their own. For example, you can use presentation software to create information points where a user is able to determine their own path through the slides of information. In other words you can use links and action buttons so the user can choose what they see next. Presentation software can also be used to create quizzes. You will also learn about how to make your presentations become more interesting by using animation, video, slide transitions and other techniques.

Contents

Tools and techniques for creating slide presentations

In this section you will be looking at some of the tools and techniques that you can use to make a variety of multimedia products. You will also learn about the tools and techniques that enable you to add multimedia features to your presentation such as adding video, sound and interactivity.

Design templates

Unless you have an artistic streak, it is hard to produce a good design for a presentation. It is easier to use a design template. A design template is an outline design providing a basic colour scheme, font type, font size, etc. You then do not need to worry about the design, so you can concentrate fully on the content of each slide (text, graphics, video, sound, etc.).

▲ Here are some of the many design templates available for a presentation.

Animation

Animation involves getting some of the content that makes up the slides to move. The simplest way of including animation is to use animation provided by the presentation software. This allows you to select certain animations for the way the material such as headings and bullet points are added to a slide. Animation is classified as follows:

- subtle
- moderate
- exciting.

Another way of including animation would be to include clip art that is animated or to produce a Flash animation and include it on the slide.

Transitions and timings

The movement from one slide to another is called a slide transition. To make your presentation more interesting you can:

- alter the way the slide appears on the screen
- alter the speed at which the slide appears
- get the computer to make a sound during the transition.

When a slide presentation is self-running it is important to leave enough time for your audience to read what is on each slide. Using the software, you can alter the timings for each slide.

Video and sound

If a picture paints a thousand words then video probably paints a whole book. There is sound and movement and you can add so much more interest than simply writing about the same thing or looking at a still picture.

There are two main ways of obtaining video for use in presentations and websites:

- By creating the video yourself using a digital video recorder.
- By using video created by someone else.

You can use a search engine such as Yahoo to search for video in a similar way to the way you search for images. There are sites such as YouTube that are huge sources of video and it is possible to link to these sites from websites and presentations.

"I think I've put together the perfect presentation
that's guaranteed to hold everyone's attention
from start to finish...all 17 seconds of it!"

Activity

Finding sound clips

Use the site http://www.
findsounds.com/ to search for the
following sound clips. You will
need to decide on the best search
condition to find the clips. When
you have found them, you should
store them in a suitable folder.

1 A car braking
2 An owl hooting
3 The sound of a helicopter
4 Rain
5 Waves

Sound files

Most people think of clip art sites as
just containing ready-made images
but many of them contain sounds as
well. Sounds and music can liven up
a multimedia product but they need
to be used with care as they can
detract from the message or content
being delivered.

As well as clip art libraries, you
can use the following sites as sources
of sound files:

- Here are some sound files
  from the movies: http://www.
  moviesoundscentral.com/
- One of the best sound sites where
  you can search for sound effects is
  at: http://www.findsounds.com/

Navigation: hyperlinks and hotspots

Navigation

Navigation is the way provided by
the software for a user to choose
which slide they want to view next.
Remember that it is possible for a
presentation to be interactive just
like a website.

Hyperlinks

A hyperlink is an icon, graphic, or word
on a document (slide or webpage)
that, when clicked with the mouse,
opens another slide or webpage.

Hotspots

As well as using text for hyperlinks,
you can create images that contain

▲ This is graphic on a slide where there are several hotspots (i.e., the different coloured areas).
When a user clicks on one of these areas they are taken to different slide about that area.

links. Images containing links are
called graphical hyperlinks, although
you will often hear them referred to
as hotspots. You can create your own
buttons and turn them into hotspots
or you can use an image. It is
important that you tell the user that
the image is a hotspot.

Sometimes you want to have an
image that contains several hotspots.
An example of this could be a map
where the towns or main tourist
areas on the map are the hotspots.
When a user moves over a town or
area, the cursor changes to a hand
indicating a hotspot and when
they click on it, they are taken to a
different page containing information
on that town or area.

Narration and speaker notes

Narration

Narration is speech that is recorded
about each slide. Narration is useful

if the speaker is not present when
the presentation is viewed. In order
to record a narration there needs to
be a microphone connected. Most
laptop computers have a microphone
built in but with desktop computers,
you will need to connect one unless
someone else has already done this.
Before starting the narration for
each slide, it is a good idea to write
down a script. You can then refine
this script and read from it when
recording the narration.

Speaker notes

We all need some sort of prompt to
help us with our presentation. Rather
than have bits of paper with prompts
written down on them, it is better to
have them with the slides. You can
see these notes with the slides but
the audience only sees the slides.

These notes may also be useful to
your audience, so they can be printed
out at the end along with the slides.

153

Tools and techniques for creating slide presentations *continued*

Printing formats

When presentations are given to an audience by a speaker it is usual for the speaker to give out copies of the slides to the audience. This enables them to take notes and refer to the material in the future.

There are several different printing formats for slides:

- You can have 1, 2, 3, 4, 6 or 9 slides on each page.
- You can print an outline view that lists what is on each slide in the presentation.

The advantages and disadvantages of presentation software

There are a number of advantages and disadvantages in using presentation software and these are summarized below.

Advantages

- The use of presentation software makes the presenter look more professional.
- It encourages the presenter to summarize what they are saying in a number of bullet points.
- The presenter can print out the slides so the audience have some information to take away and digest.
- The presenter is able to make use of full multimedia capability in their presentation.
- Presentations can be stored and transferred to people who were unable to attend the presentation.
- Presentations can be shown using a projector, whiteboard or TV or on a desktop or laptop computer screen, so the presenter has flexibility in the way the presentation is delivered.
- There is the presenter notes facility that gives a set of notes on

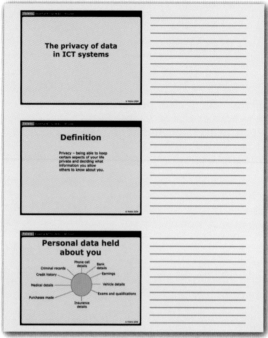

Here three slides are printed on each page and lines are left for the audience to add their own handwritten notes.

screen that the audience cannot see in case the presenter wonders what to say next.

Disadvantages

- The files for presentations containing video are extremely large and need a lot of memory and storage for them to run successfully.
- The audience can get fed up seeing all these special effects that people tend to put in their presentations.
- Good presentations can take a long time to set up.
- Sometimes people concentrate more time on presenting the information than they do on the gathering of the information in the first place. This means that the information is sometimes incorrect.
- Sometimes the sound effects and animation used in presentations can annoy the audience.

Questions A

1 A business creates a presentation to advertise its products. The presentation allows users to decide which slides of the presentation they want to look at by making use of hyperlinks.
   (a) Describe what is meant by a hyperlink. *(1 mark)*
   (b) Hotspots can be used as hyperlinks. Explain what is meant by a hotspot. *(1 mark)*

2 The creator of a presentation for children aimed at helping them learn their times tables wants to make it interesting for them. They decide to use slide transitions and animation to help.
   (a) Explain what is meant by a slide transition. *(1 mark)*
   (b) Explain what is meant by an animation. *(1 mark)*

END-OF-TOPIC REVIEW

Questions

 Test yourself

The following notes summarize this topic. The notes are incomplete because they have words missing.

Using the words in the list below, copy out and complete the sentences A to G, underlining the words that you have inserted. Each word may be used more than once.

> transition   design template   navigation
>
> bullet   hyperlink   animation   hotspots

A A _____ _____ is an outline design providing a basic colour scheme, font type, font size, etc.

B _____ involves getting some of the content that makes up the slides to move.

C You can select certain animations for the way the material such as headings and _____ points are added to a slide.

D The movement from one slide to another is called a slide _____.

E The way a user can move from one slide to another is called the slide _____.

F A _____ is an icon, graphic, or word on a document (slide or webpage) that, when clicked with the mouse, opens another slide or webpage.

G Images containing links are called graphical hyperlinks, although you will often hear them referred to as _____.

Examination style questions

1 A person is to give an important presentation in front of a large audience. They have the choice of using a design template or creating the design of their slides themselves.

  (a) Explain what is meant by a design template. *(2 marks)*

  (b) Give **one** advantage to them in using a design template. *(1 mark)*

  (c) Give **one** disadvantage in using a design template. *(1 mark)*

2 A salesperson has created a presentation to be given to customers using a laptop computer. The presentation is self-running and narration is included so all the customer has to do is watch it proceed.

  (a) Give **one** reason why it is important that the slide timings are correct. *(1 mark)*

  (b) Explain what is meant by narration and why it might be used. *(1 mark)*

END-OF-TOPIC REVIEW

Exam support

Worked example

A tourist information office decides to produce a self-running presentation of all the local attractions.

(a) Define each of the following functions of the presentation software, and explain, using an appropriate example, how each function could be used in this situation. *(4 marks)*

    (i) Templates
    (ii) Slide transitions

(b) Animations can be added to a presentation. Describe **one** type of animation that is provided as part of the presentation software. *(2 marks)*

Student answer 1

(a) (i) *Templates are designs that you can put your own work into. This means you don't have to start from scratch so it saves you time.*

    (ii) *Slide transitions are transitions that move a bit like a cartoon. They make it fun for your audience to watch and can liven up a presentation.*

(b) *The letters can appear one letter at a time to make up the title and then the bullet points are added automatically.*

◀ Examiner's comment

(a) (i) The definition is not quite clear but the second sentence makes it worth one mark as no example is given.

    (ii) The student has latched onto the word animation but does not know how it applies to presentation software. No marks here.

(b) This explains a suitable animation and two points are made so two marks are awarded here.

(3 marks out of 6)

Student answer 2

(a) (i) *Templates allow you to set out the formatting for a presentation. For example, you can specify the font and the size of the font for all the various headings and subheadings for the webpages. This means that if you decide to change them, you only have to change them in the template.*

    (ii) *Slide transitions are the way in which one side is replaced by another in a slideshow. For example, the slide can appear from the left, right, top or bottom of the page. It is also possible to animate the bullet points as they appear on the slide. The animations add interest to the slide show and will catch tourists' eyes when they are in the office.*

(b) *The letters of the heading can spin around and then make up the word.*

The bullets are then added one at a time.

◀ Examiner's comment

(a) (i) The student is getting mixed up between style sheets and templates and they have given a definition of a style sheet. Remember that style sheets determine the style (i.e. the formatting of the document) whereas a template is whole document where you can change the text, graphics and so on. No marks for this part.

    (ii) This is a clear definition of slide transitions and they have given a good example of their use so two marks are given here.

(b) Two suitable points have been made here. This is worth two marks.

(4 marks out of 6)

Examiner's answers

(a) (i) One mark for the definition and one mark for the example.

Templates are partly prepared documents/slides that contain placeholder text and graphics that you can replace with your own to save you from starting from scratch.

An example would be to have a slide containing the logo for the tourist information office, a graphic, a certain background colour and some text that can be replaced quickly when a new slide needs to be produced.

(ii) One mark for the definition and one mark for the example.

Slide transitions refer to the way slides can appear on the screen or it can refer to the way individual components such as text or graphics appear on the screen. For example, the slide for a different attraction could appear from different directions to add impact to the slide show.

(b) One mark for each point made to a maximum of two marks such as:

- One mark for explanation of animation (e.g. pinwheel, fading, etc.).
- One mark for explanation of how titles or bullet points are added.

EXAM TIPS

If you see the word 'define' in a question, you are required to give a definition of the term or concept.

If you are asked to 'give an example' of a feature or function, you will often be asked to give the example based on a particular situation or scenario. Make sure that any example refers to this.

You are often asked for definitions in GCSE ICT and students find it quite hard to make these up from what they know. Usually the definition is too vague and not worded precisely. It is therefore a good idea to simply learn certain definitions off by heart.

Do not separate the work you do in the theory from the things you do practically as they are all part of the same thing (i.e., being able to use ICT). If you are asked for an example of a particular piece of software being used, think about how you used it during your course or even in the controlled assessments completed as part of your GCSE or short course.

Current developments in the multimedia industry and their effects

You will find out

▷ **About what is meant by multimedia and what its features are**

▷ **About current developments in the multimedia industry and their effects on education, entertainment, business and society**

Multimedia is developing all the time and as the technology evolves, more uses will be developed. In this section you will be looking at current developments and their influence in certain areas of our lives.

What is multimedia?

Multimedia means many media such as text, audio, still images, animation, video and interactivity. Usually multimedia means more media than just text and graphics, so this means that a normal book or magazine would not be considered multimedia.

It is possible to have books and magazines on the Internet and these usually make use of multimedia features such as video, sound, etc.

Multimedia in education

People learn in different ways, so teachers like to have variety in the way they teach. This is why most educators think that multimedia is a good thing, because it offers so many different ways to get a message across.

Reading a book to learn a language is not ideal as you need to hear how words sound. This is why many schools have material on iPods and other MP3 players so that students can listen to lessons when they are doing other things such as walking to school.

If you are able to access a computer then you can have learning packages that make use of animations and video as well as sound. You can also have interactive links to interesting webpages.

Uses of multimedia in education include:

- interactive whiteboards to help with teaching and learning
- online tutorials
- simulations to explain how things work
- revision material.

Multimedia in entertainment

The Internet has made some big changes in the way we entertain ourselves. More and more people are using the Internet to entertain themselves by posting text, images and video on social networking sites. They are also using webcams to chat to each other.

Activity

Spotting multimedia components in websites

Look at the diagram on multimedia components to check you understand what they are. Now access the following websites in turn and write down the name of each multimedia component you spot and write a short description of its purpose.

1 http://www.ferrariworld. com/FWorld/fw/index.jsp
2 http://www.premierleague. com/
3 http://www.moremagazine. co.uk/

There has been a huge change in the way people listen to music, with people turning to downloads rather than physical CDs. In addition many people do not want just to listen to the music, they want to see video of the music being played. Television programmes are also being viewed on the Internet. There is a growing trend to actually stream the music, video, films, etc., over the Internet, which means that the person does not have to waste time downloading them. You are likely to start getting the ability to view films and TV programmes on iPods and similar devices. This means you will not have to download films and music as you simply select them on the device and the file will be streamed to your portable device or computer.

Multimedia in business

There are many different ways multimedia is used in business such as:

- websites to promote products and services
- presentations given to an audience of either your own staff or customers
- promotional videos/cartoons
- banner adverts on other organizations' websites
- adverts on the Internet.

Multimedia in society

The main benefits of multimedia to society are:

- **Flexibility** – there are so many different ways to do the same thing using multimedia. For example, you could read a story yourself, you could download it and listen to someone reading it on an MP3 player, you could watch a video of someone reading it or perhaps watch it as an animation. Which you prefer is up to you.
- **Interactivity** – the user has more control over what material they want to see, listen to, etc.
- **Integration of material** – this can be used to make the material easier to understand. This makes it easy to get a message across as it can be done in so many different ways.
- **Attention getting** – the word gets around quickly using websites. Look at the number of hits some YouTube material gets.

The use of multimedia is set to increase with the use of:

- e-books – a wafer thin device that can store hundreds of books
- streaming content such as TV programmes straight to people's portable devices or computers
- Internet access all the time from portable devices.

Activity

Finding out about e-books

E-books are starting to become really popular. Why bother having lots of dusty books on shelves when you only need a thin and light portable device that enables you to read them?

For this activity you have to find out about e-books such as:

- What can you do with them?
- How much do they cost?
- How do you get books to store on them?
- What other things can they do?

Amazon sell e-books and you can see what customers who have bought them think about their use.

Can you see a future where books are no longer needed?

Write a short piece of text explaining the answers to the points raised here.

Activity

Investigating multimedia features

Multimedia features include:

- audio
- still images
- text
- video
- animation
- interaction.

Log onto the Internet and access the following website:

http://www.nasa.gov/ multimedia/index.html

Using the above list as a guide, explain how this website makes use of each item in the list.

KEY WORD

Multimedia making use of many media such as text, image, sound, animation and video.

Questions A

1. A PowerPoint presentation can make use of multimedia. Apart from text, write down **three** different multimedia effects that a presentation can have. *(3 marks)*

2. Websites are made up of components. For example, a website may contain a search facility. Write down **three** other components of websites. *(3 marks)*

3. Everyone has their pet hates when looking at other people's websites. Write down a few sentences to describe the things that annoy you when accessing other websites. *(3 marks)*

Extension activity

Using newspapers and magazine articles as your guide produce a brief article for a school magazine that explains the latest trends in multimedia. Your article should also consider current new developments and try to predict how we are likely to use multimedia in the future.

Memory, storage and hardware needed for multimedia

You will find out

▷ **About the importance of memory size**

▷ **About the backing store needed for multimedia**

▷ **About the hardware needed for multimedia**

Because multimedia uses large files it places great demands on the computer equipment. In this section you will be looking at the requirements for running multimedia successfully.

The importance of memory size

Having a large amount of memory is important. Having more memory means:

- applications run faster on their own
- more applications are able to run at the same time
- you are able to move quickly between applications.

It is always important to know about the size of certain files because it is essential if you want to know how many of them could be stored on a particular storage device.

File size

File sizes can be a little confusing but here they are from the smallest to the largest:

> Bit
> Byte
> Kilobyte (KB)
> Megabyte (MB)
> Gigabyte (GB)
> Terabyte (TB)

The rough file size conversions are shown here:

Bit (0 or 1)	the smallest unit of measurement
Byte	8 bits
Kilobyte (KB)	1000 bytes
Megabyte (MB)	1000 kilobytes (KB)
Gigabyte (GB)	1000 megabytes (MB)
Terabyte (TB)	1000 gigabytes (GB)

The demands made by multimedia software on memory

Multimedia software demands a lot from the hardware of the computer. It is constantly driving the specification of an average computer higher. This means that computers need more powerful processors and creating multimedia products such as websites means that many different applications and files need to be open at the same time.

Backing store needed for multimedia

Backing storage is storage that is not the main memory. It is therefore storage on:

- magnetic hard drives (fixed or portable)
- optical disks (e.g., CD-ROM, DVD)
- flash drives (sometimes called pen drives, memory sticks, etc.)
- memory cards.

Hardware

Multimedia software makes use of a large number of pieces of hardware and these are looked at here.

Screens

Screen or VDU (visual display unit)

Screens are sometimes called monitors or VDUs (visual display units). Here are some facts about screens:

- They come in lots of sizes.
- They are usually in colour.
- They are useful for enquiries (When is the next train to...?, Do you have a holiday on this date...?).

TFT/LCD screens

Both desktop and laptop computers use TFT/LCD (thin film transistor/liquid crystal display) flat panel display screens. The advantages of TFT/LCD screens are:

- They are light – hence their use in laptop computers.

- They are cheaper to run – because they consume less power.
- In the case of desktop computer systems – they do not take up very much desk space.

Plasma screens

Plasma screens are large flat panel screens and are generally available in larger sizes compared to TFT/LCD screens. They have the following uses in ICT:

- used in reception areas
- used in videoconferencing systems
- used for presentations to a large audience.

Screen size and resolution

The screen size is usually determined by the type of application the multimedia is for. For example, although it is usually desirable to have a large screen for viewing video, this may not be possible, as the device may need to be portable.

Resolution is measured in pixels per cm or inch. The greater this value, then the higher the screen resolution and the clearer the image on the screen will appear.

MIDI (Musical Instrument Digital Interface) instruments

MIDI is an interface, which means a way of connecting and getting two devices to communicate with each other. MIDI can send signals to electronic devices such as keyboards, music synthesizers, guitars and drum machines. These devices can also send the signals back to the computer hardware so that the signals can be stored and modified in some way. For example, the sound from a drum might be too loud in a recording. Using MIDI you could save the sound from the drum and make it softer whilst keeping the loudness of the other instruments the same.

Input devices

Input devices are those hardware devices that input either instructions or data into the computer for

processing. Here are the main hardware devices used with multimedia systems.

Mouse

The main points about a mouse are:

- Mice are input devices because they are used to issue instructions by making selections.
- When the mouse is moved, a pointer or cursor moves on the screen mirroring the movement of the mouse.
- Selections can be made by pressing the mouse buttons.
- A scroll wheel can be used for scrolling through long documents or viewing images in detail.
- A mouse may also be used for drawing lines, sizing graphic objects such as pictures or clip art.

Graphics tablet

A graphics tablet consists of pen-like device that you use to draw or write on a tablet (it looks a bit like a flat board) and it then appears on the computer screen.

You can use a graphics tablet to design your own graphics.

Some graphics tablets contain special buttons to select shapes or special pictures.

Touch-sensitive input devices

To operate a touch screen you simply touch the item on the screen to make a selection or produce a drawing. Usually a special pen-type device, called a stylus, is used to create drawings or edit existing images. Most creative people find it much easier to draw using a stylus rather than a mouse.

Microphone

A microphone allows sound to be converted into data. Using a microphone allows you to do the following:

- You can record sounds/music.
- You can have a narration to a presentation, which saves you having to speak.
- You can tell the computer what to do (i.e., you can issue instructions).
- You can dictate letters and other documents directly into your word-processor or email package. This is called voice recognition.

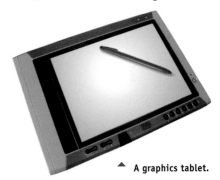

▲ A graphics tablet.

GLASBERGEN

"I spent a fortune for a 60-inch plasma TV and *now* you'd rather watch programs on a 2-inch iPod screen?!"

Memory, storage and hardware needed for multimedia *continued*

Digital still camera

A digital camera looks like an ordinary camera except there is no film and there is usually a screen on which to view the picture (called an image) when taken. Here are some facts about digital cameras:

- Digital cameras have memory where they store the image.
- The more memory a camera has, the more pictures you can store.
- There are no developing fees as with an ordinary camera.
- If the picture is not suitable (as viewed on the screen) then it can be taken again.
- You can transfer the pictures to your computer, where you can store and edit them.
- Digital cameras are more expensive than ordinary cameras.

Digital cameras produce an image made up of millions of dots. The greater the number of dots (called pixels) in the same space, the clearer the picture will appear. This is called the resolution of the image. High resolution images use more dots and take up more storage space on the computer.

Digital video camera

Digital video cameras look the same as ordinary video cameras except that they store the image digitally. Here are some other facts:

- Most digital video cameras can capture still as well as moving images.
- Images may be stored and edited on the computer.
- You can use video in websites.

KEY WORDS

Digital camera a camera that takes a picture and stores it digitally.

Web camera a digital camera used to capture still and video images.

Web cameras (webcams)

A web camera (webcam) is simply a digital camera that is used to capture still images and video images (i.e. moving images). These images can then be transmitted to a computer where they are stored in a suitable graphics format. If required, pictures can be used on a website.

▲ Webcams can be fixed to the top of the screen or in the case of some computers they are built into the screen.

Questions B

1 **(a)** Tick **five** boxes to show which of the following are input devices. *(5 marks)*

	Tick 5 boxes only
Graphics tablet	☐
Colour laser printer	☐
Mouse	☐
Microphone	☐
Speakers	☐
LCD screen	☐
Pen drive	☐
Digital still camera	☐
Magnetic hard disk drive	☐
CD-ROM drive	☐
Webcam	☐

(b) Name **two** output devices given in the table above. *(2 marks)*

(c) Give the name of a storage device in the above table. *(1 mark)*

2 Musicians often use MIDI with musical instruments. Fill in the blank:

(a) MIDI stands for Musical Instrument Digital _____. *(1 mark)*

(b) Briefly describe what MIDI is. *(1 mark)*

Interactive components, multimedia software and storing techniques

In this section you will be looking at the interactive components of multimedia software. You will also be looking at the advantages and disadvantages of multimedia software. Many of the files used by multimedia software are very large and they need large amounts of storage even though many of these files are compressed before they are stored. You will be looking at the way these files are stored along with the advantages and disadvantages of the storage techniques.

Interactive components

Key word searches

You simply type a word, series of words or a sentence and the multimedia package will find relevant content.

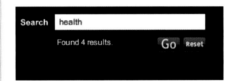

▲ Search box.

Quizzes

It is fairly easy to create quizzes on websites or quizzes using presentation software such as PowerPoint. Both types of multimedia software use the interactive features of the software to jump from the questions to the answers. Quizzes can be included to find out how much a user has learnt from using a multimedia product. They can also be used to assess how much a person already knows about a subject.

Questionnaires

People who design websites like to get user feedback, so one way of doing this is to get users to complete an online questionnaire. This is a very cheap way of finding out what users think of the site, or their online shopping experience in the case of an e-commerce site. As the answers to the questionnaires are completed, the results from all the questionnaires can be processed and analysed.

Games

Games are normally at the forefront of multimedia technology and are popular with all generations. The demands that games software makes on computer hardware are high, which results in people having much more up-to-date systems at home than they do at work.

Links

Many multimedia products, such as presentations and websites, use links to enable a user to take them to information stored in a different file or on a different website.

Advantages and disadvantages in using multimedia software

Advantages

The advantages of multimedia include:

- Offers interaction with the user – they can decide what they want to do and in which order.
- Offers different ways of presenting information other than just reading text and looking at still images.
- Can suit different learning styles. For example, people who do not like reading can use animations or listen to audio.
- It enables learning through exploration, discovery and experience.

END-OF-TOPIC REVIEW

Exam support

Worked example

Multimedia is an important aspect of ICT and it can be used in education, business, entertainment and society as a whole.

(a) Explain the meaning of the term 'multimedia'. *(2 marks)*

(b) Multimedia products, such as presentations and websites, make use of multimedia features. Give the names of **three** multimedia features. *(3 marks)*

(c) Describe **one** advantage in using multimedia software. *(1 mark)*

(d) Describe **one** disadvantage in using multimedia software. *(1 mark)*

Student answer 1

(a) *Software that does all sorts of things such as play games.*

Websites are this as well.

(b) *Sound*

Video

Music.

(c) *You can use more of your senses to take in what is being shown so you learn more.*

(d) *It is not always very good.*

▲ Examiner's comment

(a) This fails to explain that it makes use of a variety of different media to get the message across. This answer is not worth any marks.

(b) Music and sound are the same feature. Students should always ensure that the answers they give are distinctly different as this is a frequent cause of loss of marks.

(c) This is a valid answer although not completely clear. One mark is given.

(d) A very general answer. In what way is it not very good? No marks for this.

(3 marks out of 7)

Student answer 2

(a) *Software, such as presentation software or website design software, that makes use of many different types of media so as to make it easier for the user to get the benefits from it.*

(b) *Animation such as cartoons or logos that move across the screen.*

Videos such as of a holiday resort.

Music such as tracks you can listen to a bit of before you buy the CD.

(c) *It offers a variety of different methods to teach the same thing. For example, you have animation to show how something works and then you can have an interactive quiz so the user can assess how much they have learnt.*

(d) *Some people with old computers may not be able to use some of the multimedia things without upgrading their computer.*

◀ Examiner's comment

(a) This is a good answer and makes two points (the examples of types of software) and the fact that many different types of media are used. Two marks are given for this.

(b) When you are asked to 'give' an answer, then a brief answer is required and even a one-word answer may do. All the answers here are good and so full marks are given.

(c) This is a clear advantage and is worth a mark.

(d) The demands placed on hardware by multimedia is a disadvantage and may prevent a user from accessing the software. One mark for the answer given.

(7 marks out of 7)

Examiner's answers

(a) Two marks for a definition similar to the following which makes two points.

Multimedia means many media (1) such as text, audio, still images, animation, video and interactivity (1).

(b) One mark each for three of the following (single word answers are ok):

- Text
- Audio
- Still images
- Animation
- Video
- Interactivity.

(c) One mark for an advantage such as:

- Offers interaction with the user – they can decide what they want to do and in which order.
- Offers different ways of presenting information other than just reading text and looking at still images.
- Can suit different learning styles. For example, people who do not like reading can use animations or listen to audio.
- It enables learning through exploration, discovery and experience.

(d) One mark for a disadvantage such as:

- The hardware may need to be upgraded in order to run the software.

Summary mind map

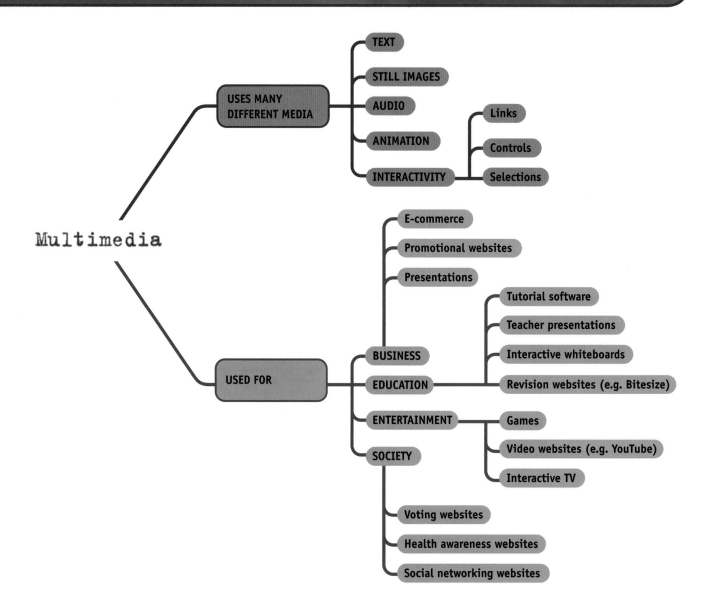

Digital imaging

The key concepts covered in this topic are:

- **Understand vector and bitmap graphics**
- **Understand the tools and techniques for creating and manipulating still images**
- **Understand common file formats**

In order that images can be used on a computer they need to be in digital form. If you only have old images such as family photographs then these will need to be converted to digital format by using a scanner. You could also consider taking a digital photograph of the printed photograph.

There are other ways of getting digital images, such as producing them directly using software. Once an image is in digital format it can be stored and manipulated by software.

In this topic you will be looking at the two main types of digital image, bitmap and vector, along with their relative advantages and disadvantages. You will also learn about the tools and techniques for manipulating still images.

Contents

Vector and bitmap graphics

▷ **About vector and bitmap graphical techniques**

▷ **About pixel dimensions, and benefits and problems with resizing images**

▷ **About screen resolution and memory requirements for different backgrounds**

There are two different types of graphics – bitmapped graphics and vector graphics.

When you design a graphic you have a choice of which type to use. If you obtain a photograph from a digital camera it will be a bitmap graphic/image.

In this section you will look at the difference between these two types of graphic and how they can be manipulated. You will also look at their relative advantages and disadvantages.

◁ This photograph is a bitmap image. A small square of this photograph has been enlarged and you can see that the image is made up of lots of coloured squares. These are called the pixels.

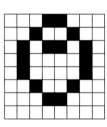

▲ The above arrangement of pixels (i.e. an 8 × 8 square) is stored as a bitmap like this:

0	0	0	1	1	0	0	0
0	0	1	0	0	1	0	0
0	1	0	1	1	0	1	0
0	1	0	0	0	0	1	0
0	1	0	0	0	0	1	0
0	0	1	0	0	1	0	0
0	0	0	1	1	0	0	0
0	0	0	0	0	0	0	0

◁ Black pixels are represented as 1 and white pixels are represented as 0.

▲ A single coloured square on the screen is called a pixel.

Vector and bitmap graphical techniques

Bitmap images are made up of millions of pixels. Normally there are many pixels and they are extremely small. This means you cannot see them in an image. If the image is enlarged, then you can start to see the pixels and the image appears blocky.

Remember: the more pixels an image contains, the greater the file size needed to store it.

In general:

- Bitmaps are big files so they take lots of space on a disk. They also take a long time to upload (i.e., put onto a website) or download (i.e., to appear on a user's screen).
- They can lose their sharpness when they are enlarged or reduced in size.
- They are made up of individual pixels that can be set to a colour.
- They are used for photographs or images with continuous colours.

Vector graphics

Vector graphics are graphics that use maths to work out the positions and lengths of lines, curves, etc. Vector images:

- can be enlarged or reduced, keeping their sharpness
- do not take up much space when stored compared to bitmap images
- are made up of objects that can be edited and filled with colour
- are used for more precise images such as: maps, technical drawings/plans or images that contain a limited number of colours (e.g., logos, clip art, lettering)
- are not good for re-creating photographic type artwork
- are uploaded and downloaded faster owing to their smaller file size.

The advantages of vector graphics over bitmapped graphics

There are a number of advantages of vector graphics over bitmapped graphics:

- Vector graphics have very small sizes. Small file size means that a viewer of the graphic does not wait long to see it appear on the screen.
- They have a low upload and download time and so are ideal for the Web.
- They are much easier to edit and can be resized without any loss in quality.
- By using software it is easy to zoom in and out on a vector image.

Screen resolution

The number of pixels per inch or pixels per centimetre determines the screen resolution. The more pixels per inch or cm then the better the resolution of the screen and the better the picture it can produce.

If a screen has a screen resolution of 300 pixels per inch then by knowing the size of the image in pixels we can work out how big it will appear on the screen.

Suppose we have an image which is 1200 pixels by 600 pixels.

We can work out how big the image will appear on a screen with resolution 300 pixels per inch (118 pixels per centimetre) like this:

$$\text{Length of image} = \frac{1200}{300}$$

$$= 4 \text{ inches}$$

$$\text{Width of image} = \frac{600}{300}$$

$$= 2 \text{ inches}$$

If the screen has a lower resolution, say 150 pixels per inch (59 pixels per centimetre) then the image size can be calculated in the same way:

$$\text{Length of image} = \frac{1200}{150}$$

$$= 8 \text{ inches}$$

$$\text{Width of image} = \frac{600}{150}$$

$$= 4 \text{ inches}$$

As you can see the screen resolution affects how big a particular image appears on the screen.

Pixel dimensions

Pixel dimensions are the horizontal and vertical measurements of an image expressed in pixels.

The benefits and problems in resizing images

Benefits of resizing images:

- You can fit the image into your design (website, presentation, etc.).
- You can alter the shape slightly.

Problems in resizing images:

- In the case of bitmap images they become blurred when resized.
- If the image is too big, you may not be able to fit it on the screen without scrolling.

Memory requirements for different backgrounds

Many pieces of clip art have a transparent background. This is just like drawing the image on a sheet of glass, so whatever is underneath is what appears as the background.

As you would imagine, the more complex the background in terms of variety of colours used, then the more memory is needed to store it. In order of increasing memory for backgrounds to images we have:

- transparent
- white
- colour.

Questions A

1 There are two types of graphic that can be used by a computer. These are bitmap and vector graphics.
   - (a) Name **one** hardware device that can be used to draw an image. *(1 mark)*
   - (b) Give the name of the type of graphic that is stored by a digital camera. *(1 mark)*
   - (c) Explain what is meant by a bitmap graphic. *(2 marks)*
   - (d) Explain what is meant by a vector graphic. *(2 marks)*
   - (e) Give **two** advantages of using vector graphics rather than bitmap graphics. *(2 marks)*

Extension activity

Many graphics packages are able to produce and edit bitmap graphics or vector graphics.

Find out about the packages that your school or college has and write down the names of the packages and find out a little about how they work.

The tools and techniques for creating and manipulating still images

You will find out

▷ **About the standard tools used for manipulating graphics**

▷ **About colour effects, colour palettes and gradient tools**

▷ **About imaging effects**

▷ **About transparency effects**

▷ **About composite patterning (repeated patterns)**

There are many tools and techniques for creating and manipulating still images and you will have used them when you did some of your Key Stage 3 work. As part of this course you will be doing a lot of practical work where you will doubtless use everything that this section covers.

Manipulating graphics using standard tools

Graphics can be manipulated in a number of different ways including:

Zoom: Allows a user to magnify or reduce the size of an image on the screen. Usually zoom is used to magnify an image so that the individual pixels can be viewed and edited if necessary.

Selection: Allows the whole of a graphic or just part of the image to be selected for editing.

Transforming: There are a number of ways you can transform an image. For example, you can:
- *Rotate* – occasionally to produce a more eye-catching display, you can rotate a graphic through a variety of angles.
- *Reflect* – you may decide that the way a graphic is facing needs to be reversed.

Sizing: The graphic will have been pre-stored at a certain size but it can have its size altered to fit any space available. This process is called sizing.

Scaling: Scaling is sizing to a certain pre-determined size. Often this is expressed as a percentage of the original size of the graphic. For example 200% would produce an image exactly twice the size of the original graphic but a scale of 50% would reduce it to half the size.

Copying: An invitation to a Christmas party could be set on paper covered by graphics of Father Christmas. The quickest way to do this would be to import one of them and copy the rest into the various positions.

Moving: If a graphic appears to be in the wrong position then it is fairly simple to select it and then move it to a new position on the screen.

Cloning: A clone is simply a replica of an original graphic.

Brush settings: In most graphics editing packages there is a tool called the paintbrush and when you click on it you will see various options appear in the options section like this:

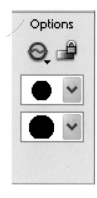

Controlling a paintbrush on a screen by moving a mouse is quite difficult and some professional artists prefer to use an alternative input device such as a light pen (where they draw directly onto the screen) or a graphics tablet.

Layering: Layering is a very useful technique. If a graphic consists of lots of smaller graphics then you can draw each small graphic on its own layer. This is a bit like drawing the graphics on a sheet of glass with each sheet being equivalent to a layer. When all the layers are placed over each other, the complete graphic is produced. It is easier to edit graphics and re-use them if they are in their own layer.

Shapes on a layer will obscure shapes on layers below them if they overlap. This is useful in animation where you could have a walking person in one layer walking past a lamp post in a different layer.

Colour effects

There are many colour effects you can apply to parts or all of a graphic. Here are some of the main tools you can use to create these.

Colour palette

Any element of a graphic can be produced in a colour using a palette of colours similar to the one shown below.

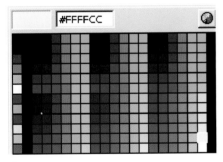

▲ Colour palette.

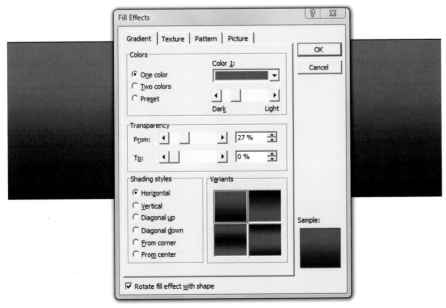

▲ The gradient effect can be altered in PowerPoint using the Fill Effects window shown above.

Gradient tools

Gradient tools allow the colour to be more intense in one area and then start to fade away as you move away from this area. Backgrounds to slides in a PowerPoint presentation can have a gradient applied.

The following graphic produced using the software Flash has a radial fill applied to it.

▲ Notice how the colour increases away from the centre.

Imaging effects

Graphics editing software has many useful imaging effects and some are detailed here:

- Altering the pixels in a photographic image/air brushing – it is possible to zoom into a bitmap image until you can see the individual pixels. It is then possible to edit the pixels by changing their colour. You can therefore remove skin blemishes, unwanted objects and even people from an image.

- Removing red eye from a photograph – this is a common problem in photographs taken using a flash. It is easily removed using graphics software.

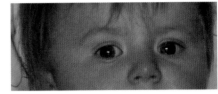

▲ You could change the colour of the red part to the colour blue or you can simply press a button to get rid of the red.

Transparency effects

When you insert a bitmap image into a webpage, there are four sides to the image. You can only see this if the background has a different colour to the background of the graphic.

▲ A graphic like this is enclosed within a rectangle.

▲ You can see the rectangle when the graphic is inserted into a document with a different background colour.

You can see from the above picture that the image does not look part of the page because of the white background. It would look better if the background colour of the graphic were the same as the background colour of the webpage. Here we need what is called transparency. Transparency involves taking the image and putting it on whatever background is used for the page. It can also be used when you want to see what is behind an image.

The tools and techniques for creating and manipulating still images *continued*

Composite patterning

Composite patterning means a pattern that can be repeated over and over. Composite patterning can be used:

- for backgrounds (e.g., for slides, webpages, etc.)
- to fill shapes.

KEY WORDS

Colour palette a selection of colours from which a user can select a colour by clicking on one.

Gradient tool a feature offered by graphics software that allows a colour to soften in different ways.

Transparency effect allows a user to see through the background to a piece of clip art so that the background takes the same colour of page the clip art is put onto.

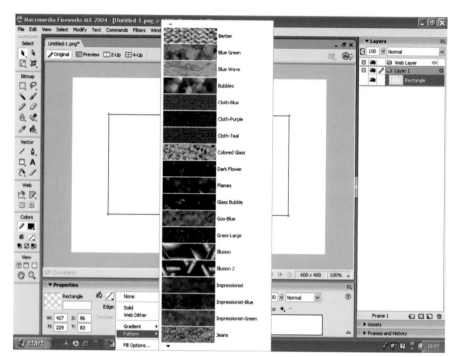

▲ Graphics software allows you to fill areas with patterns.

Questions B

1 **(a)** In a book about digital photography it says that a digital image can be scaled up or down. Explain in a sentence what this means. *(2 marks)*

(b) A photograph may be edited. Give **three** different ways of editing a photograph. *(3 marks)*

2 Here are some examples of types of image. For each one, you have to decide whether it is best created as a vector or bitmap image.

(a) A photograph taken using a digital camera. *(1 mark)*

(b) A simple logo for a company that only uses four colours. *(1 mark)*

(c) An accurate plan of your bedroom drawn to scale. *(1 mark)*

(d) A piece of clip art that will regularly need to be resized. *(1 mark)*

(e) A picture that contains continuous colours. *(1 mark)*

Extension activities

In this section you learnt about some of the tools that are available in graphics packages and some of things you can do with them.

For this activity you should investigate the tools available in a graphics package that your school/college has. Give the name of each tool and state its purpose.

Common file formats (bmp, jpeg, gif, tiff, eps, etc.)

You will find out

▷ About the use, advantages and disadvantages of common file formats (bmp, jpeg, gif, tiff and eps)

When obtaining or creating images for use in websites, presentations, multimedia products and so on, it is important to save the image in a certain file format. The file format that should be used depends on the type of medium (e.g., on-screen, Web or print) that you intend to use to display the image.

GIF files

GIF stands for graphical interchange format and along with the file format called JPEG, it is one of the two main file formats for images used on the Internet.

GIF files have the advantage that they are small in size. The original image file is compressed by removing any irrelevant data in the file. The main disadvantage with GIF files is that only 256 colours are used even though an actual image can contain 16 million colours. This means that GIF images do not quite look the same as the original image.

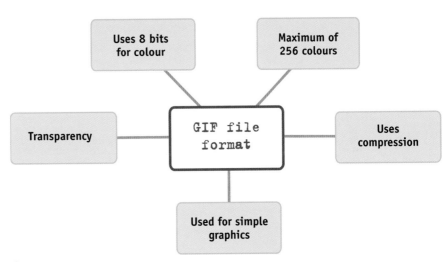

▲ Summary of the GIF file format.

GIF files are good for:

- images on the Web
- photographs on the Web.

JPEG files

JPEG stands for Joint Photographic Expert Group. With GIF, it is the main file format for images on the Web. JPEG is ideal for photographs and many digital cameras automatically create files with this file format.

Like GIF, JPEG compresses the original image. There is a slight distortion when the image is converted to a JPEG file. This is noticeable at the edges of the image. JPEG files use 16 million colours, which is why they are ideal for photographic images.

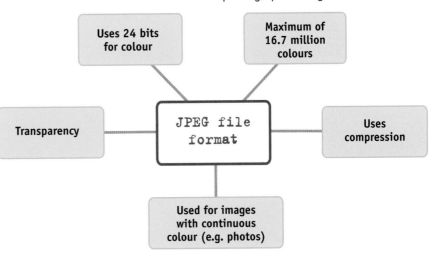

▲ Summary of the JPEG file format.

Common file formats *continued*

PNG files

PNG stands for portable network graphics. PNG files uses compression that creates a compressed image without any loss in image quality. It uses 16 million colours but the resulting file size is slightly larger than GIF or JPEG files.

When you create a graphic using the software Fireworks, you create it in this file format. You can then choose to save the file in different file formats depending on the use to which the graphic is to be put.

TIFF files

TIFF stands for Tagged Image File Format. TIFF is a bitmapped image format and is ideally suited to scanned images, images with continuous colours and photographs. TIFFs are widely used and can be easily modified and can have any number of colours.

PSD files

PSD stands for Photoshop Document. Photoshop is a popular piece of software used for creating and modifying images. PSD file format produces very high quality images but as there is no compression, the file sizes are large. This means that if you used PSD files with the Internet, they would take a while to upload and download.

BMP files

This file format saves the image as a map of pixels. It supports millions of colours but because of the very large file size the time taken to load the file from the Internet is large.

Pictures created using the package Windows Paint are saved as bmp files and of course digital photographs can be stored as bmp files.

EPS files

EPS stands for Encapsulated PostScript and is a standard format for importing and exporting PostScript files. EPS files can contain text, graphics and images and contain a small preview image. Adobe Photoshop can save bitmap images in this file format.

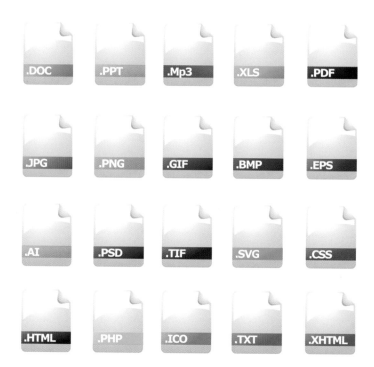

▲ You will come across a huge number of different file extensions when working with ICT.

END-OF-TOPIC REVIEW

Questions

 Test yourself

The following notes summarize this topic. The notes are incomplete because they have words missing.

Using the words in the list below, copy out and complete the sentences A to I, underlining the words that you have inserted. Each word may be used more than once.

pixel   JPEG   upload   vector   bitmap

quality   resolution   download   pixels

A A _____ is a single point in a graphics element or the smallest dot of light that can appear on a computer screen.

B A _____ graphic or image is stored as a map showing the position and colour of individual dots of light called pixels.

C Bitmaps are big files so they take lots of space on a disk and they also take a long time to _____ (i.e., put onto a website) or _____ (i.e., to appear on a user's screen from the Internet).

D A _____ graphic is a graphic that is expressed mathematically as an equation.

E Vector graphics are much easier to edit and can be resized without any loss in _____.

F If bitmap images are enlarged too much, you can start to see the individual _____ so the image appears blocky.

G The number of pixels per inch or pixels per centimetre determines the screen _____.

H The type of image obtained from a digital camera is a _____ image.

I The GIF and _____ file formats are ideal for storing images on the Web.

Examination style questions

1 A graphic has been created using graphic design software.
Give the names of **two** ways a graphic can be edited. *(2 marks)*

2 A website designer would like to use a background for a graphic they would like to include on each page as a logo.
They have a choice of the following backgrounds:
    Transparent
    White
    Colour

  (a) Which background from the above list would use the least memory? *(1 mark)*
  (b) Before the graphic can be used, it needs to be edited using standard tools.
Describe **two** standard tools for editing graphics and for each describe what changes to the graphic they can be used for. *(4 marks)*

3 There are two types of graphic: bitmap and vector. Discuss vector and bitmap graphical techniques and how they affect memory size and the ability to edit them. *(4 marks)*

END-OF-TOPIC REVIEW

Exam support

Worked example

When an image is to be published on a website the image should always be optimized.

(a) Explain why an image on a website should be optimized. *(2 marks)*

(b) Give **one** advantage for optimizing the image on a website. *(1 mark)*

Student answer 1

(a) It means making it load faster and making it appear clearer on the screen.

(b) It will be faster to appear on the user's screen.

◀ **Examiner's comment**

(a) The first answer about making it loading faster is true but the user should have said how it is made to load faster (i.e., by compressing it to reduce the file size). Reducing the file size is done at the expense of the image quality so the other part in the sentence gains no marks. No marks are given here.

(b) This answer is fine for one mark.

(1 mark out of 3)

Student answer 2

(a) The download time, which is the time taken for the image file to come from the server to the user's computer, should be kept low. This means that the file size needs to be small.

It should have enough resolution to be clear but the resolution does not have to be too high as the user will not notice and it will only make the file size too big.

(b) It will mean that the webpage with the image on will load faster onto the user's screen. It means they are more likely to stay with the website rather than click off it.

◀ **Examiner's comment**

(a) Both the answers for this part are clear so two marks are awarded.

(b) This answer is well explained so full marks for this part.

(3 marks out of 3)

Examiner's answers

(a) One mark each for two points such as:

- Optimization reduces the file size of the image *(1)*
- Usually by reducing the quality of the image *(1)*
- By reducing the resolution of the image *(1)*
- Or reducing the number of colours used to represent the image *(1)*
- Reduce the size of the image (which in turn reduces the number of pixels) *(1)*

(b) One mark for one of the following points:

- Takes less time to upload onto the website
- Takes less time to download
- Saves memory usage

Summary mind maps

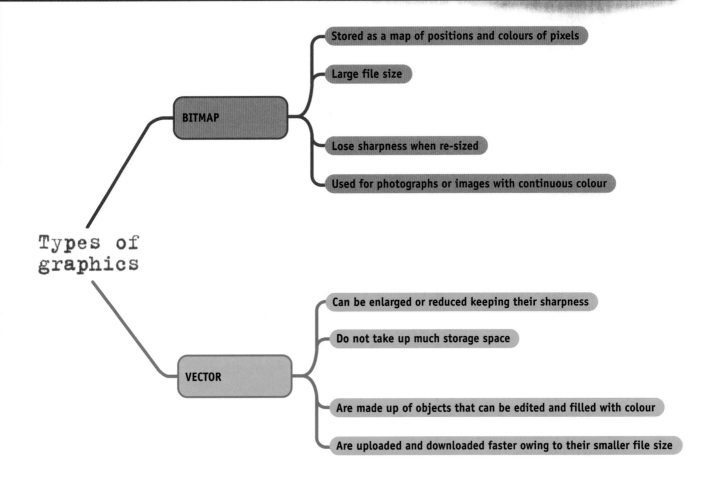

Types of graphics

BITMAP
- Stored as a map of positions and colours of pixels
- Large file size
- Lose sharpness when re-sized
- Used for photographs or images with continuous colour

VECTOR
- Can be enlarged or reduced keeping their sharpness
- Do not take up much storage space
- Are made up of objects that can be edited and filled with colour
- Are uploaded and downloaded faster owing to their smaller file size

The origins of animation and animation processes

You will find out

▷ **About the origins of animation**

▷ **About animation processes**

In this section you will be looking at the development of animations (i.e. moving images) and the various processes used to produce them using ICT.

Animation is a very important aspect of ICT and it is hard to find a website or multimedia product that does not make use of them in some way.

The origins of animation

When most people think of animation they think of cartoons. Simple animations of horses or people running were produced long before cartoons. The first cartoons used cel animation. Here each frame was painted on a piece of cellulose acetate (transparent plastic). A background was painted containing all the items that do not move. The transparent frames were laid over the background and photographed. Another cel was painted and laid over the background with a slight difference. The process was repeated until a complete scene was produced. The process was very laborious but in the early days of animation it drew huge audiences.

▲ This device was invented in 1877 and when you spin the centre part, the horse appears to gallop.

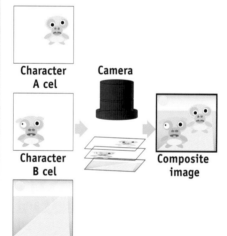

Character A cel

Character B cel

Camera

Background

Composite image

▲ How cel animation works.

Animation processes

Animation processes are those steps that need to be taken in order to produce an animation that could be as simple as a moving image or logo to a full length movie.

The following are examples of the processes involved.

Persistence of vision techniques

The human eye sees an image for one twenty-fifth of a second after the image has actually disappeared. This is called the persistence of vision. This means that it is easy to produce animations that do not appear jerky.

A series of frames can be produced, with each frame slightly different, so that the objects appear to move. Joining them up at a certain rate means that the eye sees a smooth transition from one frame to the next.

▲ Here are a series of frames used to show a man walking. When put together at the right speed, the movement of the man appears to be smooth.

Flip books

Flip books are books containing drawings, with a slightly different drawing on each page, that appear to move when the pages are flipped quickly. The persistence of vision gives the appearance of smooth movement.

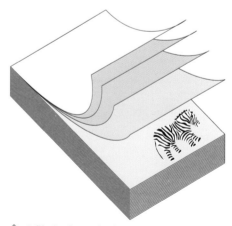

▲ A flip book – a simple low-tech animation method.

Stop motion animation

In this type of animation a model is photographed and then moved slightly and photographed again and so on. The photographs are combined and the tiny movements are joined together to show the model moving smoothly. As you can imagine, it is a slow and laborious process but it is simple to do and a good way to get into animation.

The film Corpse Bride is an award-winning example of stop motion animation.

Flash/key frame animation

You have probably heard of Flash. Lots of websites use it to produce impressive results. Flash is a piece of software used to create interactive and animated websites.

Flash has these advantages:
- Flash images are very fast to load.
- You can create interactive animated images using Flash.
- You do not need to know anything about programming to use it.

Key frames are the starting frame and the finishing frame in an animation. For example, if you had a simple animation of one shape such as a square changing into a different shape such as a circle then key frames would be:

- the start frame of the square
- the end frame of the circle.

Here are the steps you would need to take to move a red ball across the screen from left to right:

1. Draw the red ball
2. Erase it
3. Draw the red ball a little to the right
4. Erase it
5. Draw the red ball a little further to the right
6. Repeat steps 3 to 5 enough times
7. Draw the red ball in its final position.

When you use Flash (and other brands of animation software), when you want an object to move across the screen you need only to define the key frames (i.e., drawn in steps 1 and 7) where something changes. You leave it to Flash to put in the frames in between. This is tweening which you will meet on page 190. This reduces the amount of work you need to do considerably.

3D animation

You will probably have seen the film Toy Story. This is a good example of 3D animation. This technique uses very sophisticated and expensive software, which means that it is mainly used by film studios for the production of films. However, there are some less complex packages that can be used at home.

As well as the special software, you also need to use modelling techniques to make the whole thing look realistic. These modelling techniques use shaders (to show realistic shadows) and textures just like in real life.

Questions A

1. Explain what is meant by the term persistence of vision. *(2 marks)*

2. Flip books can be used to produce simple animations. Describe how an animation is produced using a flip book. *(2 marks)*

3. Describe how the technique called stop motion is used to produce an animation. *(3 marks)*

Uses of animation in commercial and learning environments

You will find out

▷ **About the film making and special effects industries**

▷ **About the uses of animation in VLEs and educational websites**

▷ **About animations for websites**

▷ **About the advantages and disadvantages of animation in commercial and educational environments**

Animation is a very important technique and there is a huge industry built around it.

Film making is one such industry but there are also many people employed creating animations for websites. Animations are also important in education, where they can be used to explain simple things from teaching young children words to enabling students to understand a complex situation.

In this section you will be looking at some of these uses of animations.

Film making and special effects industries

There is a huge film industry based around animation and many different types of animation techniques are used to keep audiences entertained.

Illusions to illustrate a film, programme, game or other computer program used to stimulate the imagination are called special effects. Now, with the use of digital cameras and video editing software, special effects are fairly easy to make.

It the olden days of films, special effects included the use of props, scale models and atmospheric effects such as rain, wind and snow. Nowadays with the use of computers and digital imagery, special effects can be made that are much more convincing and much cheaper to produce.

Uses of animation in VLEs and educational websites

Animation can be used to make a dull topic come alive. Animation is used in educational multimedia products from programs to teach young

children to read and do very basic maths to material for A-level.

Greek mythology is a subject that can be read about but look at the following website with stories that have been brought to life with the use of animation techniques: http:// www.wingedsandals.com/

Animations for websites

Adding animations to a webpage can make the webpage more interesting but you have to make sure that the images are appropriate for the content.

One quick way of adding animations to a webpage is to use an animated gif.

▷ The Wallace and Gromit films are very popular.

Identification through logos

Most organizations and companies use logos to help present an image to customers. If these logos are on paper, such as in brochures, letterheads, business cards and so on, it is impossible to use animation. However, many organizations have a website or produce presentations, so it is now possible to bring the logos to life and animate them.

Standard banners for webpages/leader boards

A web banner is a form of advertising that you will see on websites. The banners are adverts that are embedded into a webpage. If you click on one of these banners, you are taken to the website. There is a link between the banner and the advertiser's website.

Banners come in a variety of different sizes. When designing webpages it is a good idea to use one of these sizes. The reason for this is that you may want to have advertising on your site and you need to leave spaces for these. Normally advertisers will have several banners and one of them will fit the space left. Without these standard sizes it would mean redesigning the page (and possibly others) just to fit in an advertisement. These standard size banners are called standard banners.

One popular size standard banner has a name and it is called a leader board. A leader board is 728 pixels long and 90 pixels wide.

728 × 90

▲ A leader board has a fixed size of 728 × 90 pixels.

Many people do not like web banners for two main reasons:

- They can detract from the main content on the website.
- They are sometimes animated, which means they are slow to load.

However, the person who puts them into their website usually gets money if the person viewing uses the link to the advertiser and buys something. This is a useful source of income for the person who has gone to the trouble of making the site.

The advantages and disadvantages of animation in commercial and educational environments

Advantages of animation

- It can help explain a difficult concept (e.g., the greenhouse effect, the nitrogen cycle, etc.).
- It can be used to entertain young children.
- It can attract users to a website.
- It can make learning fun for young children.

Disadvantages of animation

- Good animation can be expensive to produce.
- It can distract users away from the content or the message being given.
- On a website, it can take a while to load, which can put off some visitors to the website.

Questions B

1 Banners are used on websites.
- **(a)** Explain what a banner is. *(2 marks)*
- **(b)** Give **one** reason why banners come in standard sizes. *(1 mark)*
- **(c)** Some web users do not like banners. Give **one** reason why. *(1 mark)*

2 Animations are used in many websites.
Give **one** advantage and **one** disadvantage in using an animation in a website. *(2 marks)*

Tools and techniques for creating animated images

You will find out

▷ **About planning an animation**

▷ **About the importance of awareness of audience**

▷ **About the tools and techniques for animation**

▷ **About the advantages and disadvantages of different file formats**

Animations take a lot of thought and planning before they are started. In this section you will be looking at the tools and techniques for creating animated images.

Planning an animation

Taking time to plan an animation is very important. Here are some of the things you need to do when creating an animation.

Folder trees

A folder tree is a graphic representation of a hierarchical folder structure.

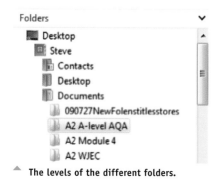
The levels of the different folders.

With any project in ICT it is very important to get organized before you start by thinking about the folder structure you are going to use and about the folders in folder structure. Being organized by creating a folder tree at the start does take time but you will reap the benefits later on because all the files will be easy to find. It is also much easier to back up the folders and files.

Storyboards

Explaining how an animation, multimedia presentation or website will work is quite difficult. It is not easy explaining the visual ideas involved. Storyboarding provides a way of communicating visual ideas.

A storyboard is a series of sketches showing the layout of drawings, still photographs or animations involved in a multimedia presentation or website. Storyboards are used to show the sequence and layout of ideas.

What should a storyboard contain?

There are no rules as to what a storyboard should or should not contain. You are completely free to use your artistic talents.

Typically, a storyboard for a website or presentation would contain:

- Rough designs showing what the menus will look like.
- What pictures are included (just a description of what needs to be on the picture).
- In an animation it can show some of the frames.
- What video is used (again you would need a description of what it shows).

Storyboard a storyboard is a story told in pictures; a bit like a comic book. It is a visual representation of everything on the presentation or website.

- What sound is included (music, sound effects, speech, etc.).
- Some detail of the text to be included.

Making a storyboard

The easiest way to make a simple storyboard of a presentation or website is to produce a rough sketch on paper.

Use a large blank sheet of paper and Post-It notes. On the Post-It notes you can sketch the content of the slides or webpages. You can then experiment with the arrangement on the paper.

Once you are happy with the design, you can produce a final design. This final design can then be used as a guide when producing the actual website or presentation using the computer.

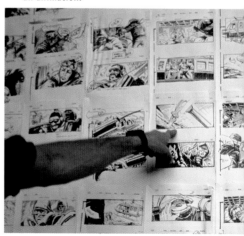
▽ An example of a storyboard used for an animation.

Awareness of audience

An animation should always be chosen or designed with the audience in mind. An animation liked by one group of people may be disliked by another group. For example, loud colours in an animation may be ideal for young children but may be annoying to an older audience. You also should take care in the choice of music you use to go with the animation.

Mood boarding

When creative people do work, they are usually asked to do so by clients who aren't that creative themselves. For example, they may be asked to produce a home page for a website for baby clothes that must contain eye-catching animations. If the designer just goes away and produces the work, the client may not like it. The secret is to get the client involved in the ideas at an early stage.

Texture

Imagery

Pastel colours
Rounded typeface
Soft shapes

◀ An example of a mood board.

A mood board is a compilation of elements that will give the look and a feel of the animation, website or multimedia product. It can include such things as examples of proposed types of animation, colour palettes used, patterns, font styles for text, etc.

The main purpose of the mood board is to prevent the designer putting lots of work into a design that the client does not like. The mood board is quick to create and allows a design to be discussed and altered.

Frame rates

In an animation each unique image used in the animation is called a frame. The frame rate is the frequency or rate at which the frames appear on the screen. The greater the frame rate, the better the quality of the movement of items in the animation. Low frame rates result in the image flickering.

Looping

The image shown below is a gif but by drawing eight slightly different images and looping them so that they go back to the beginning, the horse's legs appear to move continuously.

Vector and bitmap animation

There are two types of animation: vector and bitmap animation and their main features are described below.

Vector animation

In vector animation the motion is controlled by vectors rather than pixels. Mathematical equations are used to draw the frames in their new positions. Adobe Flash produces vector animation.

Bitmap animation

In bitmap animation the arrangement of bits on the screen changes in some way and a new bitmap is produced.

Advantages of vector animation over bitmap animation:

- The animation is cleaner (there are no blurred bits around the edges of the image).
- The animation is much smoother.

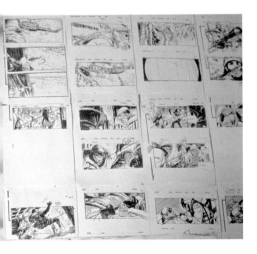

▲ Looping is frequently used in animations when a motion is repeated over and over again.

Activity

Bitmap animation

The following animation gives you a really good introduction to bitmap animation.

The site is found at:
http://www.youtube.com/watch?v=EULYbnAxJu0

Tools and techniques for creating animated images *continued*

Claymation and pixelation techniques

Claymation

Claymation is a form of stop animation. As you can probably guess, it uses an object made of a substance that is easily moulded, such as plasticine or clay. A model is made and it is photographed and then the model is altered slightly and photographed again. The process is repeated until a whole series of frames are produced and then these frames are played back producing the animation. Producing a whole animation using this technique involves a huge amount of work and time.

The Wallace and Gromit films are perfect examples of the Claymation technique.

Pixelation techniques

If you enlarge a bitmap image too much then you start to see the individual pixels that make up the image. Sometimes pixelation is added deliberately. You have probably seen these real-life police programmes where they blank out a person's face or a car number plate so that it cannot be recognized. They do this by pixelating that part of the image they do not want the viewer to see.

▲ This shows a plasticine model that has been photographed in different positions with each picture being the equivalent of a frame in the animation.

Rotoscoping

In this animation technique a piece of film with the movement of live actors is drawn over so you get an animation effect with realistic movement. Once the outline of the moving actor has been captured an artist can fill in the rest of the image.

Tweening

Tweening is sometimes called inbetweening. This is because you create a start frame and a final frame and the computer generates all the inbetween frames so that the start image changes into the final image.

Adobe Flash is a software package that many people use for animation and this package allows tweening. It allows you to specify how an object is to move or change during the tweening process.

Onion skinning

Onion skinning is a technique used in animation where several frames in an animation are superimposed over each other. If you look at the picture of the horse shown on the right, you can see the current frame as well as the previous three frames. The reason this is done is to allow the animator to keep track of the motion so they have a better idea when they create the next frame.

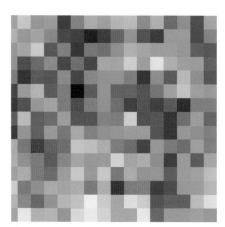

▲ Here the individual coloured pixels can be seen.

Activity

Rotoscoping

Look at the film called *Waking Life* which uses the rotoscoping animation technique.

The following website shows sections of the film: http://www.imdb.com/video/screenplay/vi2734358809/

▲ This shows the start frame (the blue circle on the left) and the final frame (the blue square on the right). The software (Flash in this case) inserts all the shapes it needs to move the object from the left to the right

▲ Onion skinning.

Claymation animation that makes use of a figure that is photographed, moved and photographed again, etc. The photographs form frames that are played in sequence to produce the animation.

Onion skinning showing several frames of an animation together so that the animator can keep track of the motion when working on new frames.

Rotoscoping films live actors and then traces over the frames to form the animation.

Tweening the process of getting the computer to fill in the inbetween frames between the start and end frames in an animation.

Grouping, cloning and backdrops

Grouping – grouping images is often done so that they are treated as a single image rather than separate ones. This makes it easier to move and size them.

Backdrop – this is the scenery against which the characters in the animation appear. For example, an animation of a talking cat might have the contents of a room as the backdrop.

Cloning – often in animations you need several items of the same thing (e.g., trees, people, cars, etc.). Rather than create each one from scratch, it is easier to create one and then copy it. The copies are identical and are called clones.

File formats and their advantages and disadvantages

As with still images, there are a number of different file formats for animated images. The main formats we will look at are:

- GIF
- CGM
- PNG.

GIF (graphics interchange format)

The main points about this format are:

- It is a bitmap image format.
- It uses compression without degrading the image quality.

Advantages

- Widespread use of format on the Internet.
- Ideal for simple images (e.g., graphics and logos).

Disadvantages

- Unsuitable for photographic quality animations.
- Limited number of colours available.

CGM (computer graphics metafile)

CGM is a file format for 2D graphics that can be represented in binary or one of two types of text. It is a series of instructions that explain how to draw the graphic and is therefore used to produce vector graphics. The main advantage of this file format is that it can be used with any system.

PNG (portable network graphics)

The main points about this format are:

- PNG was a replacement for GIF.
- It offers more features than a GIF.
- It offers more compression than a GIF.

Advantages

- PNG files are smaller than the same quality GIF files.
- More suitable for true colours than a GIF.

Disadvantage

- Older web browsers do not support some of the features of PNG.

Questions C

1 (a) Give the names of **two** file formats used for producing animations. *(2 marks)*
  (b) Explain the difference between bitmap animation and vector animation. *(2 marks)*

2 Animators often use a technique called onion skinning when producing animations. Explain what onion skinning is and how it helps the animator. *(3 marks)*

3 When some images have their size increased, they start to appear 'blocky'.
  (a) Give the name of the type of graphic that suffers from this problem. *(1 mark)*
  (b) What is the name given to the appearance of the blocks in the image? *(1 mark)*

END-OF-TOPIC REVIEW

Questions

Test yourself

The following notes summarize this topic. The notes are incomplete because they have words missing.

Using the words in the list below, copy out and complete the sentences A to H, underlining the words that you have inserted. Each word may be used more than once.

special effects   tweening   storyboard   awareness   flip

smoothly   key   inbetween   mood board   stop motion

A _____ books are books with a slightly different drawing on each page that appears to move when the pages are flipped quickly.

B Illusions to illustrate a film, programme, game or other computer program used to stimulate the imagination are called _____ _____.

C _____ frames are the starting frame and the finishing frame in an animation.

D In _____ _____ animation a model is photographed and then moved slightly and photographed again and so on. The photographs are combined and the tiny movements are joined together to show the model moving _____.

E _____ is sometime called inbetweening. This is because you create a start frame and a final frame and the computer generates all the _____ frames so that the start image changes into the final image.

F It is important to plan an animation before you start and the best way to do this is to produce a _____.

G A _____ _____ is a compilation of elements that will give a look and a feel of the animation, website or multimedia product.

H An animation should always be chosen or designed with the audience in mind and this is called _____ of audience.

Examination style questions

1 Persistence of vision is important when using computers to produce animation.
   Briefly explain what persistence of vision means and why it is important when producing animations. *(4 marks)*

2 Animations are very popular on websites and in multimedia products such as educational games.
   (a) Explain what a storyboard is. *(2 marks)*
   (b) Give **one** advantage of using animation in an educational game aimed at young children. *(1 mark)*
   (c) Give **one** disadvantage of using animation in an educational game aimed at young children. *(1 mark)*

Exam support

Worked example

There are a number of different animation techniques such as stop motion and rotoscoping.

(a) Describe what is meant by stop motion. *(2 marks)*

(b) Describe what is meant by rotoscoping. *(2 marks)*

Student answer 1

(a) *Stop motion means making a model of a person and then taking a picture of it every now and again to show movement.*

(b) *Rotoscoping means using film footage of humans moving and then drawing around them to get the outline and movement right. The artist can then add the detail of the actual person.*

▲ Examiner's comment

(a) This student probably understands stop motion but they have failed to make it clear to the examiner. Some of these animation techniques are quite difficult to explain, so students are advised to memorize the definitions or practise explaining them.

In this answer the student has failed to mention that the model is actually moved slightly and then the picture is taken. One mark is awarded for this answer.

(b) This is a good answer for a process that is quite difficult to explain. Full marks are given for this part.

(3 marks out of 4)

Student answer 2

(a) *This is where a model is used such as a plasticine model of a person. A photograph is taken and the model is moved slightly and another photograph is taken. The process is repeated many times. When played back the model appears to move.*

(b) *This is where real people move a certain way and are filmed. The animator then draws around certain frames to get the movement right. Once the outline of each frame is drawn they can add the solid bits. When played back, the movement is very realistic.*

▲ Examiner's comment

(a) This has been well explained. This student has clearly described each stage.

Two marks are given for this answer.

(b) Again this is a very good answer so full marks are given again.

(4 marks out of 4)

Examiner's answers

(a) One mark for each of two points such as:

- You use a model and take a photograph of it *(1)*
- You move it slightly and take another photograph and repeat *(1)*
- The photographs are joined up and the motion appears smooth *(1)*

(b) One mark for each of two points such as:

- You use a real-life person to move and take a video of it *(1)*
- You use frames to draw around the person in different positions *(1)*
- You fill in the outline and then join the frames up *(1)*

Summary mind map

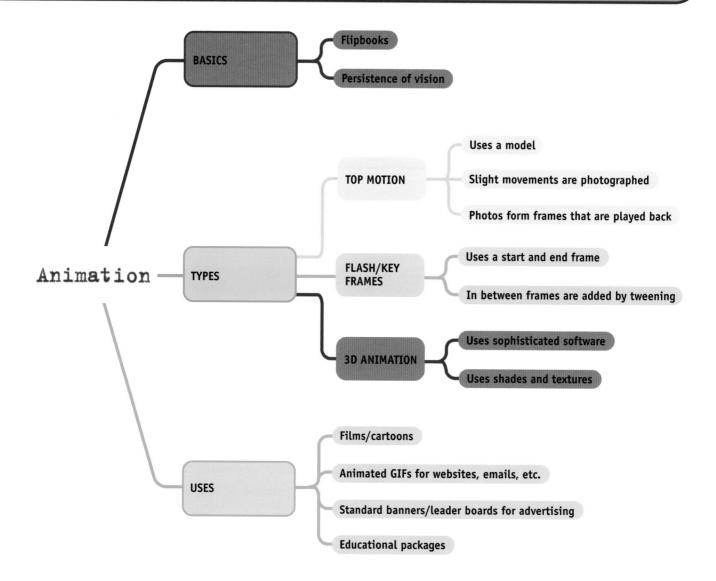

Animation

- BASICS
  - Flipbooks
  - Persistence of vision
- TYPES
  - TOP MOTION
    - Uses a model
    - Slight movements are photographed
    - Photos form frames that are played back
  - FLASH/KEY FRAMES
    - Uses a start and end frame
    - In between frames are added by tweening
  - 3D ANIMATION
    - Uses sophisticated software
    - Uses shades and textures
- USES
  - Films/cartoons
  - Animated GIFs for websites, emails, etc.
  - Standard banners/leader boards for advertising
  - Educational packages

Sound and music

The key concepts covered in this topic are:

- **The hardware used for sound**
- **The software used for sound**

The increase in portable media players and downloads has revolutionized the music industry. Not many people would dream of having to take a CD player and their favourite CDs away on holiday with them, yet it is only a few years ago that people did this. Many mobile phones can act as portable media players and many people would not dream of buying a CD, preferring instead to pick tracks and download them off the Internet. ICT has not only revolutionized the storing and playing of music, it has also changed the way in which the music is produced and edited by musicians.

In this topic you will be looking at the various technologies that have revolutionized the way we listen to sound and music.

Contents

The hardware, software and techniques used for sound

You will find out

▷ **About sound storage devices**

▷ **About sound cards**

▷ **About input and output devices**

▷ **About sound conversion**

▷ **About sequencers, notators and sound wave editors**

Sound is an essential part of ICT and most computers come with a sound card and speakers. Many websites use sound and most computer users store digital music on their computers. Some more musical users are able to use ICT to edit sound that they have produced on musical instruments.

In this topic you will be looking at the hardware, software and techniques used for sound.

Sound storage devices (e.g. MP3 players)

MP3 is a file format used to compress CD-quality music to about a tenth of the file size compared to a normal CD. One minute of music takes about one megabyte of storage capacity.

Once the music has been downloaded from a site, it may be stored on a hard disk. Of course it could then be copied onto a CD using a CD writer and this is where the problems start. Although some of the music that you can download off the Internet can be copyright free, the majority of the material is copyright. This means that you are not allowed to copy or distribute it without the permission of the copyright owner.

As MP3 files are compressed compared to normal sound files, it means that about 14 hours of music can be stored on a single CD.

© Randy Glasbergen.
www.glasbergen.com

GLASBERGEN

"THERE'S NOTHING WRONG WITH YOUR IPOD, DAD. IT'S JUST TOO EMBARRASSED TO PLAY THE KIND OF MUSIC YOU LIKE!"

MP3

MY BAND
MY ALBUM

my favorite song

02:17

▲ Portable music players play music in MP3 file format.

Sound cards

A sound card is an electronic circuit board containing chips and other components and circuitry that enables high quality sound to be produced. Most people use their computer to produce sound, so all computers have a sound card installed. However, people do replace these with more expensive cards that are able to produce higher quality sound.

▲ All computers now come with a sound card.

Input devices

Input devices are used to get music into a form that can be stored, processed and output by the computer.

Microphone

A microphone allows sound to be converted into data. Special software called voice recognition software is used to interpret the sounds into words.

Here is what a microphone allows you to do:

- You can tell the computer what to do (i.e., you can issue instructions).
- You can dictate letters and other documents directly into your word-processor or email package. This is called voice recognition.
- You will need a microphone if you want to send voice mail or take part in videoconferencing.
- You can record a live music performance.

KEY WORD

Voice recognition the ability of a computer to 'understand' spoken words by comparing them with stored data.

MIDI (Musical Instrument Digital Interface)

MIDI enables a computer and a musical instrument to communicate with each other. For example, when a keyboard is played, the music is transferred using MIDI to the computer where it can be edited if needed and stored. The MIDI converts the music in analogue format (i.e. a complex wave) from a musical instrument into a digital format that the computer can manipulate and store.

The process can be reversed by the music stored on the computer being fed back and using MIDI it can play the music back on the keyboard or other instrument.

Output devices

▲ The main output devices used with sound are loudspeakers and headphones.

Sound conversion (analogue to digital and digital to analogue)

Sound is a continuous wave and is therefore analogue. As computers can only work with digital data (i.e., data stored as numbers), it is necessary to convert the analogue data to digital data. This process is called analogue to digital conversion. Once the data is in digital format, the computer can store it, edit it, transfer it to another computer and play it back.

Loudspeakers and headphones use analogue signals, so when these devices are used to output sound from the computer, the digital data/signal from the computer has to be changed to an analogue signal. This is done using a digital to analogue converter.

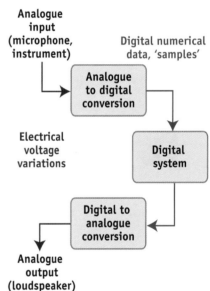

Analogue input (microphone, instrument) → Analogue to digital conversion

Digital numerical data, 'samples'

Analogue to digital conversion → Digital system

Electrical voltage variations

Digital system → Digital to analogue conversion

Digital to analogue conversion → Analogue output (loudspeaker)

▲ Signals are converted using a digital to analogue converter.

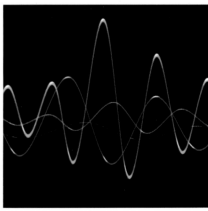

▲ A sound wave is analogue.

The hardware, software and techniques used for sound *continued*

Creating music

By using the latest technologies it is possible for home users of ICT to compose and hear their own music.

Sequencers (multitrack recording studios)

Sequencers are hardware or software used to create and manage electronic music. Examples of sequencers include:

- Drum machines – these are electronic musical instruments that simulate the sound of a drum and sometimes other percussion instruments. Drum machines are sequencers because they create and manage the drum beats.
- Music workstations – a single piece of electronic equipment that allows a musician to create electronic music. Music workstations consist of the usual computer but with a large screen with all the controls such as knobs, sliders, buttons and sampling information. Some music workstations make use of touch screens.

Notators (music composition software)

A notator is a piece of software that allows you to compose your own music and you do this by entering notes into the computer via:

- the keyboard
- a MIDI system
- or scanning a piece of music on paper using a scanner.

Once the notes are entered into the system, the musician can experiment by changing notes, loudness, tempo, etc. The main advantage is that the notator allows the musician to experiment. The notator can also be used to create the music for individual musical instruments that can then be played together to produce the final piece of music.

◄ Using ICT equipment to edit sound in a studio.

Sound wave editors

Sound wave editors are software that allows the editing of sound waves. Using the software sound waves can:

- be edited
- be cut, copied and pasted
- have effects like echo, amplification and noise reduction applied.

Sound wave editors can also be used to alter a person's speech pattern, so it can be used to disguise a person's voice or even simulate another person's voice. You may have seen this being used on the news when a witness or victim speaks but does not want to be identified.

Questions A

1 Copy and complete the sentences below by filling in the missing word in each case. *(3 marks)*
   (a) Sound is an _____ wave which means it is constantly varying.
   (b) Computers can only store and process _____ signals.
   (c) This means an _____ to _____ _____ is needed to change the sound signal for processing by the computer.

2 Give the names of **two** hardware devices used to output sound from a computer. *(2 marks)*

Extension activity

To understand sequencers and how they work, use the Internet to investigate the following sites. Look at any online videos that will help you understand how sequencers are used.

- http://www.musicsequencersoftware.com/
- http://www.socc.ie/~midiclass/sequencers.htm
- http://www.musiconmypc.co.uk/art_which_compose_tool.php

File formats, downloading music and the problems it causes

The widespread increase in the use of portable music devices and downloadable music has been brought about by advances in methods of compressing files so the file sizes are small. This means that as well as more tracks being stored on the same sized storage media, the files can be downloaded more quickly.

Downloading music is great because it gives the listener so much flexibility but there are a number of copyright issues that will be looked at in this section.

File formats for music and their advantages and disadvantages

If you want to store and play sound, there are a lot of file formats to choose from. No single file format is perfect which is why so many different ones exist. Here you will be looking at different file formats and their advantages and disadvantages.

wav

This file format retains every bit of audio information, which means that when you play it back, it will sound exactly the same as when it was created. This is perfect if you want the highest quality sound but the file sizes needed to store the files are very large. This means you wouldn't be able to store many tracks on a portable player and if you download them it will take a lot longer.

MP3

This is the best known format and the most popular. It uses compression so the files are only about one-tenth of the size compared to a wav file or a music file on CD. This means you can store around 10 times the amount of music in the same space. The quality is still very good but not as good as with wav format. MP3 files need to be decoded when used, which means they are not as fast to load.

wma

wma stands for Windows Media Audio and is a file format used with Windows that offers high quality sound at high compression. This enables music files to be decoded, stored and distributed at high speed.

Downloading music

Most singles are purchased as downloads off the Internet but albums are usually bought as physical CDs.

Downloads have become very popular owing to:

- the ease with which they can be obtained
- the ability to just download tracks that you want – you do not need to buy the whole album
- you can still burn the tracks to a CD provided they are only for personal use
- the ease with which they can be loaded onto portable players such as iPods, MP3 players and mobile phones.

There are a number of problems with downloads including:

- Many people use file sharing sites to avoid having to pay for downloaded music tracks.
- People who download music or films illegally could be cut off from the Internet by their Internet service providers.
- You do not have a physical CD that can be sold at a car boot sale or on e-Bay.

DOWNLOAD

199

File formats, downloading music and the problems it causes *continued*

Copyright problems

There are copyright problems with sounds and music in the same way as there are with text and images. Here is some advice:

- You cannot use music on a website without the copyright owner's permission.
- Do not copy samples of voices or sounds without permission.
- Do not make copies of music tracks to share with your friends.
- Do not use illegal file sharing sites as your use of the Internet may be affected.

All sound and music is produced by someone and this person has to make a living. All sound and music is protected by the Copyright, Designs and Patents Act 1988.

▲ Many people are guilty of copying copyrighted material without permission.

▲ Illegal copying is often called piracy.

KEY WORDS

MP3 there are lots of ways to compress a music file but the most popular way is by using MP3.

Download to copy files from a distant computer to the one you are working on.

Questions B

1 There are many different file formats used for music.
   (a) Give the names of **two** different music file formats. *(2 marks)*
   (b) Most music files are compressed. Explain what this means. *(1 mark)*
   (c) Give **one** reason why music files are compressed. *(1 mark)*

2 Downloads are a popular way of obtaining music.
   (a) Explain what is meant by a download. *(1 mark)*
   (b) Give **two** advantages of downloading music rather than obtaining the music on CD. *(2 marks)*
   (c) Explain **two** problems caused by downloading music. *(2 marks)*

Extension activity

- You have produced some original work such as music, photographs, graphics, etc., on a website. This work took you a long time to produce and you hope to be able to sell some of the work to others.
- Present a written argument to explain to others why they should not copy your work without your permission or without paying for it.

Questions

 Test yourself

The following notes summarize this topic. The notes are incomplete because they have words missing.

Using the words in the list below, copy out and complete the sentences A to J, underlining the words that you have inserted. Each word may be used more than once.

loudspeakers	MP3	microphone	analogue	notator
wav	digital	sound card	sequencers	wma

A _____ is a file format used to compress CD-quality music to about a tenth of the file size compared to a normal CD.

B A _____ _____ is an electronic circuit board containing chips and other components and circuitry that enables high quality sound to be produced.

C A _____ allows sound to be converted into data.

D The output device from an ICT system used to store and process sound is usually headphones or _____.

E Sound is a continuous wave and so is _____.

F Sound needs to be changed to a _____ signal before it can be stored on the computer.

G A _____ is a piece of software that allows you to compose your own music.

H _____ are hardware or software used to create and manage electronic music.

I The _____ file format retains every bit of audio information which means that when you play it back it will sound exactly the same as when it was created.

J _____ is a file format used with Windows that offers high quality sound at high compression.

Examination style questions

1 Many musicians use ICT to help them compose music, create and edit music and distribute music. Explain how each of the following helps a musician.
   (a) Notator *(2 marks)*
   (b) Sequencer *(2 marks)*
   (c) Sound editor *(2 marks)*

2 MP3 is a file format used with many portable music players, media players and mobile phones.
   (a) Give **one** advantage and **one** disadvantage of the MP3 file format. *(2 marks)*
   (b) Music tracks in MP3 file format can be downloaded from music sites on the Internet.

   (i) Give **one** advantage of downloading music tracks using the Internet. *(1 mark)*
   (ii) Give **one** disadvantage of downloading music tracks using the Internet. *(1 mark)*

3 The use of the Internet has opened up a whole new source for music: music downloads.
   (a) Explain how the use of ICT has made it possible to load, store and transfer music files. *(4 marks)*
   (b) Storing music files in digital format has led to a number of legal and ethical issues. Explain **one** legal issue and **one** ethical issue that music downloads present. *(2 marks)*

Types of network

If more than one computer is used in the home or in a business, then it makes sense to network them. Networking means that devices such as printers and scanners can be shared between all the computers on the network. It also means that all the computers can share an Internet link that will allow all computers access at the same time. There is also the ability to share programs and data.

What is a network?

A network is two or more computers that are linked together so that they are able to share resources. These resources could be a printer, scanner, software or even a connection to the Internet. You can also share data using a network. For example, a pupil database in a school could be accessed from any of the computers connected to the network.

Peer-to-peer and client–server networks

There are two ways of operating a network: peer-to-peer and client–server. Large organizations would use a client–server network because it is more powerful and can do a lot more. Peer-to-peer networking is fine for home networks or small businesses where a simple inexpensive network is all that is needed.

Whether an organization chooses peer-to-peer or client–server is mainly determined by the size of the network.

Peer-to-peer networks

Here are the main features of peer-to-peer networks:

- Each computer on the network has equal status.
- All computers can share each other's resources (e.g., data, an Internet connection, printers, scanners, etc.).

- They are only suitable for small networks with fewer than ten users.
- Only very basic knowledge is needed to set one up and use it.
- As more people use the network, the whole network slows down considerably.

Client–server networks

Here are the main features of client–server networks:

- One more powerful computer, called the server, is used to store the data and the programs needed by the whole network. The server is in control of the network.
- Software and data is stored on the server, so it can be accessed by all the computers on the network.
- The network is totally dependent on the server. If the server breaks down, the network cannot be used.
- They are the popular choice for networks that need lots of computers.

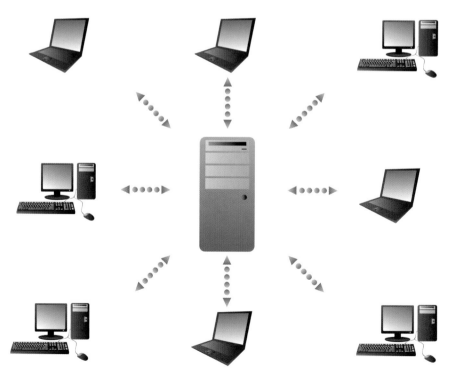

The server in a client–server network is in control of the network.

LAN (local area network)	WAN (wide area network)
Confined to a small area	Cover a wide geographical area (e.g., between cities, countries and even continents)
Usually located in a single building	In lots of different buildings, cities, countries, etc.
Uses cable, wireless, infrared and microwave links that are usually owned by the organization	Uses more expensive telecommunication links that are supplied by telecommunication companies
Cheap to build	Expensive to build
Cheap to run	Expensive to run

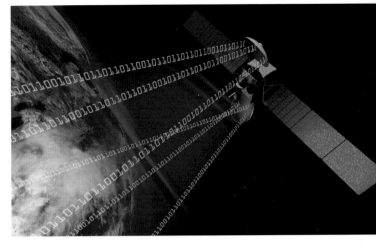

▲ Wide area networks often make use of satellite links.

The two types of network: LAN and WAN

There are two types of network: a local area network (LAN) and a wide area network (WAN).

Basically a WAN is much bigger than a LAN and spread over a much wider area. The table above gives you the main features of each type of network.

Network topologies

The devices in a network may be arranged in different ways. Each way is called a topology.

It is important to note that in a wired network the topology would show how the wires are connected. However, many networks are now set up without wires, making use of radio, infrared or satellite links. The topologies in this case will show the communication links between the devices.

There are three main topologies:

- ring
- bus
- star.

The ring topology

This is a ring network that is also a peer-to-peer network because there is no server. With the ring topology:

- All the computers are arranged in a circle.
- Data sent by one computer passes around the ring until it reaches the correct computer.

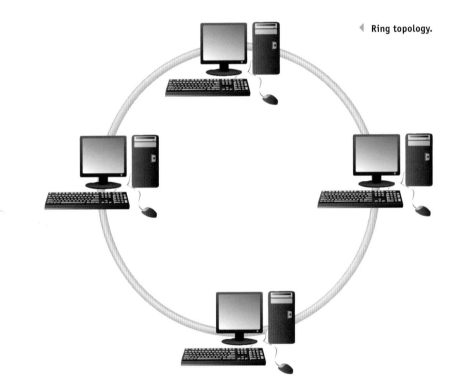

◀ Ring topology.

Advantages of ring networks

- It is easy to add extra devices.
- Each computer has the same access as the others, so no one computer can 'hog' the network.

Disadvantages of ring networks

- If there is a break in the connection (wire or wireless), then the whole network fails.
- Faults are difficult to locate.
- It is impossible to keep the network running whilst equipment is added or removed because there is only one path for the data to follow.

KEY WORDS

LAN (local area network) a network of computers on one site.

Network a group of computers that are able to communicate with each other.

WAN (wide area network) a network where the terminals/ computers are remote from each other and telecommunications are used to communicate between them.

Types of network *continued*

The bus topology

With a bus topology:

- All the devices connected to the network are connected to a common shared cable called the backbone.
- Signals are passed in either direction along the backbone.

Advantages of bus topology networks

- They are cost effective because of the small amount of cable needed.
- Simple cable runs makes them easy to install.
- It is easy to add extra devices to the network.

Disadvantages of bus topology networks

- If more than about 12 devices are connected to the network, then the performance of the network is poor.
- If there is a break in the backbone cable, then the network cannot be used.

Star topology

The star topology uses a central connection point for all the devices on the network. The central connection point can be a server, or inexpensive devices called hubs, routers or switches.

Advantages of star topology networks

- They are fault tolerant – if one of the cables fails, then the other computers can still be used.
- They are load tolerant – extra computers can be added without much loss in performance because all computers have their own path to the hub/router/switch/server.
- It is easy to add extra computers – extra computers can be added without disturbing the network.

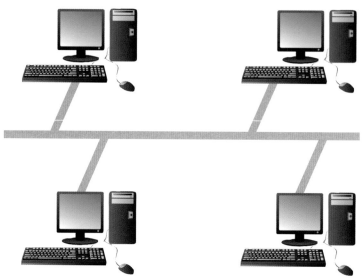

▲ Bus topology.

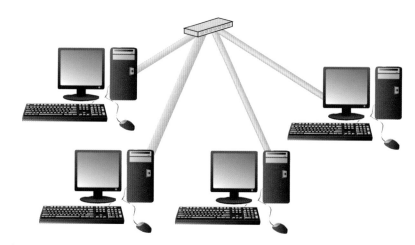

▲ Star topology.

Disadvantages of star topology networks

- Higher cost – the large amount of cabling needed makes it a more expensive topology.
- Dependence on the central hub/switch/router/server – if the device at the centre of the network fails, then the whole network will fail.

The Internet, intranets and extranets

You will hear the terms Internet, intranet and extranet used a lot when talking about network services. Here are some definitions:

Internet – the Internet is a huge group of networks joined together. Each of these networks consists of lots of smaller networks. This means that the Internet consists of hardware.

Intranet – a private network that uses the same technology as that used by the Internet for the sending of messages/data around a network. The main use of an intranet is to share organizational information and share resources.

▲ The Internet is formed by millions of computers being connected together. It is the largest network in the world.

Extranets – an intranet is restricted to employees of the organization, whereas with an extranet, customers, suppliers and other partners as well as the employees of the organization, can access the information. Extranets are not accessible by the general public and this is ensured by the use of usernames and passwords.

▲ Extranets are networks that can be accessed by customers and suppliers.

Questions A

1 Write down what the abbreviation LAN stands for. *(1 mark)*

2 Describe what is meant by a computer network. *(1 mark)*

3 A business with six computers is using them as stand-alone computers.
   (a) What is meant by the term 'stand-alone computers'? *(2 marks)*
   (b) The manager decides to network the computers together. There are two types of network: peer-to-peer and client–server. Describe **one** main difference between these two types of network. *(1 mark)*
   (c) The firm decides to use a client–server network. Give **one** reason why they may have made this choice. *(1 mark)*

4 There are two main types of local area network (LAN): peer-to-peer and client–server.

   (a) Describe **four** features of a peer-to-peer network. *(4 marks)*
   (b) Describe **four** features of a client–server network. *(4 marks)*

5 In computer networking the word topology means the layout of the connected devices on the network. A local area network is to be set up. Give the names of **two** topologies that could be used for this LAN and draw a diagram to illustrate each one. *(4 marks)*

6 Most schools use networked computers to form a LAN rather than using stand-alone computers.
   (a) Explain the difference between computers in a LAN and stand-alone computers. *(2 marks)*
   (b) Describe **two** advantages to the students in using a LAN rather than using stand-alone computers. *(2 marks)*
   (c) Describe **two** disadvantages to the students in using a LAN rather than using stand-alone computers. *(2 marks)*

Extension activity

LANs are often connected to WANs. Use the Internet to find a diagram that shows one or more LANs being connected to a WAN.

Computer network operation

The importance of being able to transfer data is the most important advantage in using a network and it is why networks are used in organizations of all sizes such as banks, schools, hospitals and shops as well as homes.

In order for computers to be networked some new hardware and software may be required. This allows the transfer of data between the computers on the network.

Hardware and software needed for data transfer

This section looks at the hardware and software that are needed to create a network.

Data transfer medium

Data transfer medium is the material through which data travels from one computer to another in a network. For small, simple networks this is usually wire, but many networks work wirelessly. Wires add considerably to the cost of a network, especially the cost of installing them.

The main forms of data transfer media are:

- metal wires
- fibre optic cable

▷ Metal wires can be used to transfer data.

▲ Wireless Internet is available in many public places.

Network cards

Before a computer can be connected to a network, it will need to have a network card. Most modern computers have these when you buy the computer.

▲ The end of a fibre optic cable. Fibre optic cables can transmit data faster than metal cables.

▲ A network card allows a connection to be made between the network cables and the computer.

Hubs, switches and routers

All these devices allow the computers in a network to be joined so they are able to share files and an Internet connection.

Hubs – are simple devices used to join computers in a network so they are able to share files and an Internet connection.

Switches – are like hubs in that they are used to join computers in a network but they are more intelligent. Switches look at each packet of data and then send it to the computer it was intended for. This reduces the amount of data travelling around the network and makes it work faster.

Routers – are devices that join several wired or wireless networks together. They are often used in the home to enable several computers to access the Internet using a single connection.

Bridges – are devices that connect separate LANs together to form one large LAN.

For example Sales and Human resources may have their own LANs and the bridge allows data to pass between them and therefore run as if it were just one big LAN.

Network software

Small networks can be run using existing Windows software. For larger client–server networks, specialist network operating systems software is needed.

This software includes facilities to:

- keep track of the software being run on each computer
- keep all applications software up-to-date
- check that all computers have and are kept up-to-date with the latest virus checker
- check that a user has not loaded software illegally onto their computer
- check what hardware each computer has (e.g., processor, memory, size of hard drive, etc.).

Connecting networks together

Many networks are connected together. For example, you might have a couple of computers networked together in the home, that share a connection to the Internet using a router. You therefore have a small network connected to the largest network in the world (i.e., the Internet).

Connecting LANs and WANs together using a gateway

Often a LAN is connected to a WAN. For example, the LAN might be located at the head office of an organization with lots of computers in small branches around the country. To connect a LAN to a WAN a device called a gateway is needed and this allows a computer in the LAN to communicate with a computer in the WAN and vice versa.

KEY WORDS

Network a group of computers that are able to communicate with each other.

Networking software this is systems software that allows computers connected together to function as a network.

Gateway the device/software that translates between two different kinds of computer networks (e.g., between a WAN and a LAN).

Questions B

1 A company is thinking of installing a new network. They have the choice of a wired network, where cables are used to transmit the data, or a wireless network, where no cables are needed. Describe the relative advantages and disadvantages in using a wireless network. *(4 marks)*

2 Data may be transferred between the computers in a network in different ways. Give the names of **three** ways of transferring the data between computers in a network. *(3 marks)*

3 Give the name of the device that is used so that several computers in a home can all share a single Internet connection. *(1 mark)*

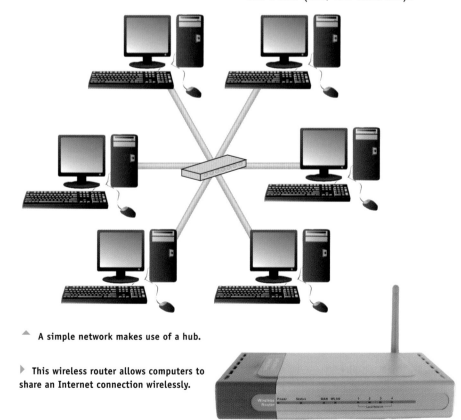

▲ A simple network makes use of a hub.

▶ This wireless router allows computers to share an Internet connection wirelessly.

211

Advantages and disadvantages of network systems

You will find out

▷ **About the advantages and disadvantages of network systems in comparison to stand-alone computers**

▷ **About integrated point of sale (PoS) systems**

Nowadays most computers are connected to a network. If you connect your personal computer at home to the Internet then your computer becomes part of a network.

The advantages and disadvantages of network systems compared to stand-alone computers

Advantages

- You can share hardware – you can just have one printer and one scanner, as any of the computers connected to the network can use them.
- Software can be installed in one place – you do not need to install software on each computer. This makes it faster to install and easier to maintain. If the software needs to be upgraded, then this is much easier if only one copy is used.
- Improved security – work can be saved on the network. The network manager will make sure that the work is backed up. Passwords make sure that other people cannot access your work unless you want them to.
- Speed – it is very quick to copy and transfer files.
- Cost – when software is bought, the school can buy network versions. These are much cheaper than buying a copy for each stand-alone computer.
- Email facilities – any user of the network will be able to communicate using electronic mail. This will be much more efficient compared to paper-based documents such as memos, etc.
- Access to a central store of data – users will have access to centrally stored data.

Disadvantages

- A network manager will need to be employed – this can be quite expensive.
- Security problems – a virus could get onto the system and cause problems, or hackers may gain access to the data on the network.
- Breakdown problems – if the network breaks down, users will not have access to the important information held.
- Expensive – a server and cables and/or other communication devices will be needed. The installation costs of a network are also high.

Integrated point of sale (PoS) systems

Point of sale terminals are where you pay for your goods in a store. PoS terminals are networked together. This means when an item is sold and its bar code is scanned, the system looks up the price and description details to print out an itemized receipt. At the same time the system will deduct the item from stock so that the stock control system is updated.

Point of sale terminals consist of the following hardware:

- Bar code reader/laser scanner – this is used to input a number that is coded in the bar code as a series of light and dark lines.
- Keyboard – the keyboard is used to enter codes on items if the bar code is damaged.
- Touch screens – these are often used in restaurants where there are no goods to scan.
- Swipe card readers – these are used to swipe the magnetic strips on loyalty cards.
- Chip and pin readers – these are used by customers to insert their credit/debit cards containing a chip. The system then asks them to enter their PIN (personal identification number) which is a number only they know and this proves to the system that they are the genuine owner of the card.

Point of sale terminals are connected via networks to other systems such as:

- Payment systems – where the customer can pay using credit/ debit card.

This reader can read chip and pin as well as swipe cards.

◁ Touch screens are used as input devices in restaurants and bars.

- Loyalty card systems – where customers are given loyalty points according to how much they spend.
- Accounts systems – where the money coming into the shop is accounted for.
- Automatic stock control systems – the system knows what has been sold, so that it can automatically reorder more once the stock falls below a certain amount.

Automatic stock control

When an item is sold at the PoS terminal the number of that particular item in stock is reduced by one. This means that the computer knows how many items are in stock. Once the number of items has fallen below a certain level, the computer system will automatically order more stock from the supplier. This means that stores should not run out of fast-selling items.

Good stock control systems are very important in supermarkets as customers will go elsewhere if the shop keeps running out of key items such as bread, milk, etc.

KEY WORD

Stand-alone computer if a computer is used on its own without any connection (wireless or wire) to a network (including the Internet), then it is a stand-alone computer.

Questions C

1 Give **three** advantages of a network over stand-alone computers. *(3 marks)*

2 A dentist's surgery has four stand-alone computers. They want to network these computers together.
(a) Give **two** advantages of these computers being networked. *(2 marks)*
(b) The computers on the network contain personal information about patients including their medical details.
Give **four** rules that the staff who work in the dental practice must obey when using the network. *(4 marks)*
(c) Give **one** advantage and **one** disadvantage in allowing the staff in the dental practice access to the Internet. *(2 marks)*

3 Give the names of **three** devices whose resources may be shared using a network. *(3 marks)*

4 A school is thinking of installing a network system throughout the school. The school network is to be linked using metal wires. The school already owns all the computers they need. At the moment the computers are being used as stand-alone machines.
(a) Give **two** other ways computers can be linked without the need for metal wires. *(2 marks)*
(b) Explain what is meant by a stand-alone machine. *(1 mark)*
(c) Give **two** items of hardware or software that the school will need in order to turn their computers into a network. *(2 marks)*

Extension activity

Produce a poster to be put up in the computer room entitled:

The Advantages and Disadvantages of Networks

Use the Internet and information contained in the topic as your sources of information. You have to choose suitable software for this task and make it as eye-catching as you can.

Summary mind maps

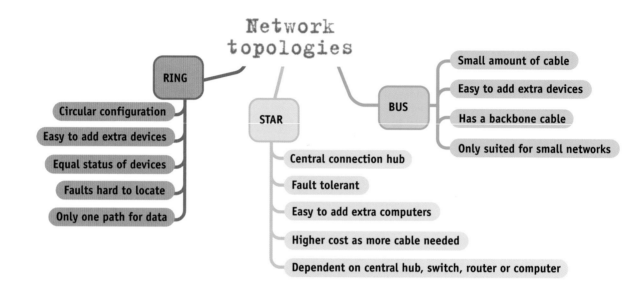

Network topologies

RING
- Circular configuration
- Easy to add extra devices
- Equal status of devices
- Faults hard to locate
- Only one path for data

STAR
- Central connection hub
- Fault tolerant
- Easy to add extra computers
- Higher cost as more cable needed
- Dependent on central hub, switch, router or computer

BUS
- Small amount of cable
- Easy to add extra devices
- Has a backbone cable
- Only suited for small networks

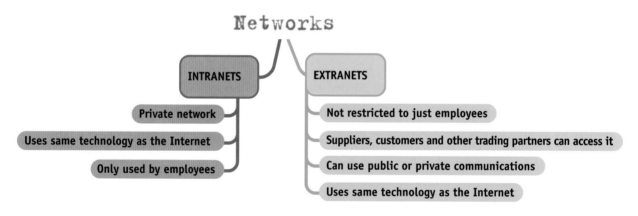

Networks

INTRANETS
- Private network
- Uses same technology as the Internet
- Only used by employees

EXTRANETS
- Not restricted to just employees
- Suppliers, customers and other trading partners can access it
- Can use public or private communications
- Uses same technology as the Internet

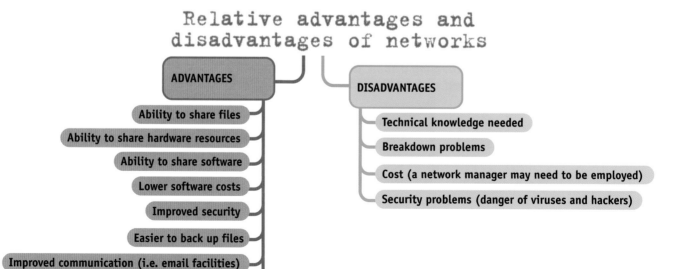

Relative advantages and disadvantages of networks

ADVANTAGES
- Ability to share files
- Ability to share hardware resources
- Ability to share software
- Lower software costs
- Improved security
- Easier to back up files
- Improved communication (i.e. email facilities)
- Access to central store of data

DISADVANTAGES
- Technical knowledge needed
- Breakdown problems
- Cost (a network manager may need to be employed)
- Security problems (danger of viruses and hackers)

Topic 20

Human–computer interfaces

The key concepts covered in this topic are:

- Understand the functions of an operating system

- Recognize and describe the features and uses of the different types of user interface

- Discuss the advantages and disadvantages of each type of human–computer interface

Software is the general name given to all the programs that can be run on computer hardware. They all give the hardware instructions and can be divided into two main categories: operating systems and applications software.

Human–computer interfaces are important because having a good one means the computer is easier to use. Human–computer interfaces are being developed all the time and many of the new interfaces are making more use of touch screens and voice recognition.

In this topic you will be learning about the function of the operating system as well as the range of human–computer interfaces that are available.

Contents

The functions of an operating system, and the different user interfaces

You will find out

▷ **About the functions of an operating system**

▷ **About the features and uses of the different types of user interface**

In order for ICT hardware to do a useful job it needs two types of software: systems software and applications software. The applications software performs a particular job or application but the system software is needed to control the hardware directly. Both these two types of software are essential components of any ICT system.

Any software has to interact with the user and this is through the human–computer interface or sometimes just the user interface. The main aim is to make this interface as easy to use as possible.

The functions of an operating system

Operating systems are programs that control the hardware directly. The operating system supplies the step-by-step instructions that tell the computer hardware what to do.

Operating systems have the following functions:

- Manage and control any devices such as printers, scanners, webcams, etc., that are attached to the computer.
- Provide a user interface that makes it easy for the user to load programs, search for files, copy files, etc.
- Hide the complexity of the hardware from the user.
- Deal with any errors that occur while the computer is working on tasks.
- Provide the interface between the application packages being run and the hardware.
- Allow new hardware or software to be installed using installation programs.
- Contain various utilities such as disk formatter, virus checking, encryption, etc.
- Handle the storage of data by keeping track of all the files and directories/folders on the disk drives.
- Maximize the use of computer memory by the operating system deciding where in the memory the program instructions are placed.
- Recognize new hardware such as a pen drive, camera, portable hard drive, etc., has been attached to the computer and load the software needed to control it.
- Organize resources (e.g., processing time and memory) when the computer user is running several programs at the same time.

Brands of operating system software include:

- MS Windows
- Macintosh OS-X
- UNIX
- Linux.

The features and uses of different types of user interface

An interface is where two things meet, so a user interface in ICT is the point where the human user meets or interacts with the ICT system. This is commonly called the user interface or sometimes the human–computer interface (HCI).

User interfaces have seen huge changes over the years and are being developed all the time so that ICT systems are made as easy to use as possible.

In this section you will be looking at the range of user interfaces used by ICT systems and their relative strengths and weaknesses.

The different user interfaces and their features

When you turn on the computer you see a user interface. The cursors, prompts, icons, menus, etc., allow you to get things done with your computer. They are all part of the user interface. A user interface can make your computer either hard or easy to use. You will probably have experienced software that is frustrating to use.

There are three main types of interface:

- **Command line/driven interface** – here you have to type in a series of commands. This type of interface is very hard to use.
- **Menu-driven interface** – here you are presented with a list of things to do and you have to choose one of them by typing in either a number or a letter. These are easy to use but are limited in the sorts of things you can do with them.
- **Graphical user interface (GUI)** – these are very easy to use and have all the features such as windows, icons, menus, pointers, etc.

List Employee No, Surname
For Job = "Production"

▲ Command line interface.

▲ Menu-driven interface

KEY WORDS

Hardware the physical components of a computer system.

Operating system software software that controls the hardware of a computer and is used to run the applications software. Operating systems control the handling of input, output, interrupts, etc.

Software programs that supply the instructions to the hardware.

GUI (graphical user interface) interface that allows users to communicate with the computer using icons and pull-down menus.

Graphical user interfaces and WIMP

Graphical user interfaces (GUIs) are very popular because they are easy to use. Instead of typing in commands, you enter them by pointing and clicking at objects on the screen. Microsoft Windows and Macintosh operating systems use graphical user interfaces.

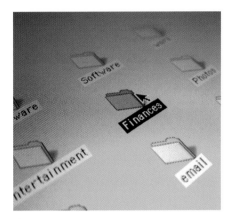

▲ The icons (small pictures) representing folders in a GUI.

The main features of a GUI include:

Windows – the screen is divided into areas called windows. Windows are useful if you need to work on several tasks.

Icons – these are small pictures used to represent commands, files or windows. By moving the pointer and clicking, you can carry out a command or open a window. You can also position any icon anywhere on your desktop.

Menus – menus allow a user to make selections from a list. Menus can be pop-up or pull-down and this means they do not clutter the desktop whilst they are not being used.

Pointers – this is the little arrow that appears when using Windows. The pointer changes shape in different applications. It changes to an 'I' shape when using word-processing software. A mouse can be used to move the pointer around the screen.

Notice that the first letter of each feature in the above list spells out the term WIMP (i.e. **W**indows, **I**cons, **M**enus, **P**ointers).

Office assistants

Office assistants are features of GUIs and they provide assistance or help when a user wants to do something using the software. When the office assistant is asked for, the system tells them how to complete the task.

Online tutorials

Online tutorials are used to:

- explain how to use the computer
- show the new features of a new version of the software.

Customized desktops

You will know from your work in Topic 6 that you are able to customize the desktop environment. There are many ways you can do this and here are just some of them:

- You can alter the size of the icons.
- You can alter the way the mouse works.
- You can alter resolution, brightness and contrast on the computer screen.

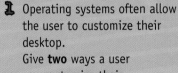

Questions A

1 Operating systems often allow the user to customize their desktop.
Give **two** ways a user can customize their desktop. *(2 marks)*

2 All computers need an operating system.
   (a) Explain what an operating system is. *(2 marks)*
   (b) List **three** different functions of an operating system. *(3 marks)*
   (c) Windows is one operating system. Give the name of **one** other operating system. *(1 mark)*

More features and uses of different types of user interface

There are many new ways of interacting with a computer and many of these ways replicate the way humans communicate with each other.

Voice driven applications

We are used to communicating with each other using voice, so it makes sense to communicate with ICT devices such as computers, mobile phones, MP3 players, etc., in a similar way.

Voice driven applications, also called voice recognition, can be used to:

- issue commands to the software
- enter data into the software.

Voice driven is a popular interface because manufacturers are trying to make devices small, but if there is a small keyboard, then it is hard to use.

Menu/dialogue boxes

A dialogue box is a window used with a graphical user interface (GUI) that displays a message to the user or requests that a user types in some information it needs. It is called a dialogue box because there is a constant interaction between the user and the computer. Sometimes the dialogue box simply informs the user about something such as the printer running out of paper and the user only has to acknowledge they have seen the information and click on OK to get rid of the box.

▲ **An online booking form for a holiday company shows a dialogue box.**

Touch sensitive applications

Many portable devices use touch screens. This enables the device to be kept small but the screen can still be almost the same size as the device, as a keyboard is no longer needed. You use your fingers to interact with the interface. You will have seen this type of interface used in some mobile phones such as the Apple iPhone.

Windows 7 provides a touch screen interface that can be easier to use than a keyboard and mouse.

Many devices used by the general public have touch screen interfaces and these include:

- portable music players
- mobile phones
- information kiosks (at airports, train stations, visitor attractions, etc.)
- notebook computers
- point of sale systems in supermarkets and restaurants
- learning aids.

Biometrics

Biometrics make use of features of the human body that are unique to a particular person. Usually this is a person's fingerprint or the pattern on the back of the eye (called the retina).

Rather than have to log-in to a computer by providing a username and a password, a user can now simply put their finger into a scanner. The system automatically recognizes who it is that is using the computer and gives them the network resources allocated to them.

▲ Fingerprint scanner.

▲ Retinal scanning.

There is also a biometric method that can identify a person from behind by the way they walk. This is a new method and can be used for access control for buildings and can help police catch criminals who think they cannot be identified from behind.

Advantages and disadvantages of each type of HCI

Advantages of a command line interface

- Quicker – in some instances you can do a task more quickly by typing a command line rather than using the mouse and all the features of Windows.

Disadvantages of a command line interface

- Very difficult for beginners to use – you have to learn the structure (called the syntax) of commands.
- You have to remember instructions – hard to remember the instructions/commands you need to do a particular task.

Advantages of GUIs

- No language needed – in the past you had to type in certain instructions to communicate with the computer.
- Use of icons – novice users can simply select programs or things they want to do by pointing and double clicking.

- Easier to use a mouse – most users would prefer to use a mouse to point and click rather than use the keyboard.

Disadvantages of GUIs

- More memory is needed – sophisticated GUIs have large memory requirements, so older computers may need upgrading or new computers bought.
- Increased processing requirements – faster and more powerful processors are needed to run the latest GUIs. This could involve upgrading the processor or buying new computers.

Questions B

1. Give **two** different features of a voice driven application by explaining each feature with an example. *(4 marks)*

2. UNIX is a make of operating system and it uses both a GUI and a command line interface.
   (a) Explain the meaning of the term operating system. *(2 marks)*
   (b) What does the abbreviation GUI stand for? *(1 mark)*
   (c) Briefly explain **one** difference between a GUI and a command line interface. *(1 mark)*
   (d) New users tend to prefer a GUI, whilst an experienced user may prefer to use a command line interface. Give **one** reason for this. *(1 mark)*

3. Touch sensitive applications have become very popular, especially with portable devices.
   (a) Explain what is meant by a touch sensitive application. *(2 marks)*
   (b) Give **one** example of a touch sensitive application. *(1 mark)*

Extension activity

Produce a mind map showing the advantages and disadvantages of the following types of user interface. You may have to do some research using the Internet to do this.

Here is a list of what you need to cover:

- **Menu/dialogue box**
- **Voice driven**
- **Touch sensitive**
- **Biometrics**

Questions

 Test yourself

The following notes summarize this topic. The notes are incomplete because they have words missing.

Using the words in the list below, copy out and complete the sentences A to J, underlining the words that you have inserted. Each word may be used more than once.

line	storage	printers	interface
system	voice	hardware	recognizes
	errors	menu–driven	GUI

A Software is the general name given to all the programs that can be run on computer _____ and there are two types: applications software and operating _____ software.

B One purpose of an operating system is to manage and control hardware devices such as _____ and scanners.

C The operating system also deals with _____ that occur when the computer is working on tasks.

D Keeping track of the _____ of data on the magnetic hard disk drives is another function of the operating system.

E When you attach a device such as a pen drive or portable hard drive, the operating system _____ it and loads the software to control it.

F An _____ is where two things meet so a human–computer interface is where the human user and the computer meet.

G One interface where you issue instructions to the computer as a series of commands is called a command _____ interface.

H Making selections from a series of menus to accomplish a task is called a _____ interface.

I The user interface that is very easy to use and uses windows, icons, menus and pointers is called a _____.

J Some interfaces use _____ where a user simply issues instructions by speaking a series of commands.

Examination style questions

1 Choose the **three** tasks from the list below that are carried out by all operating systems. *(3 marks)*

   A   Underlining text in a word processing program
   B   Supervising the running of other programs
   C   Storing data into a database structure
   D   Transferring data between memory and the hard drive
   E   Maximizing the use of the computer's memory
   F   Changing the size of a picture

2 In order to communicate with users, ICT systems need a user interface.
   Give the names of **three** different types of user interface. *(3 marks)*

3 Place a tick in the correct column to show whether each of the following statements about operating systems is true or false. *(4 marks)*

Statement	True	False
An operating system is always software		
Operating systems supervise the running of other software		
Operating systems must be loaded before the computer can do a useful job		
Operating systems handle outputs but not inputs		

4 Personal computers (PCs) make use of a graphical user interface (GUI) that allows humans to communicate with the computers.
   (a) Give four features of a GUI. *(4 marks)*
   (b) There are other types of interface a user can use.
      (i)   Give the names of **two** other types of interface. *(2 marks)*
      (ii)   Give an advantage for each of the interfaces you have named in part (i). *(2 marks)*

5 Here is a list of tasks. Put a tick next to those tasks that are performed by the operating system. *(4 marks)*

Task	Tick here if performed by the operating system
Searching for a record in a database	
Allocating space for files on the disk drive	
Issuing an instruction to the printer to start printing	
Formatting text in a word-processed document	
Managing the flow of data from a keyboard	
Controlling the security of a system	
Altering the margins in a package	

END-OF-TOPIC REVIEW

Exam support

Worked example

User interfaces are important because they allow humans to communicate with ICT systems.

One type of user interface is called a graphical user interface (GUI).

(a) List **four** features of a GUI. *(4 marks)*

(b) Give **one** disadvantage in using a GUI. *(1 mark)*

(c) Give the names of other different types of user interface and give an advantage for each type. *(4 marks)*

Student answer 1

(a) Windows

Icons

Menus

Pointers

(b) Users have to learn it.

(c) Command driven interface. It has the advantage you can just type in the commands rather than have to pull down a whole load of menus and make selections.

Menu driven. It is very easy to use as the user does not have to remember a list of commands.

▲ **Examiner's comment**

(a) All of these are correct so four marks for this part.

(b) Users have to learn any interface so no marks here.

(c) For the first answer the student has not spelt out the advantage, which is time saving. There is enough detail here so the student is given the two marks for this answer.

The second answer has the correct name for the interface and it is clear what the advantage is, so full marks are given here.

(8 marks out of 9)

Student answer 2

(a) WIMP

Help screens with search facilities.

Allows a user to customize the desktop.

(b) Takes a while to load because it is a big program.

(c) Touch screen – it is good in portable devices where there is no room to put a keyboard because it would be too small.

Command driven interface – it is a powerful interface because using just a couple of commands you can complete a complex task.

▲ **Examiner's comment**

(a) Only three features are given here so only three marks are awarded. Students should always check that they have given the right number of answers as it is easy to miss an answer out.

(b) This is a correct answer so one mark here.

(c) Both of these are acceptable answers so full marks for this section.

(8 marks out of 9)

Examiner's answers

(a) One mark for each of four correct features such as:

- WIMP
- Windows
- Icons
- Menus
- Pointers
- Online tutorials
- Ability for user customization of the desktop.

(b) One mark for one disadvantage such as:

- Demands a lot of memory so computers may need upgrading or replacement.
- May need to replace the processor as GUIs need fast processors.
- The software takes time to load.
- The colour combinations can be a problem to some people who might be colour blind.

(c) Command driven – you can accomplish a complex action simply by entering a few words thus saving you time.

Voice driven – you use ordinary language and spoken commands to issue commands and data into the software, which makes it easier to use.

Menu driven – you use a series of pull-down menus so you do not have to remember any commands or syntax (i.e., the way the commands are structured).

Forms driven/dialogue box – you enter into a 'conversation' where the software asks you to enter certain data and you enter the data. This interface is ideal because it guides the user though a series of steps so the user does not have to remember the steps.

EXAM TIPS

For your revision, why not create mind maps showing the features for each type of user interface?

You may be asked to make a comparison between the features of two different user interfaces. You must refer to both types of interface in your answers.

If you are asked to give or list the features, then writing one word or a couple of word answers is ok.

Always check, after you have written your answers, that you have actually answered the question you have been asked and not the question you would like to have been asked.

Check also that you have the right number of answers. So, for example, if the question asks for two advantages you need to check that you have at least two advantages.

It is always important to check that your answers to questions are distinctly different. Check that you have not simply explained the same point in a different way.

END-OF-TOPIC REVIEW

Summary mind map

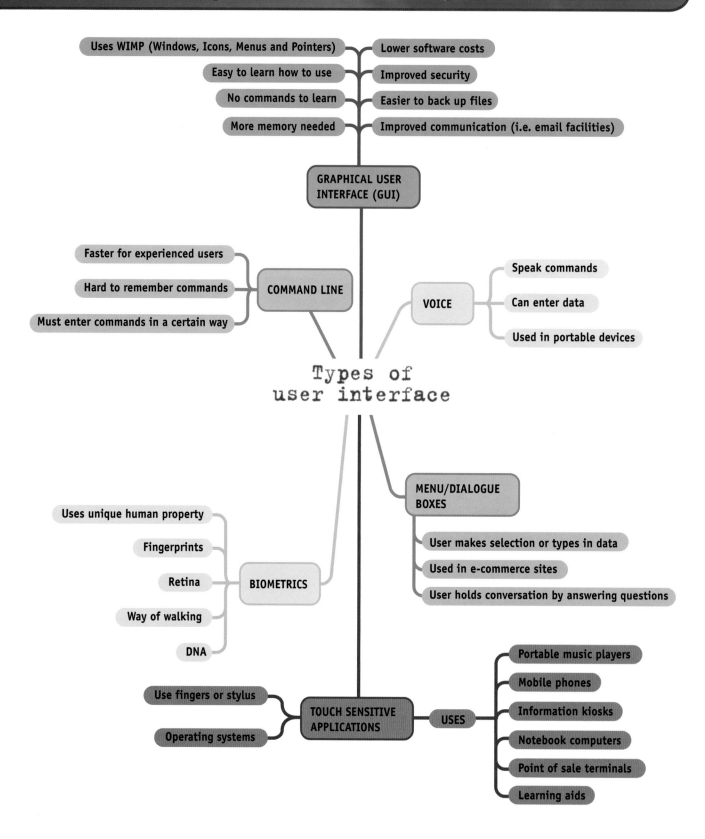

Uses WIMP (Windows, Icons, Menus and Pointers)

Easy to learn how to use

No commands to learn

More memory needed

Lower software costs

Improved security

Easier to back up files

Improved communication (i.e. email facilities)

GRAPHICAL USER INTERFACE (GUI)

Faster for experienced users

Hard to remember commands

Must enter commands in a certain way

COMMAND LINE

VOICE

Speak commands

Can enter data

Used in portable devices

Types of user interface

Uses unique human property

Fingerprints

Retina

Way of walking

DNA

BIOMETRICS

MENU/DIALOGUE BOXES

User makes selection or types in data

Used in e-commerce sites

User holds conversation by answering questions

Use fingers or stylus

Operating systems

TOUCH SENSITIVE APPLICATIONS

USES

Portable music players

Mobile phones

Information kiosks

Notebook computers

Point of sale terminals

Learning aids

Topic 21
Organizations

The key concepts covered in this topic are:

- The use of ICT in a variety of applications

- The use of ICT in a variety of different organizations

- The data protection methods used in the different organizations and in the different applications

In this topic you will be looking at different applications of ICT in a range of organizations. Some of the material in this topic will be new but some of it has been covered in previous topics. You will be looking at a variety of computer applications and all the aspects of ICT used in these applications. You will also be looking at data protection methods such as backups, using biometric access, passwords and so on.

Contents

E-commerce systems

You will find out

▷ **About the advantages and disadvantages of e-commerce systems**

▷ **About data capture and checking**

▷ **About type of processing**

▷ **About output from the system**

Buying goods and services over the Internet has really caught on despite people being worried about keying in their card details. Many busy people buy their groceries online and have them delivered, and the rise in low cost airlines has meant that many people now book flights and accommodation online.

In this section you will be looking at aspects of e-commerce systems.

The advantages and disadvantages of e-commerce systems

E-commerce means using the Internet to conduct business. When you buy a CD, DVD or book off a website you are involved in e-commerce.

Anyone can create a website and sell their goods and services to anyone in the world who has Internet access. This has allowed very small businesses to grow rapidly.

Years ago no-one would have thought of buying goods from abroad even though they might be cheaper. Now there are international parcels companies that make deliveries to anywhere in the world, so distance is no problem.

The running costs of an e-commerce business are much less and there are other benefits as well, which are summarized in the following diagram:

Data capture and checking

Data capture is how the data gets into the system. E-commerce systems use the customer to enter data. They allow the customer to select items to put in the virtual trolley (shopping basket) and then go to the checkout where they enter their personal details such as name and contact details. These are entered into an online form using the keyboard. They are then connected to a secure site where they enter their payment details such as credit/debit card number.

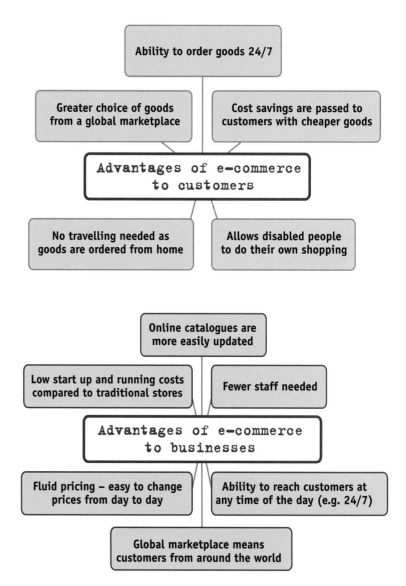

Ability to order goods 24/7

Greater choice of goods from a global marketplace

Cost savings are passed to customers with cheaper goods

Advantages of e-commerce to customers

No travelling needed as goods are ordered from home

Allows disabled people to do their own shopping

Online catalogues are more easily updated

Low start up and running costs compared to traditional stores

Fewer staff needed

Advantages of e-commerce to businesses

Fluid pricing – easy to change prices from day to day

Ability to reach customers at any time of the day (e.g. 24/7)

Global marketplace means customers from around the world

Disadvantages of e-commerce to customers
- Problems with fraudulent sites
- Customers worried about security of credit/debit card details
- Sometimes more hassle when returning goods
- Hidden costs of postage or duties (e.g. VAT)
- Harder to assess the quality of goods before ordering
- Loss of the social pleasure of shopping

Disadvantages of e-commerce to businesses
- Network downtime can be very expensive
- Increased competition from abroad offering cheaper goods
- Cost of delivery may make goods more expensive
- Reliance on third party delivery companies who may be unreliable

KEY WORD

Data capture term for the various methods by which data can be entered into the computer so that it can be processed.

Checking is by performing a visual check. This involves the customer checking carefully all the details they have entered. There are also validation checks on many of the fields on the online form that the customer uses to enter their details. There are presence checks to ensure important fields are not left blank.

Type of processing

Real-time (transaction) processing is used. This means that the transactions are processed as they occur (i.e., when customers place orders). It is important that processing takes place as soon as details are entered so that the goods or services can be reserved for that customer.

Output from the system

Once an order has been entered, the system will automatically acknowledge receipt of the order by sending the customer a copy of the order by email. This will also show that payment has been made. Order confirmations can be output on screen or printed out.

Questions A

1 Credit and debit cards are often used when purchasing goods using the Internet.
   (a) Many people are worried about entering their credit card details into e-commerce sites. State **one** reason why they might be worried. *(1 mark)*
   (b) Explain what the e-commerce company can do to ensure that card details remain safe. *(2 marks)*
   (c) Some shoppers might be worried that a site they are thinking of buying something from is not a genuine site.
   Explain **one** way they might check that a site is genuine. *(1 mark)*

2 Many people now buy goods and services from an e-commerce site.
   (a) Explain the methods of data capture used to place an online order. *(2 marks)*
   (b) Describe **two** different checks that are performed on the data to minimize the introduction of errors. *(2 marks)*
   (c) Give **one** method of output used with an e-commerce system. *(1 mark)*

Extension activity

Investigate a number of e-commerce sites, which must include a service site (e.g., holidays, flights, insurance) and one that is a retail site.

For each one, write down a list of the main features of the e-commerce site.

Banking

In banking, millions of transactions take place each day and they all have to be recorded. It is therefore not surprising that the banks take as much benefit from ICT developments as they can.

In this section you will be looking at how banks make use of ICT to deal with the huge volume of transactions and how many more people now choose to bank online.

Cheque clearing using magnetic ink character recognition (MICR)

Cheques are still used and many millions of them go through a process called cheque clearing each day. Check clearing uses input methods that use magnetic characters printed on the cheque.

⌐:,'**¦¦**⊫ **···· 0123456789**

▲ **Example of magnetic ink characters.**

With MICR, the numbers are printed onto the cheque in a special magnetic ink, which can be read at very high speed by the magnetic ink character reader. Most of the data (cheque number, bank sort code and account number) are pre-printed onto the cheque but the amount is not known until the person writes the cheque.

When the cheque is presented for payment, the amount the cheque is for is then printed onto the cheque, again in magnetic ink.

All the cheques are batched together at a centre operated by all the banks called a clearing centre. All the cheques are read and processed in one go by the machine, so this is an example of batch processing.

Advantages

Advantages of magnetic ink character recognition include:

- Accuracy – the documents (usually cheques) are read with 100% accuracy.
- Difficult to forge – because of the sophisticated magnetic ink technology used, it would be difficult to forge cheques.
- Can be read easily – cheques are often folded, crumpled up, etc. Methods such as OCR or OMR would not work with these. MICR uses a magnetic pattern, so this is unaffected by crumpling.

- Speed of reading – documents can be read at very high speed and this is particularly important for the clearing of cheques.

Disadvantages

Disadvantages of magnetic ink character recognition include:

- Expense – the high-speed MICR character readers are very expensive.

ATMs (automated teller machines) (cash points)

ATMs, commonly called cash points, are the 'hole in the wall' cash dispensers that many people use when the bank is not open or when they do not want to queue inside the branch. In order for you to use the service the machine needs to check that you are the card holder. You are asked to enter a PIN (personal identification number) that only you should know. If the card is stolen then the thief should have no way of finding this, unless of course you have stupidly written it down!

Here are some of the things you can do using an ATM:
- You can get cash out.
- You can find out the balance in your account.
- You can change your PIN (personal identification number).

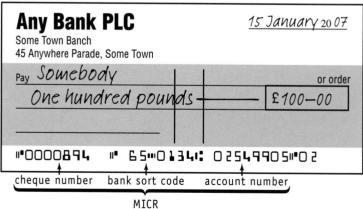

Any Bank PLC
Some Town Banch
45 Anywhere Parade, Some Town

15 January 20 07

Pay _Somebody_   or order

One hundred pounds ———— £100—00

⊫**0000894** ⊫ **65··0134⊫ 02549905··02**

cheque number   bank sort code   account number

MICR

▲ An ATM, commonly called a cash point.

- You can make deposits (i.e., put cash, cheques or both into your account).
- You can obtain a mini statement listing your recent transactions (i.e., money in and out of your account).

Type of processing used with ATMs

Real-time transaction processing is used with ATMs. This means that as soon as a customer gets the money out of their account, their balance is updated. This only takes a short amount of time but is not real-time processing because real-time processing takes place instantly.

Benefits to banks in using ATMs

There are some benefits to the banks in the use of ATMs and these include:

- Staff are freed from performing routine transactions so that more profitable sales-oriented work can be done.
- Fewer staff are needed, since the computer does much of the routine work.
- A 24-hour per day service is provided to satisfy their customers' demands.
- The system makes it impossible for a customer to withdraw funds from their account unless they have the money in their account or an agreed overdraft.

Benefits to customers in using ATMs

- Some customers prefer the anonymous nature of the machine since it cannot think you have stolen the cheque book or think that you are spending too much.

- It is possible to use the service 24 hours per day; ideal for those people who work irregular hours.
- It is possible to park near the dispenser of an evening, so getting cash is a lot quicker.
- Fewer queues, since the transactions performed by the ATM are a lot faster.

Online banking

Many of the tasks you would have had gone to a bank branch to do, you can now perform at home using Internet or online banking. Using online banking you can:

- view bank statements
- transfer money between accounts
- make payments for bills
- apply for loans.

Online banking uses the Internet to enable a customer at home to connect to the bank ICT systems and interact with them. In order to do this the customer has to enter log-in details (username and password) and answer some other security questions.

▲ When you access a secure link, the web address should start with https not just http.

Any details passed between the bank and their customers are encrypted to ensure hackers cannot access banking details.

Backup systems

Most large organizations operate 24/7, so their systems must be capable of running continuously. Here are the main points about backups:

- Backups are normally taken remotely (e.g., away from the main computer centre).
- Many systems use dual computer systems – so if one breaks down, the other one takes over.

- Uninterruptible power supplies are used to power the ICT systems, which means there will not be a problem with power cuts.

Questions B

1 Plastic cards, such as the one shown, are often issued to bank customers.
  (a) Give the names of **two** different types of plastic card that are used by bank customers. *(2 marks)*
  (b) These plastic cards often contain data in a magnetic strip on the card but many of the new cards use chip and pin.
  Explain why these new chip and pin cards were introduced and what advantages they offer over the older cards. *(4 marks)*

2 One problem in using credit cards is that they can be used fraudulently.
  (a) Explain **two** ways that a credit card could be used fraudulently. *(2 marks)*
  (b) State **one** way such frauds can be prevented. *(1 mark)*

Extension activity

Banking online

Many people use their home computers in order to bank online but many people are put off banking online and using their credit/debit cards for online purchases because of all they have heard about identity theft and fraud.

You have been asked to produce an A4 poster that explains and illustrates what people can do to avoid becoming a victim of online fraud or identity theft.

Payroll and modern mail handling methods

You will find out

▷ **About what payroll entails**

▷ **About the method of data capture, the type of processing and the outputs from the system**

▷ **About modern mail handling methods**

Most organizations employ staff who need to be paid and the system for paying them is called a payroll system. Many organizations do their own payroll and they use ICT for this. Payroll processing is similar between organizations so it is possible to purchase a software package to do this.

In this section you will be looking at the ICT systems that are used for payroll.

Organizations send and receive a huge amount of mail each day and in this section you will also look at modern mail handling methods.

What payroll is

If you work for someone, you expect to be paid the correct amount and on time. Payroll is an application that deals with all the information needed to pay employees.

Some staff are paid monthly and others are paid weekly according to the number of hours they work. Some staff may get paid overtime and their hourly rate may increase if they work nights, weekends, etc. Some employees may have part or all of their pay dependent on commission or bonuses. As you can see, payroll can get a bit complicated.

Not all employees get the same pay, even if they are doing identical jobs. Some may be given more pay because they have worked longer in the organization. Some people's pay may differ because the amounts deducted vary, for example the amount of tax. This depends on a person's tax code, which in turn is determined by an individual's circumstances. Each employee is supplied with a detailed breakdown of the amount they are paid, including deductions, in the form of a payslip.

In addition to the money paid to employees, an organization has to send money to many other organizations such as the HM Revenue and Customs for income tax and National Insurance contributions, pension agencies for the payment of pension contributions, trade unions for the payment of subscriptions and so on.

Because of the security and cost problems of dealing with the transfer of large amounts of cash, many organizations use electronic funds transfer (EFT) to transfer the money between the organization's bank account and the employees' accounts. They can also use the system to make payments of income tax and National Insurance contributions that have been deducted from employees' pay.

Data capture, checking and type of processing

There are lots of ways in which data is captured and these include:

- Employees clock in and clock out using a card or key – this records the hours they have worked and these are input into the computer directly.
- Employees fill in timesheets that are read automatically – sometimes these use techniques such as OMR (optical mark recognition) where the employee shades in boxes on a form. Other methods use OCR (optical character recognition), where the reader is able to read numbers and letters the employee fills in on a form.
- Employees fill in timesheets that are input manually using a keyboard.

▼ Some employees may have to fill in a timesheet and the details are then typed in using a keyboard.

Processing timesheets

Both types of form can be collected and batched together to be read automatically at the end of the week or month. They are then input into the computer, which processes them in one go. This type of processing is called batch processing.

Checking

When forms are processed, it is important that every timesheet is processed. Batch totals and hash totals (see Topic 1 for further details) are used to ensure that all the forms are processed.

Output from a payroll system

After the pay has been calculated a document called a payslip is printed. As most payrolls are processed in a batch, the payslips are also printed in a batch. The payslip provides confirmation of the hours worked, the pay, the tax, National Insurance and other deductions and the net pay. These are provided so that the employee is able to check them.

Modern mail handling methods

Although you may think that email is replacing traditional mail, all you have to do is look at the amount of traditional mail arriving through your door. Much of this is junk mail and is opened and quickly discarded. Other mail tends to be bills, although to reduce the costs many companies, such as credit card companies and utilities (gas, electric, water, etc.), prefer to send email bills.

Mail merge letters target individual potential customers and these can be produced using word-processing software.

People in organizations receive huge amounts of email each day and it takes time to sort. Much of the email is advertising goods or services that have not been asked for. Luckily email software is able to identify this type of email and can place all the spam email in a separate folder. The user can then quickly glance at the emails to check none have been trapped by the spam filter by mistake. They can then be deleted.

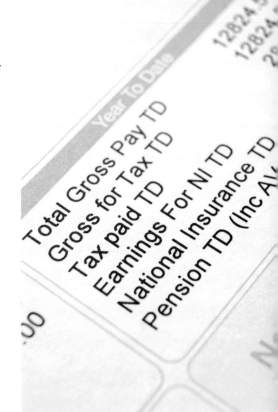

▲ Payslips are the output from a payroll system.

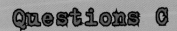

Questions C

1 A veterinary surgery uses computers throughout the practice.
One important task the computer system does is performing the payroll.
  (a) Explain the meaning of 'performing the payroll'. *(1 mark)*
  (b) Some staff are hourly paid and they work a variety of different hours. At the end of the week they are required to fill in a timesheet that shows the hours they have worked each day.
    (i) Give **two** ways the data on these forms could be input into the computer system. *(2 marks)*
    (ii) Once the payroll has been completed some information is output. Give the name of the printed document that is given to employees outlining their pay and deductions. *(1 mark)*

2 A large organization has hundreds of timesheets to process each week. They use pre-printed forms where the employees record the hours they work by shading in boxes on the form. The organization processes all the timesheets in one go at the end of the week
  (a) Give the name of the data capture method used to input the data held on the forms into the computer. *(1 mark)*
  (b) Give **one** advantage of this method of capturing the data on the timesheets. *(1 mark)*
  (c) Give the name of the type of processing used in this application and give **one** reason why it is used. *(2 marks)*

Control systems, robots and bionics

Control systems are all around us and we could hardly do without them. We have many control systems in the home controlling the heating, washing machines, dishwashers, showers, burglar alarms and so on. Once you are in a car the number of control systems shoots up. There are control systems to control the management of the engine, the braking system, the airbags and so on.

There are many ICT systems in use in the home but not many homes have robots. The main problem is that at the moment most robots perform fairly routine tasks.

In this section you will be looking at robots and their use in industry.

Control systems

Simple control systems were looked at in Topic 5 and here we will be looking at control systems that incorporate something called feedback. Basically, having feedback makes the control system more intelligent and more useful.

The importance of feedback

A computer can be used to control a robot arm. If we want the robot arm to move through a certain angle, we can give an instruction to a special motor that moves small steps at a time. When the command has been issued, the arm will move to the required position. If there is an object in the way of the arm, it will stop. The problem is that if this happens, it will assume that it has reached its desired position. The computer can no longer be sure of its position.

What is needed is a way for the arm to relay its actual position back to the computer. It can do this by making use of sensors. The sensors continually send data about the position of the arm back to the computer. If the robot arm is not in the correct position then remedial action can be taken to put it in the correct position. Here, output from the system directly affects the input. Such a system is said to use 'feedback'.

Example of process control making use of feedback

Here is a simple example of process control.

In a chemical process a container is filled with water to a certain level and heated up to a temperature of 80°C.

1. The computer issues a control signal to the motorized tap instructing it to turn the tap on and let the water into the container.
2. As the water enters and the level rises, the water pressure is continually fed back to the computer.
3. As soon as the pressure reaches a certain value the water is up to the correct level. A control signal is sent back to the tap to turn the water off. At the same time a signal is fed back to the computer from the temperature sensor. If the temperature of the water is less than 80°C, a control signal is sent to the heater to turn it on.
4. The temperature is continually measured and sent back to the computer, which compares the temperature with its set level (i.e. 80°C). At soon as the temperature reaches this level, a control is issued to the heater to turn it off. At any time the temperature drops below 80°C, the heater is switched on again so that the temperature remains constant at 80°C.

The type of processing used for process control

Process control always uses real-time processing because the system needs to react instantly to changes so that the system being controlled is safe.

What is bionics?

Bionics is where you apply biological methods and systems found in nature to the study and design of robots and computers.

What is a robot?

A robot is a device that can be programmed to perform a sequence of actions.

Robots can be re-programmed with a new set of instructions so that they are able to carry out a completely different task. For example, a robot arm can be programmed to hold equipment for welding and the same robot arm holding a different tool can be re-programmed to spray cars with paint.

Sometimes the programs are entered into the computer directly and in other cases, such as paint spraying, an experienced operator will guide the robot through the actions it needs to take. It will then remember these actions so that it can perform the task on its own.

Robots

Robots are often seen in factories doing routine jobs such as assembling, welding and paint spraying.

The advantages of using robots

There are a number of advantages in using robots such as:

- No time taken off sick and robots do not take holidays.
- Possibility of robots working 24/7.
- Ensures consistency in the quality of the job.
- Robots do not need paying (although the start-up costs are high).
- Robots are able to carry out boring or dangerous jobs.

Robots are used in hazardous situations. Here are some situations where they might be used:

- Using them to investigate bombs to make them safe.
- Using them to search for wreckage of aircraft that have crashed into the sea.
- Using them to investigate underwater structures such as the feet on drilling platforms.

Problems caused by robots

Robots in factories do replace people; however, people are needed to build, program and repair them.

▲ Car factories use lots of robots.

▶ If you are going to make a robot arm it makes sense to study how the human arm works.

Questions D

1 Robots are used in car manufacturing as they speed up the production process.
Give **two** other advantages of using robots in car manufacturing. *(2 marks)*

2 Robots are used in industry for assembly work, paint spraying and picking and packing goods into boxes. Define the word robot. *(2 marks)*

237

Artificial intelligence (AI) and expert systems

Artificial intelligence (AI) seeks to build computers so they can think and learn the way we do. As you can imagine, as the brain is so complex, building a computer that can think for itself is not going to be easy. We do have a range of computer systems that can appear intelligent and they have been developed to become experts in a certain area such as medicine. Such systems are able to mimic a human expert and are called expert systems.

In this section you will be looking at artificial intelligence and expert systems.

What is artificial intelligence?

Artificial intelligence is a reasoning process performed by computers that allows the computer to:

- draw deductions
- produce new information
- modify rules or write new rules.

The computer, just like a human, is able to learn as it stores more and more data.

What is an expert system?

An expert system is an ICT system that uses artificial intelligence to make decisions based on data supplied in the form of answers to questions. This means that the system is able to respond in the way that a human expert in the field would to come to a conclusion. A good expert system is one that can match the performance of a human expert in the field.

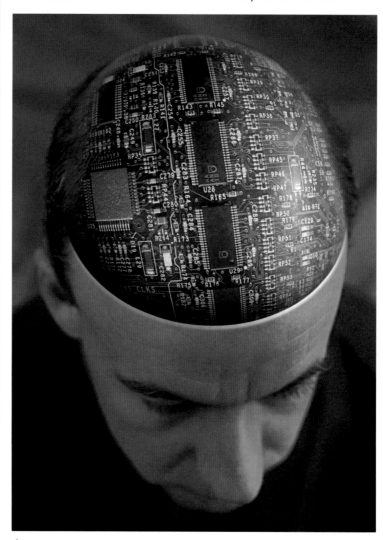

▲ Artificial intelligence seeks to get computers to work and think like the human brain.

The three components of an expert system

Expert systems consist of the following components:

- **Knowledge base** – a huge organized set of knowledge about a particular subject. It contains facts and also judgemental knowledge, which gives it the ability to make a good guess, like a human expert.
- **Inference engine** – a set of rules on which to base decisions and most of these rules have the 'if-then' structure. It is the part of the expert system that does the reasoning by manipulating and using the knowledge in the knowledge base.
- **User interface** – the user interface presents questions and information to the operator and also receives answers from the operator.

Uses for expert systems

Here are three uses for expert systems:

- For making a medical diagnosis or giving medical advice.
- Used by oil companies for deciding where is the most likely place to find oil.
- For giving tax advice to individuals and companies.

Advantages and disadvantages of expert systems

There are a number of advantages and disadvantages of expert systems and these are outlined here.

Advantages of expert systems

- Fewer mistakes – human experts may forget but expert systems don't.
- Less time to train – it is easy to copy an expert system but it takes many years to train a human expert.
- Cheaper – it is cheaper to use an expert system rather than a human expert.

Disadvantages of expert systems

- Lack common sense – humans have common sense so they are able to decide whether an answer is sensible or ridiculous. Human experts can make judgements based on their life experiences, and not just on a limited set of rules as in the case of computers.
- Lack senses – the expert system can only react to information entered by the user. Human experts have many senses that they can use to make judgements. For example, a person describing a type of pain might use body language as well that would not be detected by an expert system.

▲ **There are many examples of medical expert systems.**

Questions E

1. Expert systems are used in medicine to help diagnose illnesses.
   (a) Explain what is meant by an expert system. *(2 marks)*
   (b) An expert system consists of three components. Name **two** of these components. *(2 marks)*
   (c) Give **one** benefit to the patient in using an expert system. *(1 mark)*
   (d) Give **one** benefit to the doctor in using an expert system. *(1 mark)*
   (e) Give **one** possible disadvantage in using this type of expert system. *(1 mark)*

2. Expert system shells are important in the development of medical expert systems.
   (a) Describe the three main parts of every expert system. *(3 marks)*
   (b) Describe, using examples, **two** advantages of using an expert system in medicine. *(2 marks)*

Extension activity

Use the Internet to do some research on the uses of expert systems. For each use you find, write a short paragraph to explain how the expert system is used and what advantages it offers.

Data protection methods

You will find out

▷ **About how data can be made secure on networks**

▷ **About the use of passwords, encryption, backups, file access rights and transaction logs**

If you want to gain access to a stand-alone computer (i.e., one not connected to a network) then you physically need to be there. You could not access it at a distance. With networks, including the Internet, this has all changed. For example, once you are connected to the Internet other people can access your computer unless you take certain precautions. This section looks at data protection issues for stand-alone computer systems as well as networks.

Copyright 2004 by Randy Glasbergen.
www.glasbergen.com

GLASBERGEN

"I'm sure there are better ways to disguise sensitive information, but we don't have a big budget."

▼ When encrypted data is sent to a person, they need a key/password to read it.

KEY WORD

Hackers people who try to break into a computer or computer network.

Protecting a network

Because so many people use a network it is important to ensure that the system is secure. If there is access to the Internet via the network then there needs to be protection against hackers. These hackers could simply intercept and read email or they could alter data or collect personal details and credit card numbers to commit fraud.

Encryption is used to protect data from prying eyes by scrambling data as it travels over the Internet. Encryption is also used when saving personal data onto laptops or removable storage devices. If any of these gets lost or stolen then the data cannot be read.

Encryption should be used for:

- sending credit card details such as card numbers, expiry dates, etc., over the Internet
- online banking
- sending payment details (bank details such as sort code numbers, account numbers, etc.)
- confidential emails
- sending data between terminals where confidentiality is essential
- storing sensitive personal information on laptops and portable devices and media.

Identifying the user to the system: usernames

A username is series of characters that is used to identify a certain user to the network. The person who looks after the network will use this to allocate space on the network for the user. It is also used by the network to give the user access to certain files.

The network manager can also keep track of what files each user is accessing for security reasons.

Preventing unauthorised access to the system: the use of passwords

A password is a string of characters (letters, numbers and punctuation marks) that the user selects. Only the user will know what the password is. When the user enters the password, it will not be shown on the screen. Only on entry of the correct password will the user be allowed access to the network.

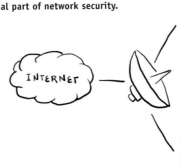

▲ Usernames and passwords are an essential part of network security.

Transaction logs

When transactions (bits of business) are performed on the computer, there may not be any paperwork to go with the system. So that the system can be audited, the software produced will have a function built in that provides an audit trail. The audit trail provides evidence of what has happened in the system. For example, if a record has been deleted, it will provide evidence of the record before the deletion along with the date and time and the name of the member of staff who performed the deletion and even the reason the record was deleted.

Transaction logs are a deterrent to people who might be thinking of committing computer fraud, as they will know they are likely to be found out. It also provides evidence for the police to prosecute computer fraudsters.

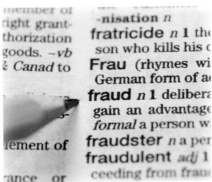

▲ Transaction logs deter computer fraudsters.

Firewalls

Firewalls are software, hardware or both used to filter out unauthorized requests from outside users to gain access to a network. This keeps hackers out. Firewalls also filter data so that only allowable data is allowed into the system.

All networks that have access to the Internet should have a firewall.

▲ Firewalls are used to protect networks from hackers.

"For security purposes, the information should make no sense at all to spies and hackers. We'll bring in someone later to figure out what you meant."

"I know a lot of highly-confidential company secrets, so my boss made me get a firewall installed."

Data protection methods *continued*

▲ Credit/debit card details are encrypted before being sent over the Internet.

File access rights

Access rights restrict a user's access to only those files they need in order to perform their job. Their rights are initially allocated to them by the network manager and when they log on, by giving their username/user-ID and password, these rights are allocated by the computer.

A user can have a number of different levels of access to files including:

- Read only – a user can only read the contents of the file. They cannot alter or delete the data.
- Read/write – a user can read the data held in the file and can alter the data.
- Append – they can add new records but they will be unable to alter or delete existing records.
- No access – they cannot open the file so cannot do anything to it.

▼ Flash/pen drives can be used for backing up small amounts of data but they are easily lost.

Physical protection

Physical protection is all the types of protection that involve the use of actual devices or media to ensure the security of the data held. For example, having key pads on doors to computer rooms to prevent unauthorized access is physical protection.

Here are some other methods of physical protection:

- Attaching computers to desks to prevent them from being stolen.
- Keyboard locks to prevent keyboards being used.
- Locking backups away in fireproof safes.
- Using biometric devices such as retinal scanning, fingerprint scanning to gain access to rooms and the computers themselves.

Backups

Backups are copies of data and program files kept for security reasons. Should the originals be destroyed then the backups can be used. Using a file server and storing both programs and data on it, means that backups can be taken in one place. Backups should be held on removable devices

KEY WORDS

Encryption the process of coding files before they are sent over a network to protect them from hackers. Also the process of coding files stored on a computer so that if the computer is stolen, they cannot be read.

Firewall a piece of software, hardware or both that is able to protect a network from hackers.

Password a series of characters chosen by the user that are used to check the identity of the user when they require access to an ICT system.

Username or User-ID a name or number that is used to identify a certain user of the network or system.

or media that are taken off site each day. The individual users do not need to take their own backups. The person in charge of the network (i.e., usually the network manager) will take the backups needed.

Many systems now take backups automatically at a certain time of the day and send the data using the Internet to a company that specializes in storing backups.

Questions F

1 Networks can suffer from security problems.
Describe briefly **two** security problems that networks suffer from. *(4 marks)*

2 Explain how a network can be protected from the following:
(a) Loss of data *(2 marks)*
(b) Unauthorized access *(2 marks)*

3 Explain briefly how each of the following helps improve the security of a network.
(a) User-ID *(2 marks)*
(b) Password *(2 marks)*
(c) Encryption *(2 marks)*
(d) Transaction log *(2 marks)*
(e) Firewall *(2 marks)*

END-OF-TOPIC REVIEW

Questions

 Test yourself

The following notes summarize this topic. The notes are incomplete because they have words missing.

Using the words in the list below, copy out and complete the sentences A to I, underlining the words that you have inserted. Each word may be used more than once.

feedback   debit   encrypted   sensors   payroll   control

intelligence   hackers   Internet   expert system

A E-commerce systems use the _____ for the purchase of goods and services.

B In order to pay for online purchases a customer must enter their credit or _____ card details and many customers worry that this information could be accessed by _____.

C When making online payments the card details are _____, which means if they are intercepted by hackers then details will be meaningless and useless.

D Processing the payments for workers for the work they do and printing the payslips is called processing the _____.

E To ensure that all the timesheets have been read and processed by the computer a _____ total can be used.

F Artificial _____ is a reasoning process performed by computers.

G An _____ _____ is an ICT system that uses artificial intelligence to make decisions based on data supplied in the form of answers to questions.

H Control often makes use of _____ where the output has some influence on the input.

I The input to control systems is usually obtained from _____.

Examination style questions

1 The data on a card is encoded in the magnetic strip on the back of the card. A typical card is shown in the following diagram:

   (a) Give **three** items of data that would be encoded on the magnetic strip. *(3 marks)*

   (b) This card can be used to obtain cash from a cash point (or ATM).

      (i) Give **two** advantages to customers in being able to use cash points rather than go into the bank to obtain the cash. *(2 marks)*

      (ii) Explain **two** other services that an ATM (cash point) is able to offer the bank customers. *(2 marks)*

2 Online banking is very popular with home users of ICT.

   (a) Give **three** services offered by online banking. *(3 marks)*

   (b) Some people are sceptical about online banking. Describe **two** worries that people might have with online banking. *(2 marks)*

   (c) Describe **one** way that the banks can address **one** of the worries you have described in part (b). *(1 mark)*

Exam support

Worked example

(a) Define what is meant by a robot. *(2 marks)*

(b) Robots are used in industry for a variety of tasks.

Give **two** tasks that robots are often used for in industry. *(2 marks)*

(c) Give **three** advantages in using robots in industry. *(3 marks)*

Student answer 1

(a) A robot is a device like a human which walks around and talks.

(b) For spraying cars.

For welding panels on cars.

(c) You do not need to pay them so they are cheaper.

They can do the job better than a person because they do not have off days.

They work hard all the time not like humans who can be lazy.

◀ Examiner's comment

(a) This sounds more like the type of robot seen on Star Wars or in children's toys. Students are best advised to remember definitions of key words like the word robot.

No marks are given for this answer.

(b) The student should have given more detail and mentioned 'for spraying cars with paint'. However, they were not penalized for this.

Both of the answers here were awarded a mark.

(c) All the answers here are correct so this part gains full marks.

(5 marks out of 7)

Student answer 2

(a) It is a device that can be programmed to do a particular task such as assemble parts of a car engine. If you want the robot to do a different task, then you have to reprogram it.

(b) For welding the spouts on electric kettles.

For packing goods in boxes ready to be sent to customers.

(c) Robots can work continuously for long periods.

The robots can work 24 hours a day 365 days per year.

Once you have paid for them, the cost to keep them working is very low compared to employing staff.

◀ Examiner's comment

(a) This is a good answer that tells the examiner that robots can be programmed and that they are capable of being reprogrammed. The fact that robots can be reprogrammed makes them robots and not simply automatic devices such as a washing machine. Full marks are given for this answer.

(b) Both are jobs performed by robots so full marks are given again.

(c) The first two points made are almost the same so only one mark is given. It is always worth checking that your answers are distinctly different.

The third point is worth a mark.

(6 marks out of 7)

Examiner's answers

(a) One mark for each of two points such as:

A machine that can be programmed *(1)* to perform a series of actions *(1)* and is capable of being reprogrammed to carry out different actions or a different task *(1)*.

(b) One mark for each task to a maximum of two marks.

- Paint spraying.
- Welding panels.
- Assembling components.
- Moving goods around a factory.

(c) One mark for each advantage to a maximum of three marks.

- Robots do not get tired or distracted.
- Robots do not have to be paid.
- They are capable of working 24/7.
- They can work in dangerous conditions.
- They are consistent and produce high quality work.
- They can create some new jobs such as the people who maintain or program them.

EXAM TIPS

It is quite hard to define a term such as a 'robot', so it is sometimes best to simply learn the definition off by heart rather than to try to explain it yourself.

Use the Glossary at the back of the book to practise your knowledge of key words. Get a friend to ask you questions from the Glossary and then swap around.

Produce a mind map on robots and use this for your revision. Make sure that you mark on this mind map a definition for a robot, the advantages and disadvantages of using robots and also some tasks for which they are suited.

Avoid science fiction type descriptions of robots in your answers. Think instead of the robots used in industry used for welding panels of cars, paint spraying, etc.

Summary mind maps

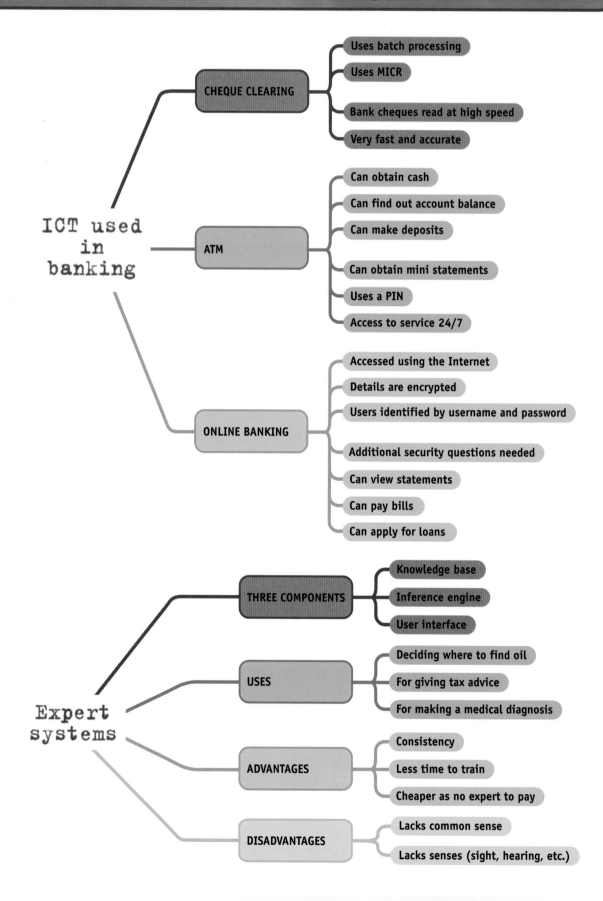

ICT used in banking

CHEQUE CLEARING
- Uses batch processing
- Uses MICR
- Bank cheques read at high speed
- Very fast and accurate

ATM
- Can obtain cash
- Can find out account balance
- Can make deposits
- Can obtain mini statements
- Uses a PIN
- Access to service 24/7

ONLINE BANKING
- Accessed using the Internet
- Details are encrypted
- Users identified by username and password
- Additional security questions needed
- Can view statements
- Can pay bills
- Can apply for loans

Expert systems

THREE COMPONENTS
- Knowledge base
- Inference engine
- User interface

USES
- Deciding where to find oil
- For giving tax advice
- For making a medical diagnosis

ADVANTAGES
- Consistency
- Less time to train
- Cheaper as no expert to pay

DISADVANTAGES
- Lacks common sense
- Lacks senses (sight, hearing, etc.)

Topic 22

Social and environmental impact

The key concepts covered in this topic are:

- Issues relating to employment patterns

- Issues relating to retraining

- Issues relating to changes in working practices such as collaboration

- Teleworking

- Videoconferencing

- The environmental impact of ICT

- The impact of ICT on rich and poor communities

In this topic you will learn about some of the many impacts that ICT has on our lives. Most of these impacts are for the good but there are some negative aspects as well.

You will be looking at the way ICT has changed employment and the way that we work and you will look at the impact that using the Internet has had on people being able to work from home. You will also be looking at videoconferencing and how it is used to help minimize the environmental impact of using computers.

Contents

The impact of ICT

You will find out

▷ **About the impact of ICT on your own and others' lives**

▷ **About the social, economic, political, ethical and moral issues**

The UK is one of the most avid users of ICT but there are many countries in the world where the use of ICT is in its infancy. ICT has brought huge benefits to those countries that have the money and the skills to exploit it. Although ICT solves many problems, there are issues created with its use that need to be looked at.

The impact of ICT on people's lives

The impact of ICT on our lives is huge. Think about all the ICT systems you use in the course of a day. How would you manage without mobile phones, the Internet, your MP3 player, communication systems such as email and being able to shop from home?

Here are a few things that have had a huge impact on our lives:

- Portable computing – owing to computers getting smaller and lighter.
- The Internet – with huge amounts of information that can be accessed almost anywhere.
- Digital music – music is no longer confined to a living room or a car.
- Video – can access video using digital TV as well as by using the Internet.

- Changes in the way we shop – many people prefer to shop online.
- Communication systems – this includes the use of text messages, emails, instant messaging, etc.
- Huge databases – keep our medical details, which can be accessed by medical staff anywhere in the country. They also help fight crime.
- Cyber crime – we have to be much more careful about revealing personal information such as bank and credit card details.
- VOIP (Voice Over Internet Protocol) – enables cheap international phone calls to be made using the Internet.
- Use of ICT systems to help people with disabilities be more independent.

Social, economic, political, ethical and moral issues

This section looks at the many different issues that the use of ICT raises.

▼ Digital music has completely changed the way we buy and listen to music.

Social issues

The use of ICT causes a number of social issues such as:

- Lack of privacy due to CCTV cameras, face recognition systems, loyalty cards, fingerprint databases and DNA databases, etc.
- Addiction to games, chat rooms, social networking sites, etc.
- Addiction to gambling as there are many casino, bingo, horse racing, etc., betting sites.
- Addiction to pornography.
- Deserted city centres as shops close down because they cannot compete with Internet shopping.
- Paedophiles look for young children using the Internet.
- Health issues such as back ache, RSI, stress, etc.
- Identity theft, where people steal your bank details to commit fraud.
- Starting rumours on the Internet. You only have to start a rumour in a chat room, a blog or on a social networking site and it soon spreads.
- Misinformation. Many sites have been set up containing wrong information.

Economic issues

There are a number of economic issues concerning the use of ICT such as:

- Jobs being transferred abroad because wage costs are lower in some other countries.
- Internet shopping has caused many small shops to go out of business.
- Globalization means it is hard to compete against the huge big businesses.

Political issues

There are a number of political issues including:

- More people would vote in elections if you could vote online.
- People are able to use the Internet to get stories out about corrupt governments around the world.
- Blogs allow people to vent their feelings on current issues.
- Some countries with dictators (i.e., they are not run democratically) control their subjects by not allowing them access to part or all of the Internet.
- There are ways of setting up online petitions.

Ethical issues

There are a number of ethical issues including:

- Employers sometimes look at profiles of job applicants on social networking sites to see if they are suitable for a job.
- Employers often monitor the use of the Internet by their staff and they may read their emails and check what they have been looking at.
- Social networking sites get users to reveal lots of personal information about themselves and their friends, which is an invasion of privacy.
- The use of cookies. Internet 'cookies' without you knowing, record details of the websites you have visited.

Moral issues

There are a number of moral issues including:

- Many people copy CDs, software, pictures off the Internet, etc., even though it is illegal to do so.
- ICT widens the gap between the rich and the poor countries.

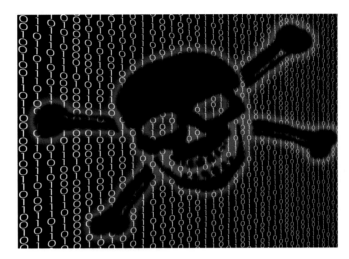

- Widens the gap between rich and poor people. Poor people often cannot get credit, which means it is hard for them to make purchases of goods and services over the Internet.
- The use of essay banks. Although many students use them as a guide, some simply copy them.

◁ Copying digital material illegally (i.e. piracy) is a moral issue as well as being a crime.

Activity

Essay banks good or bad?

John is under pressure because he has an essay to write. He heard from a friend that there is a site where people submit essays and coursework that they have done to help others. It is free to use the site.

> Take a look at the site at:
> www.essaybank.co.uk

Discuss with your friends and your teacher the moral implications of such a site. Is it a good or a bad thing? Think about the following issues:

- What are the dangers if John simply copies one of the examples on the site and passes it off as his own work?
- What would be the likely consequences if the work is submitted as coursework and it is spotted by the assessment board?

Activity

Producing a mind map on 'The impact of ICT'

The use of ICT has had a huge impact on society.

For this activity you have to produce a mind map entitled 'The impact of ICT'.

You can use specialist mind mapping software if it is available or you can draw it on a piece of paper. Think about all the things that you do in your life that use an ICT system. Your teacher may allow you to work on this activity in a small group.

Issues relating to employment

You will find out

▷ **About employment patterns**

▷ **About retraining**

▷ **About changes in working practices**

Most jobs have changed with the introduction of ICT systems but some jobs have disappeared completely. In this section you will look at the ways employment has changed and at the jobs that have disappeared.

▲ Filing clerks kept files organized but now with online databases they are no longer needed.

Employment patterns

Because of ICT, some jobs have been created and some have disappeared. Jobs that have disappeared include:

- Filing clerks – many organizations use computer databases so no paper files are kept. Records can be obtained easily by anyone connected to the network, so there is no need for filing clerks.
- Welders, paint sprayers, fabricators (who assemble products) – most of these boring repetitive jobs have been replaced by robots. It is safer to use robots in some environments.
- Packers – many large mail order/ e-commerce organizations use automated picking and packing machines to select items off shelves and pack them ready for delivery to customers.
- Typists – most people choose to type their own correspondence. Much of the routine correspondence is automated. Many people use voice recognition systems that allow a user to dictate letters, etc., into a word-processor.
- Stock takers in shops/till staff – fewer staff are needed in supermarkets as more of the tasks are automated. There is no need to price individual articles as the bar code along with a database can give all the information needed such as price, description, etc.
- Bank employees – many customers now bank online and use cash dispensers to take cash out. Also many more people use debit and credit cards to pay for goods.

New jobs that have been created through ICT include:

- Network managers/administrators – these are the people who keep the networks running for all the users, see to the taking of backup copies kept for security purposes, etc.
- Website designers – these are the people who design and create websites for others, as well as keep them up-to-date by added new and deleting old material. The work involves design skills as well as programming and other technical skills.
- Development staff – these include systems analysts (who design new ICT systems) and programmers who write the step-by-step instructions (i.e. the programs) that instruct the computers what to do.

Retraining

In the past the pace of change was slow. When you started a job, you tended to do more or less the same thing throughout your working life. Things are very different in the workplace now. The pace of change is rapid and the workforce has to adapt to new ICT systems, new ways of working, new codes of practice and new laws.

In order to equip employees with new knowledge and skills, employers need to continually train and re-train staff.

Changes to ICT systems that result in retraining include:

- New software – for example, a new database package is being used.

- New hardware – for example, a new printer that can print on both sides of the page is being introduced.
- New laws – these could be introduced to cope with misuses of new technology.
- New ways of working (i.e. procedures) – for example, the use of email rather than letters to communicate with customers.

Changes in working practices

The use of ICT has produced many changes in the way people work. Here are some of them:

- Greater collaboration – it is much easier for people to work collectively on a project and transfer work between team members.
- Businesses have to be staffed 24/7 – because business is often done globally (i.e., all over the world).
- More people are working whilst they are travelling – many business people use laptops, mobile phones, PDAs whilst they travel so they can be more productive.
- Blurring of boundaries between work and play – people can do work at home because it is easy to access the data they need using the Internet.
- They are also contactable at any time using mobile phones, PDAs and laptops with wireless Internet access.
- Fewer journeys to meetings as meetings can be conducted at a distance using videoconferencing technology.

Teleworking

If you have an Internet connection then you can communicate easily with people all around the country or even the world. Many people who use computers for their work are able to do their work at home. Working from home using ICT equipment and telecommunications is called teleworking.

The advantages of teleworking to the employee are shown in this diagram:

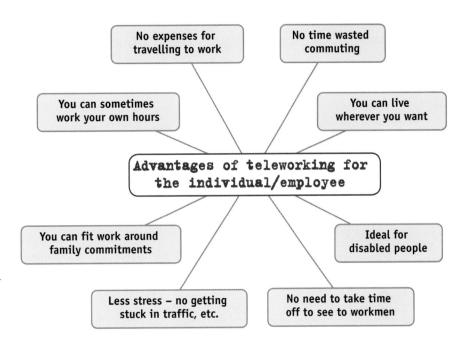

There are a number of disadvantages of teleworking to the employee and these are shown here:

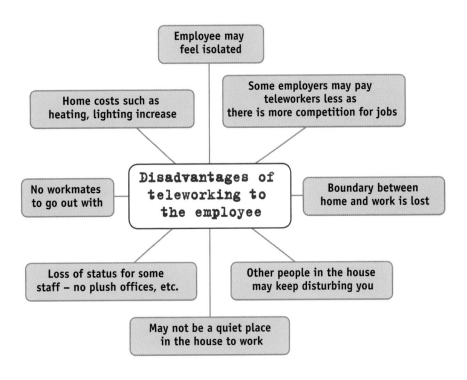

Issues relating to employment *continued*

Why do employers allow staff to telework? You can see the advantages that teleworking offers to employers in the following diagram:

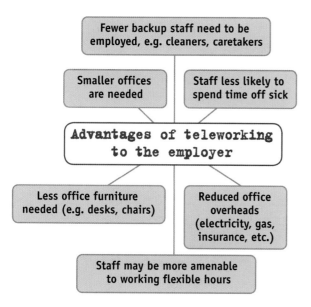

There are also a number of disadvantages of teleworking to employers and these are summarized in the following diagram:

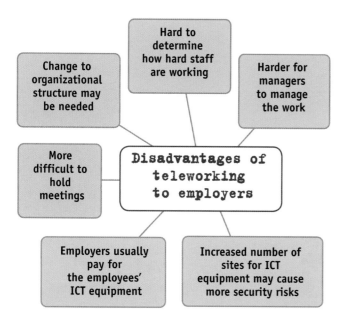

There are advantages to society in teleworking and these are summarized here:

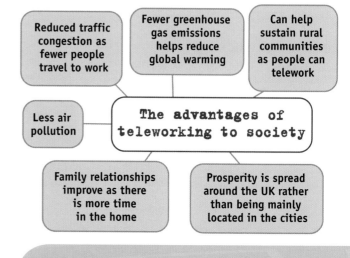

Questions A

1 ICT has replaced or changed many jobs.
  (a) Give the names of **two** types of job that have been replaced by ICT. *(2 marks)*
  (b) Some jobs have changed their nature due to the introduction of ICT. Name **two** jobs where this has happened. *(2 marks)*
  (c) The increase in high speed broadband links has led to cheaper international telephone calls using the Internet. Name **one** job that has been lost from this country to abroad as a result of this. *(1 mark)*

2 The widespread use of ICT has had a huge impact on society. One benefit that it has brought is the creation of new and interesting jobs.
  (a) Give **three** examples of jobs that have been created owing to the introduction of ICT. *(3 marks)*
  (b) Many people have had to be retrained to cope with the introduction of new ICT systems. Explain why regular retraining is needed in the workplace. *(2 marks)*

3 ICT systems and facilities mean that many employees can telework.
  (a) Explain what is meant by 'telework'. *(3 marks)*
  (b) Describe **two** advantages to the employer of teleworking. *(2 marks)*
  (c) Describe **two** disadvantages to the employer of teleworking. *(2 marks)*

Videoconferencing, the impact of ICT on the environment and communities

In this section you will learn about videoconferencing, which enables people to have virtual meetings, saving time and benefiting society in the process.

You will also be looking at the environmental aspects of ICT. Unfortunately we live in a throw away society and everyone wants to have the latest technology but we need to upgrade and recycle where we can.

Finally in this section you will be looking at how ICT affects both rich and poor communities.

Videoconferencing

Videoconferencing allows face-to-face meetings to be conducted without the participants being in the same room or even the same geographical area. You will probably have seen videoconferencing systems used to interview people in distant locations on the TV news.

▲ Videoconferencing allows virtual meetings where delegates are not at the same location.

Videoconferencing allows people to hold a 'virtual' meeting. The people at the meeting can see and speak to each other. They are also able to share documents, presentations, etc.

Advantages of using videoconferencing

There are many advantages in using videoconferencing and these include:

- Less stress as employees do not have to experience delays at airports, accidents, roadworks, etc.
- Improved family life, as less time spent away from home staying in hotels.
- They do not have to put in long working hours travelling to and from meetings.
- Saves money as business does not have to spend money on travelling expenses, hotel rooms, meals, etc.
- Improves productivity of employees, as they are not wasting time travelling.
- Meetings can be called at very short notice without too much planning.
- Greener, as there are fewer people flying to meetings. This cuts down on carbon dioxide emissions.
- Roads will not be clogged up with traffic and this will cause less stress and cut down on pollution.

Disadvantages of using videoconferencing

There are many disadvantages in using videoconferencing and these include:

- The cost of the equipment, as specialist videoconferencing equipment is expensive.
- Poor image and sound quality.
- People can feel very self-conscious when using videoconferencing and may fail to come across well.
- Although documents and diagrams in digital form can be passed around, an actual product or component cannot be passed around.
- Lack of face-to-face contact may mean a discussion may not be as effective.

Videoconferencing, the impact of ICT on the environment and communities *continued*

The environmental impact

The production of ICT equipment produces lots of carbon dioxide and the use of the equipment produces lots as well. Carbon dioxide is a greenhouse gas and causes global warming, which is bad for all of us.

▲ The production and use of ICT produces lots of emissions.

In order to help the environment there are a number of actions we can all take:

- Recycle hardware, as this reduces the greenhouses gases.
- Print preview so you only print your final copy.
- Reduce the amount of printouts you make.
- Recycle paper – printouts and other paper documents should not be thrown away with general rubbish. Instead it should be collected for recycling.
- Switch off computer equipment rather than leave it on stand-by.
- Homeworking or teleworking – this will reduce congestion and pollution and cut down on greenhouse gas emissions.
- Recycle printer cartridges by having them re-filled with ink.
- Recycle mobile phones as your old phone can be someone's new phone.

Many ICT systems help the environment in some way. Here are some examples:

- Environmental control systems – here the heating can be controlled accurately in each room in a building. If a room is not being used, then the heating can be turned off. This helps reduce fuel bills as well as carbon dioxide emissions.
- Satellite navigation systems – ensure people do not get lost and therefore use more fuel and create more pollution.
- Traffic management systems – these coordinate traffic lights, which ensures that the main body of traffic keeps moving.
- Pollution monitoring systems – monitor the environmental conditions in rivers and lakes and produce alerts if there are problems.

The impact on rich and poor communities

The use of ICT is essential if a country is to remain or become prosperous in the world. Here are some of the impacts on rich and poor communities:

Widening the gap between rich and poor countries – the use of ICT makes already rich countries richer. As many poorer countries do not have reliable electricity or telecommunications, they cannot take advantage of the financial benefits of ICT.

ICT widens the gap between the 'haves' and the 'have nots' – there are large savings to be made on the Internet. You can buy cars, CDs, books, electrical goods, take part in online auctions and so on. All this is fine, but you need one thing to take part; a valid credit card. This credit card gives you an electronic identity. If you do not have a credit/

debit card, then it is hard to take advantages of Internet savings.

Getting a credit/debit card is not that easy if you do not have a job or have a bad credit history.

Questions B

1 (a) A company has decided to use videoconferencing. Explain what is meant by videoconferencing. *(2 marks)*

(b) Other than a computer, what equipment would the company need to supply to enable videoconferencing? *(2 marks)*

(c) Write down **one** advantage and **one** disadvantage of videoconferencing. *(2 marks)*

2 Explain **one** way in which ICT increases the divide between rich and poor people. *(2 marks)*

Extension activity

For this activity you have to find out more about videoconferencing.

Use the Internet to find answers to the following and produce a brief set of notes for future reference:

- **The benefits of videoconferencing to society.**
- **The hardware needed.**
- **The software needed.**
- **Some typical applications of videoconferencing.**

Questions

 Test yourself

The following notes summarize this topic. The notes are incomplete because they have words missing.

Using the words in the list below, copy out and complete the sentences A to J, underlining the words that you have inserted. Each word may be used more than once.

political	commitments	Internet	moral
teleworking	distractions	videoconferencing	
social	power	rich	

A VOIP (Voice Over Internet Protocol) enables cheap international phone calls to be made using the _____.

B Addiction to chat rooms, social networking sites, games and pornography is a _____ issue caused by ICT.

C The availability of online voting in elections is a _____ issue.

D The use of essay banks is a _____ issue caused by the use of ICT.

E _____ means working from home by making use of computers and communications equipment.

F One big advantage with teleworking is that you are able to work around family _____.

G A disadvantage of teleworking is that there are many _____ at home.

H _____ uses cameras and microphones in addition to computers and special software in order to conduct a virtual meeting.

I ICT can widen the gap between _____ and poor communities.

J ICT uses a lot of energy to make the equipment and also to _____ the computers.

Examination style questions

1 ICT developments in organizations have caused changes to working patterns.
   Describe **three** such changes to working patterns. *(3 marks)*

2 The use of ICT has enabled many staff to work from home. Working from home has both advantages and disadvantages.
   Give **two** advantages and **two** disadvantages to an employee in working from home. *(4 marks)*

3 Teleworking is a very popular way of working in certain jobs.
   Give the names of **two** jobs that are particularly suited to teleworking. *(2 marks)*

4 Describe **one** way in which ICT is used in manufacturing in order to reduce the number of people needed to produce goods. *(3 marks)*

END-OF-TOPIC REVIEW

Exam support

Worked example

There are many ways in which ICT has had an effect on the way people work. Two such ways are teleworking and videoconferencing. Describe the benefits that each of these technologies has brought to people. *(6 marks)*

Student answer 1

With videoconferencing you can see who you are talking to. People with relatives abroad can chat to them as if they were all together. They do not need to travel to see each other. Also meetings can be set up at the last minute, so everyone can meet. The people who are attending do not have to waste time travelling and there aren't the costs of travelling as well.

Teleworking is good because you can get to work at home. You have no boss standing over you telling you what to do and if you come in late no-one notices. You may be able to work your own hours, which is great if you need to take a holiday.

◄ **Examiner's comment**

In the part of the answer for videoconferencing the student seems to have got confused between using webcams on home computers and professional videoconferencing. Videoconferencing equipment is expensive, which means its use is usually restricted to businesses, although it is sometimes used for distance learning in schools, colleges, etc. The part about meetings probably means businesses, so marks are given from here on.

The other parts were better and four points were awarded marks.

(4 marks out of 6)

Student answer 2

With teleworking there are lots of advantages such as:

- *You can work more flexibly, so by working harder you may be able to free up time to take time off later.*
- *As long as the work gets done, it does not matter when it is done. This means you can work at a time that suits you best.*
- *You do not have the time to spend commuting, which is unproductive and it can also be expensive in terms of petrol and car parking.*
- *It suits people who are self-motivated and like to work on their own.*

With videoconferencing there are lots of advantages such as:

- *You do not waste time driving to meetings and the company does not have the cost of this.*
- *You do not need to spend time away from your family, which is good for family life.*
- *There is also the environmental aspect to consider. Fewer journeys means less pollution and less global warming.*

◄ **Examiner's comment**

This is a well-structured and factually correct answer. The student has carefully explained many answers worthy of marks and there are more points made than were actually needed for this question. As six marks had been given the student needed to make six points but this is not a complaint because there is nothing wrong with writing more, because if one of the points is not quite right then the mark can be made up with one of the extra points.

(6 marks out of 6)

Examiner's answers

- One mark each for a benefit of teleworking to a maximum of three marks and the same for videoconferencing. Points should be made in complete sentences.

- Benefits of teleworking – no time spent travelling, greener/less pollution, can fit around family commitments, ideal for disabled/housebound, lower costs for teleworkers, etc.

- Benefits of videoconferencing – less time spent away from home, less cost as no travel and hotel costs, more productive as less time wasted on the move, greener as fewer journeys are made, etc.

Summary mind maps

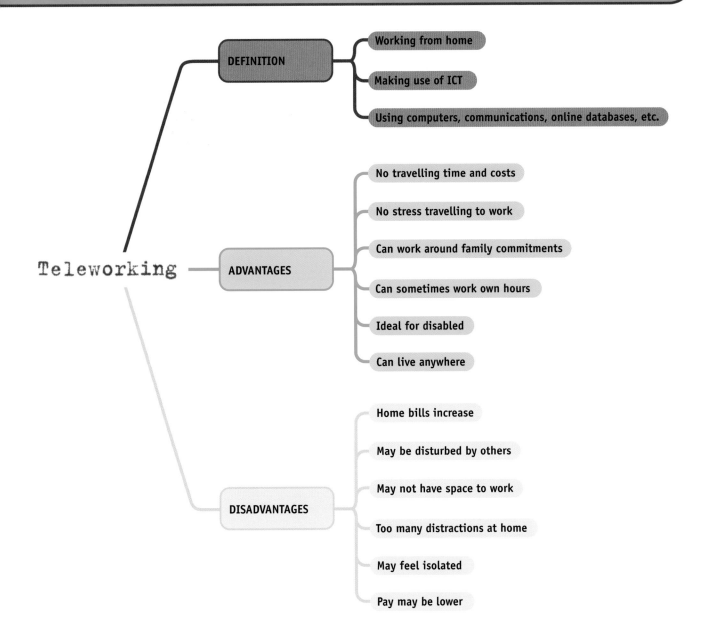

Summary mind maps *continued*

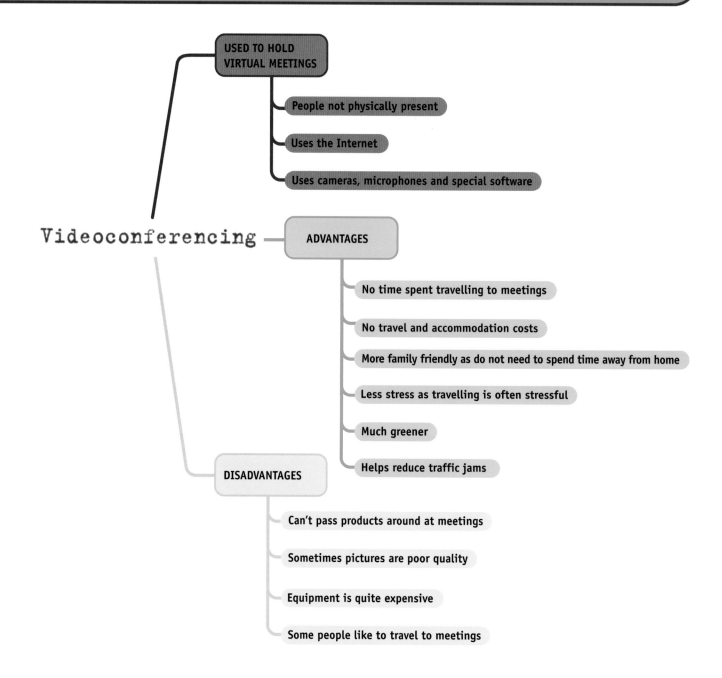

USED TO HOLD VIRTUAL MEETINGS

People not physically present

Uses the Internet

Uses cameras, microphones and special software

Videoconferencing

ADVANTAGES

No time spent travelling to meetings

No travel and accommodation costs

More family friendly as do not need to spend time away from home

Less stress as travelling is often stressful

Much greener

Helps reduce traffic jams

DISADVANTAGES

Can't pass products around at meetings

Sometimes pictures are poor quality

Equipment is quite expensive

Some people like to travel to meetings

Topic 23

Legal and ethical issues

The key concepts covered in this topic are:

- **Provisions of the Data Protection Act (DPA) 1998**

- **The Computer Misuse Act 1990**

- **The Electronic Communications Act 2000**

- **The Regulation of Investigatory Powers Act 2000**

- **Health and safety legislation**

- **Issues concerning copyright misuse**

At one time information systems/ICT systems were only used by organizations and businesses but now almost everyone uses them. The way we use our working time and leisure time has completely changed with the introduction of ICT.

The rise in the number of uses for ICT has also led to a number of problems. Most of these problems are caused by people who misuse the ICT systems in some way. These misuses can range from simple misuses such as the sending of spam (unwanted email advertising things) to serious fraud.

Legislation (laws) needed to be made to prevent people from doing certain things using ICT.

Contents

Provisions of the Data Protection Act (DPA) 1998

It is hard to keep information about yourself private. Everyone seems to want to store it and process it on ICT systems. Each time you fill in a form or complete a questionnaire you are supplying data about you which can then be processed by organizations. Finding out as much as they can about you enables companies to target their marketing. Privacy is a term used to describe keeping your personal details private.

The problems with organizations holding personal data

The DPA concerns personal data which means data:

- about an identifiable person (i.e., the data must be about someone who can be identified by name, address, etc.)
- about someone who is living
- that is more personal than name and address (e.g., medical records, criminal record, credit history, religious or political beliefs, etc.).

There are a number of problems with organizations holding personal data:

- The personal data might be wrong, which means wrong decisions could be made.
- The organization may not take care of the personal data it holds, so others may find out about it.

Examples of the effect of wrong information:

- Your medical details could be wrong, meaning you get the wrong treatment – which could be life threatening.
- Wrong decisions might be made. For example, you could be refused a loan.
- Wrong exam results could affect you getting a job.

The provisions of the Data Protection Act 1998

ICT makes it easy for organizations and businesses to store and process information about individuals. This processing can build up a complete profile about someone. Much of this is done without the person being aware it is done.

To protect individuals against the misuse of personal data, in 1998 the government brought out a law called the Data Protection Act.

Rights of the data subject and the data holder

The person about whom the personal details are held is called the data subject by the Act. The person in the organization who is responsible for the personal data held is called the data holder.

The Data Protection Act 1998 protects individuals by placing obligations on the organizations who collect and process the data (i.e. the data holders) in the following ways.

Registration (also called notification)

It requires anyone who uses personal data to register with the Information Commissioner, who is the person who is in charge of the Act/Law. They must say what data they intend to hold and what they intend to do with it.

Individuals can see their own personal data

Anyone can apply to see the personal data held about them. Organizations have to show it and if there is any wrong information, then it must be corrected.

Data must be kept secure and up-to-date

Data subjects (the people who the data is about) can sue an organization that does not keep their personal data secure.

The right for a person to claim compensation

If data is processed unlawfully by an organization then the person can take them to court and claim compensation.

Exemptions from the DPA

There are a number of exemptions:

- When the data is used for personal, family, household affairs or recreational use.
- Where the data is being used for preparing the text of documents (e.g., the writing of references using a word-processor).
- Where the data is used for producing accounts, wages and pensions.
- Where data is used for mail shots.
- Where the data is used by a sports or recreational club that is not a limited company.
- Where the data is used for the prevention or detection of crimes.
- Where the data is used for catching or prosecuting offenders.
- Collecting taxes or duty.
- Medical records or social worker reports.

The Data Protection Principles

The holder of the information has eight obligations (called Principles) placed on them by the Data Protection Act and these are summarized below. The Data Protection Principles state that personal data should be:

1 processed fairly and lawfully
2 obtained only for specified purposes
3 adequate, relevant and not excessive
4 accurate and kept up-to-date
5 not kept any longer than is necessary
6 processed in accordance with the rights of the data subject
7 kept secure
8 not transferred to a country outside the EU unless they have a comparable data protection law.

Questions A

1 Some people are not happy about organizations storing and processing personal information about them.
   (a) Explain, by giving **two** examples, what is meant by personal information. *(3 marks)*
   (b) Give **one** reason why a person might object to an organization storing personal information about them. *(2 marks)*

2 All schools use computer systems to store details about past and present students.
   Schools are required to notify the use of the personal data they hold under the terms of the Data Protection Act 1998.

   (a) Give **three** items of personal information the school is likely to store about their students. *(3 marks)*
   (b) Students in the school are given certain rights under the Data Protection Act.
   Explain **two** of these rights. *(2 marks)*
   (c) One student is worried that the personal information the school holds about them might be incorrect. Explain, with an example, how incorrect information could affect a student. *(2 marks)*

EXAM TIP

Many questions ask you about the Data Protection Principles, so you should try to remember them off by heart.

Extension activity

Find out more about the DPA by accessing the Information Commissioner's Office website at http://www.ico.gov.uk/

The Computer Misuse Act 1990 and issues concerning copyright misuse

You will find out

▷ **About the Computer Misuse Act 1990**

▷ **About issues concerning copyright misuse**

There are a number of different misuses that arose as ICT systems became widespread. For example, hacking and the spreading of viruses became more of a problem. The use of digital media led to an increase in copyright misuses. All these had to be dealt with by laws so in this section we will look at these.

The Computer Misuse Act 1990

The Computer Misuse Act 1990 was passed to deal with a number of misuses as the use of computers became widespread.

The Computer Misuse Act makes it an offence to:

- deliberately plant or transfer viruses to a computer system to cause damage to programs and data
- use an organization's computers to carry out unauthorized work
- hack into someone else's computer system with a view to seeing the information or altering it
- use computers to commit various frauds.

Issues concerning copyright misuse

Many people spend a lot of time and money creating original work such as a piece of music, a picture, a piece of software, a photograph, a newspaper article, etc. Many of these people do it for a living, so it is only fair that their work should not be copied without permission.

The Copyright, Designs and Patents Act 1988 protects intellectual property from being copied such as:

- software
- text (e.g., books, magazine articles, etc.)
- a new innovative human–computer interface
- hardware (e.g., a flexible screen, the design of a power-saving chip, etc.)
- books and manuals
- images on websites.

Here are some actions that are illegal:

- copying software and music illegally
- copying images or text without permission
- copying sections of websites without permission
- sharing digital music illegally using peer-to-peer file sharing software
- running more copies of software than is allowed by the site licence.

Extension activity

Someone has said to you that as many people copy software and music illegally, it is morally OK even though it is illegal. Produce a word-processed magazine article putting both sides of the argument. You can use the Internet to provide you with information for this article.

Questions B

1 Give the name of the Act that is designed to allow organizations to prosecute anyone accessing their ICT systems illegally. *(1 mark)*

2 Explain, by giving an example, what is covered by the Computer Misuse Act 1990. *(2 marks)*

3 Passwords are one method used to protect against unauthorized access to ICT systems. Give **one** other way in which unauthorized access can be prevented. *(2 marks)*

4 Briefly explain the term software piracy. *(2 marks)*

Data security legislation, regulatory powers and health and safety legislation

To be able to conduct e-commerce it is necessary to use encryption and digital signatures. Encryption means that data is kept secure when it is passed over the Internet or stored on computer. Digital signatures ensure that a document is from the person it says it is from and not from someone pretending to be that person. Laws needed to be produced to regulate and allow the use of these two technologies.

It also became necessary for laws that allowed certain surveillance to take place in order to prevent and detect crime and terrorism.

In this section you will be looking at all of this and also the regulations and laws that govern the use of computers and screens in the workplace.

The Electronic Communications Act 2000

There are two main things dealt with in this Act which are:

- The Act regulates the use of cryptographic services, i.e. services that allow data to be encrypted, such as services for sending credit/debit card details to make online purchases.
- The Act also made digital signatures legally binding in the same way that handwritten signatures are legally binding.

Both of these things were important when dealing with e-commerce where banking details and the transfer of money needed to be kept secure. It was also important that digital signatures could be used on documents such as contracts even though there was no actual signature from a real person.

▲ Encryption ensures that data passing over a network is secure.

The Regulation of Investigatory Powers Act 2000

The Regulation of Investigatory Powers Act 2000 is concerned with the regulation of public bodies such as the police, MI5, etc., to carry out surveillance and investigation.

The main purposes of the Act are to:

- detect and prevent terrorism
- prevent and detect crime.

Most people would agree that the above are important but some people are against this Act because it is being used in all sorts of more trivial ways such as: a local authority using it to conduct surveillance to check whether parents whose child attended a popular school actually lived in the catchment area or just said they did to gain their child's admission.

They reckon the Act is a 'snoopers' charter for public bodies to check up on us all. Under the act the police, MI5, councils and other government departments can:

- demand access to your emails, instant messages, etc., from your Internet service provider without you knowing
- listen in secret to phone calls and see all your text messages
- monitor all your searches made on the Internet.

◀ If you are sent a signed letter, you can check that it is authentic by comparing the signature on the letter with a stored one. Digital signatures are used in a similar way.

Data security legislation, regulatory powers and health and safety legislation *continued*

Health and safety legislation

Under the Health and Safety at Work Act 1974, employers have a duty to minimize the risk of injury to employees in the workplace. The more detailed regulations concerning the use of computers are contained in the Health and Safety (Display Screen Equipment) Regulations 1992.

These regulations state that health and safety policies must be in place to protect employees and these include:

- Inspections of chairs, workstations, desks, keyboards and computer screens to ensure they meet the regulations. This must be done on a regular basis.
- Putting in working practices and procedures to allow staff to change task in order to reduce repetitive strain injury (RSI).
- Ensuring staff are properly trained to minimize the risk to their health. This training would include ensuring they understand how to adjust their chair and screen, the need for regular breaks, the adjustment of the human–computer interface, etc.
- Paying for eye tests and any glasses needed for those staff using computer screens.
- Ensuring that any software created is not frustrating or stressful to use.

KEY WORD

Digital signature a way of ensuring that an email or document sent electronically is authentic. It can be used to detect a forged document.

▲ Many government departments use surveillance to check up on us.

Questions C

1 (a) Give the name of the health and safety regulations that cover working with display screens. *(1 mark)*
(b) The regulations lay down certain steps that employers must follow to protect their workers when they are working with computer equipment.
　(i)　Give **two** features that a display screen must have when being used in the workplace. *(2 marks)*
　(ii)　Give **two** features a workstation must have when being used in the workplace. *(2 marks)*

2 A person uses a computer in the course of their work.
In order for that employee to work safely, state with reasons:
(a) **Two** design features that the chair the employee sits on should have to minimize health problems. *(2 marks)*
(b) **Two** design features that the screen the employee uses should have to minimize health problems. *(2 marks)*

3 The Regulation of Investigatory Powers Act 2000 is an important Act.
(a) Give **one** purpose of this Act. *(1 mark)*
(b) The Act allows surveillance to take place. Describe **two** ways in which this surveillance can take place using ICT. *(2 marks)*

Extension activity

The Health and Safety Executive (HSE) are the government department responsible for health and safety in the workplace. Part of their job is to promote good health and safety practice in the workplace and they produce many leaflets (both online and paper) to this effect. Look at this publication, which provides information on health and safety aspects of working with VDUs: http://www.hse.gov.uk/pubns/indg36.pdf

Use the information contained on this leaflet to produce a summary on A4 paper that can be put up as a notice in the computer room.

END-OF-TOPIC REVIEW

Questions

 Test yourself

The following notes summarize this topic. The notes are incomplete because they have words missing.

Using the words in the list below, copy out and complete the sentences A to J, underlining the words that you have inserted. Each word may be used more than once.

hacking	Principles	Data Protection
	register	Information
personal	deleted	accurate
up-to-date	viruses	Computer Misuse
	surveillance	privacy

A _____ is about keeping aspects of your personal life private.

B The _____ _____ Act 1998 was passed to protect individuals from the misuse of personal data

C The Data Protection Act is enforced by the _____ Commissioner.

D The people who hold and use personal data have to _____ their use of data and they have to make sure that the data is kept _____ and _____.

E There are eight Data Protection _____ one of which says that personal data must be accurate and kept up-to-date.

F Anyone can apply to see the _____ data held about them and if the information is wrong then they can have it corrected or _____.

G The Computer Misuse Act makes it an offence to deliberately plant or transfer _____ on to a computer system to cause damage to programs and data.

H The process of unauthorized use of an ICT system with a view to seeing or altering the data is called _____.

I Hacking is made a criminal offence under the _____ _____ Act.

J The Regulation of Investigatory Powers Act 2000 is concerned with the regulation of public bodies such as the police, MI5, etc., to carry out _____ and investigation.

Questions *continued*

Examination style questions

1 Put a tick if the statement is one of the Principles of the Data Protection Act 1998. *(4 marks)*

Statement	Tick
Data is adequate, relevant and not excessive	☐
Personal data should be adequate and kept up-to-date	☐
Software should not be copied	☐
Personal data should only be used for one or more specified and lawful purposes	☐
There must be sufficient security to cover the personal data	☐
Hacking is illegal	☐

2 The use of ICT systems can lead to a number of health problems. Because of this, certain items need to have features that will help prevent these health problems. State **one** feature for each item that will help prevent health problems.
- **(a)** Chair. *(1 mark)*
- **(b)** Keyboard. *(1 mark)*
- **(c)** Software packages. *(1 mark)*

3 The Data Protection Act 1998 protects people from having their personal data misused.

There are eight Data Protection Principles that are regulations that an organization must adhere to when collecting, storing and processing personal information.
- **(a)** State **three** of the Data Protection Principles. *(3 marks)*

(b) Tick **two** boxes to show which of the following have partial exemption from the Data Protection Act 1998. *(2 marks)*

	Tick *two* boxes
Word-processed documents	☐
Insurance company data	☐
A database of friends' names and addresses	☐
A database of doctors' patients	☐
Files stored on paper	☐

(c) The Data Protection Act 1998 gives certain rights to data subjects.
- (i) Explain what is meant by a data subject. *(2 marks)*
- (ii) Give **two** rights that are given to data subjects under the Act. *(2 marks)*

4 Protection of your privacy is essential if you bank or shop online.
- **(a)** Give the names of **three** different pieces of personal information you would need to supply in order to complete an online purchase. *(3 marks)*
- **(b)** Give **one** item of personal information (that you would not want others to know) that you need to supply in order to complete an online purchase. *(1 mark)*
- **(c)** Give **one** method by which the item of personal information in your answer to (b) can be kept private. *(1 mark)*

END-OF-TOPIC REVIEW

Case studies

Case study 1

Cyber warfare

Most developed countries are totally dependent on their ICT systems and the loss of such systems could do serious damage to the infrastructure of countries.

For example, could you imagine the loss of the Internet for a lengthy period or the loss of the entire mobile phone network. What about the erasure of all the health information on the NHS computers or the erasure of tax information, so that the government could not collect money to pay for schools, hospitals, the police, etc.

In many ways damage to ICT systems could do a lot more damage than a series of terrorist bombs or even a war using conventional weapons.

Many terrorist groups use the Internet for recruitment, propaganda and communication purposes. They may also conduct cyber attacks against their enemies.

Some countries have started to investigate the use of the Internet to cause damage to the infrastructure of other countries. Targets would typically involve key businesses, the national power grid (for electricity supply), financial markets and government departments. The government has decided to set up a new office for cyber security. This department will monitor, analyse and counter any cyber attacks.

It is interesting to note that as well as protecting against cyber warfare, Britain is investigating the potential of using cyber warfare itself should the need arise.

The government has turned to hackers who have the experience to know how to get past security methods and break into networks.

Cyber attacks from other countries have already occurred. For example, there was an attack on the Foreign Office's computer from China and also an attack on the House of Common's computer system that temporarily closed it down.

Questions

1 **(a)** Explain what hacking is and why it is so important to keep hackers out of key networks. *(3 marks)*

   (b) Networks can be protected using firewalls. Explain how a firewall can be used to prevent unauthorized access. *(2 marks)*

2 Give **two** examples of systems that could be hacked into and deliberately damaged as part of a cyber attack. *(2 marks)*

3 Some people think it is morally wrong to give good well-paid jobs to hackers who have deliberately broken the law. State, with reasons, whether you agree or disagree with this. *(2 marks)*

4 Hacking is made illegal under a law. Give the full name of the law. *(1 mark)*

5 Terrorists use encryption to ensure the privacy of communication and to avoid being detected and caught.

   (a) Explain what encryption is and how it ensures the privacy of communication. *(2 marks)*

   (b) Some countries are worried that encryption of data causes as many problems as it solves. Explain why a country might ban encryption. *(2 marks)*

Case studies *continued*

Case study 2

Hackers destroy a flight simulation site

Many people are interested in flying a plane but do not have the money to do this in reality. Instead they fly the planes virtually using flight simulation software.

A very popular website that covered all aspects of flight simulation has been destroyed by hackers. The hackers took down the site's two servers. The problem was that there was no external backup system. This meant that each server was used to back up the files on the other server. This meant that because both servers were affected, all the data was lost.

The person who founded the site said that the site would be down for the foreseeable future and that it might not be possible to set the site up again. One user of the site was really annoyed and said, 'there's a special place in hell for hackers who pull stunts like this'.

Questions

1 **(a)** Explain what is meant by the word 'hacker'. *(2 marks)*

(b) There is a law which makes hacking illegal. Give the name of this law. *(1 mark)*

2 It is essential for security purposes that all files are properly backed up.

(a) Give the names of **two** different media on which files can be backed up. *(2 marks)*

(b) It is important that data is backed up off site. Give **one** reason why data should be kept off site. *(1 mark)*

3 One or more servers are used in networks. Explain the purpose of a server. *(2 marks)*

Case study 3

The NHS losing patient medical records

You would think that your personal medical details are safe in the hands of the NHS, but they are not. The Information Commissioner, the person who is in charge of the Data Protection Act, has been forced to take action against the NHS many times for breaching data protection regulations.

Here are some of the things they did:

- One GP downloaded a complete patient database containing medical histories of 10,000 patients onto an unsecured laptop. The laptop was then stolen and never recovered.
- A memory stick containing around 6000 patient details was lost. Although the details were encrypted, the password was written on a piece of paper attached to the memory stick.

The Assistant Information Commissioner said that procedures were laid out by the NHS but were not being followed. He also commented that 'medical history is very sensitive personal information which is likely to cause harm and distress'. He went on to say that 'the law dictates that they must keep this information confidential'.

◀ Medical details are personal data and need to be protected.

Questions

1 What could a person do who has suffered harm and distress when their medical details were revealed through negligence? *(1 mark)*

2 One data protection regulation (called Data Protection Principles in the Data Protection Act) is that 'Personal data shall be accurate, and where necessary, kept up-to-date'. Give another **two** of the Data Protection Principles. *(2 marks)*

3 The Deputy Information Commissioner mentioned 'sensitive personal information'.
Give **three** items of sensitive personal information that you might find as part of a medical record. *(3 marks)*

4 All disks containing personal information should be encrypted.
(a) Explain what is meant by encrypted. *(2 marks)*
(b) If a laptop is stolen and the laptop has stored personal information that is encrypted on its hard drive, explain how this protects the information. *(1 mark)*
(c) Describe **two** ways in which medical details could be misused. *(2 marks)*

Exam support

Worked example

The Data Protection Act (DPA) 1998 protects the individual against the misuse of their personal information. The DPA has eight principles.

(a) List **four** of the principles. *(4 marks)*

(b) The DPA covers personal data. Give **two** different examples of types of information that would be considered as personal. *(2 marks)*

(c) Give **two** rights individuals have regarding the personal data held about them on computer. *(2 marks)*

(d) Give **two** exemptions from the DPA. *(2 marks)*

Student answer 1

(a) *Data should not be sent out of the country.*

The data should be up-to-date and accurate.

You cannot use data collected for another purpose.

You must hold the data securely.

(b) *Details of your name and address.*

Your medical details.

(c) *They can see the information held about them.*

They can ask for the data to be put right if it is wrong.

(d) *If the data is being used by the police and they do not want you to see it.*

If the data is too personal.

◀ **Examiner's comment**

(a) The first answer about data not being sent out of the country is not strictly true. It cannot be sent to a country that does not have proper data protection laws. All the EEC countries have these laws so there is no problem in passing personal data to these countries. No marks for this part.

The other three answers are all correct Data Protection Principles and are awarded a mark each, so three marks for this part.

(b) Name and address are not classed as personal information, so no marks for this.

Medical details are personal information, so one mark for this part.

(c) Two points are made here but they are actually part of the same point in the sense that the only point in seeing the data is to have it corrected if it is wrong. Only one mark is given here.

(d) The first answer is correct and gains a mark. The second answer is incorrect.

(6 marks out of 10)

END-OF-TOPIC REVIEW

Exam support *continued*

Student answer 2

(a) Data should not be kept longer than is necessary.

Data should be adequate, relevant and not excessive.

Data should not be transferred to other countries outside the EU if they do not have adequate data protection provision.

Data should be accurate and kept up to date.

(b) Health details.

Credit history.

(c) They can see the data and have it corrected or deleted if it is wrong.

They can sue for damages if they have suffered harm as a result of the data being incorrect.

(d) If you do not want them to store the information about you it is possible to opt out.

Where data is held for family use such as a list of birthdays, Christmas card list, etc., held on your home computer.

◀ Examiner's comment

(a) All these are correct DP principles so full marks for this part.

(b) Both of these are examples of personal data so full marks again.

(c) The student has explained both these answers well, so full marks again.

(d) The first answer is wrong but the second is correct. One mark is awarded here.

(9 marks out of 10)

Examiner's answers

(a) One mark each for four of the Data Protection Principles:

- Data should be processed fairly and lawfully.
- Data should be obtained for only specified purposes.
- Data should be adequate, relevant and not excessive.
- Data should be accurate and kept up-to-date.
- Data should be not kept any longer than is necessary.
- Data should be processed in accordance with the rights of the data subject.
- Data should be kept secure.
- Data should not be transferred to a country outside the EU unless they have a comparable data protection law.

(b) One mark for each distinctly different example to a maximum of two marks.

- Medical details.
- Details of qualifications.
- Criminal records.
- Credit history.
- Details of political beliefs.

(c) One mark for each of the following (2 marks in total)

- They can see the personal data held about them and demand that it be corrected or deleted if it is incorrect.
- They can sue for damages if the wrong information has caused them harm (e.g., stopped them getting a job).

(d) One mark each for two of the following:

- Data held in the interests of national security.
- Data held by the police during a police investigation.
- Data held by HM Revenue and Customs for the collection of tax or VAT.
- Small clubs.
- Data held to perform a company payroll.
- Data for home use such as a Christmas card list held on the computer.
- Mailing lists.
- Family history.
- References produced using word-processing software.

Summary mind maps

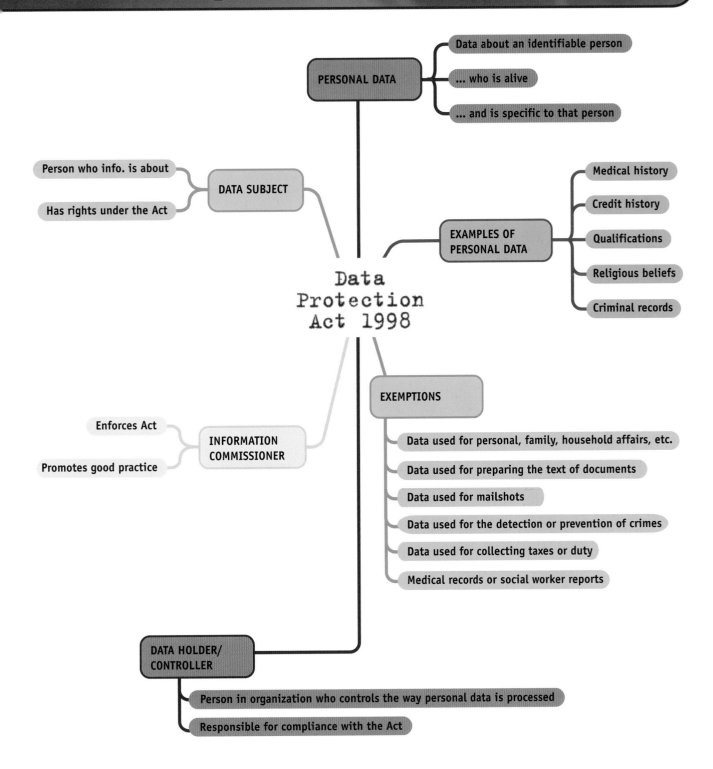

PERSONAL DATA
- Data about an identifiable person
- ... who is alive
- ... and is specific to that person

DATA SUBJECT
- Person who info. is about
- Has rights under the Act

EXAMPLES OF PERSONAL DATA
- Medical history
- Credit history
- Qualifications
- Religious beliefs
- Criminal records

Data Protection Act 1998

EXEMPTIONS
- Data used for personal, family, household affairs, etc.
- Data used for preparing the text of documents
- Data used for mailshots
- Data used for the detection or prevention of crimes
- Data used for collecting taxes or duty
- Medical records or social worker reports

INFORMATION COMMISSIONER
- Enforces Act
- Promotes good practice

DATA HOLDER/ CONTROLLER
- Person in organization who controls the way personal data is processed
- Responsible for compliance with the Act

Summary mind maps *continued*

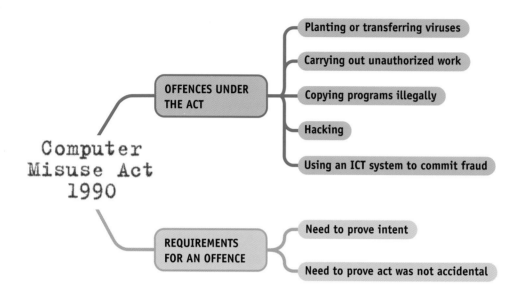

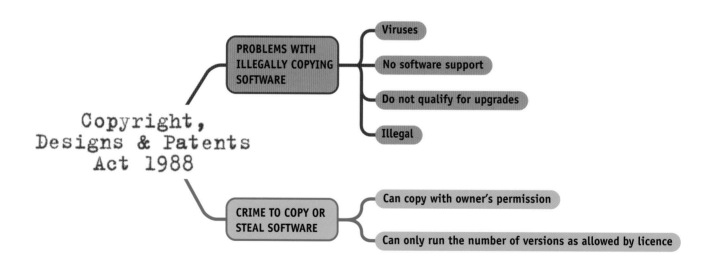

Topic 24

Staying safe online

The key concepts covered in this topic are:

- Understand the dangers associated with the disclosure of personal data, misuse of images and using inappropriate language

- Understand codes of conduct for personal protection

- Discuss appropriate steps to avoid inappropriate disclosure of personal information

In this topic you will be looking at the very important topic of staying safe online. You frequently read in newspapers about young people going missing after meeting someone in a chat room. Unfortunately not all of these stories have happy endings, so everyone needs to be aware of the dangers that lurk in cyberspace.

You will also learn about how you need to ensure that you do not reveal personal data or data from which you can be identified to strangers. You will learn about how people can misuse the images that you post on social networking sites.

Contents

Staying safe online

You will find out

▷ **About the dangers associated with disclosure of personal information, misuse of images and using inappropriate language**

▷ **About the codes of conduct for personal protection**

▷ **About taking appropriate steps to avoid inappropriate disclosure of personal information**

The Internet is a great thing and brings tremendous benefits for us all. It is not, however, without its dangers. In this section you will be looking at the dangers lurking in many corners of the Internet. If you are aware of the dangers then at least you can take precautions to ensure that you are not put at risk.

The dangers of disclosing personal information

You should never ever give out personal information when you are online.

You may be chatting to someone who seems genuine but you could be chatting to anyone. If you reveal your personal information or even worse meet them then you could meet someone who wants to do you harm. There are lots of weird people out there, and they may contact you and you may meet them thinking they are a nice person.

The misuse of images

As you know it is very easy to copy an image off a website or social networking site. Images sent to one person can be passed to others without their permission.

It is very easy to misuse an image so you need to be very careful where you put your images and what sort of images you send. Here are some ways in which an image can be misused:

- You may be identified from your image even though there are no other contact details.
- You may encounter stalkers or be pestered by email or worse still they may find where you live and your phone numbers.
- Your image might be posted on an inappropriate website.
- Your image might be edited using image editing software. For example, an innocent image of a person's face could be put on someone else's body. You can imagine what images could be produced.
- Paedophiles use school and athletic club websites to obtain images. Again these images can be edited and put onto pornographic websites.

Using inappropriate language

When you post messages on a blog or message board or use a chat room it is important to realise that this will be viewed by people of all different ages and backgrounds. You therefore need to ensure:

- You do not use swear words.
- You do not use racially offensive words.

- You do not use words likely to offend certain groups of people.
- That your material can be read by people of all ages.
- You do not engage in cyberbullying (i.e. bullying using the Internet, mobile phones, etc.).

Some services, such as chat rooms, message boards, blogs, etc., are moderated. This means that a person is appointed to view the material and remove any inappropriate content. Sometimes the services are regulated automatically, which means that the computer will pick out inappropriate words. For example, your network software may pick out certain words used in emails sent to your friends. These emails will not reach their destination and will instead be sent to the network manager or head of department for them to read. How embarrassing might that be?

Some systems may suspend you from the network service for a certain period. In serious cases you could be suspended from the service permanently.

▲ Social networking sites are great fun but they are not without their dangers.

Codes of conduct for personal protection

1 Do not give out personal information such as your address or phone number on a message board, blog, chat room, social networking site.
2 Do not use your real name when using chat rooms, etc. People may be able to identify you and find where you live.
3 Always report abuse or bullying.
4 Never reveal personal details (e.g. bank details) in response to an official-looking email.
5 Avoid publishing pictures of yourself, as they can be misused.

6 Do not open attachments to emails from people you do not know. They may contain inappropriate material.
7 Never meet strangers unless you are with an adult you trust.

Parental control

If you had young children, you would not want them to have full access to the Internet. If they had full access, they could see pornographic images and talk to adults (who could be paedophiles). All Internet service providers have parental controls that restrict a child's access to parts of the Internet.

Many parents will choose to sit with their children while they use the Internet or monitor what they have looked at by looking at the History (which gives the website addresses of all the recent websites visited).

▲ Parental controls are controls set by browser software to control what children can or cannot view using the Internet.

▲ Social networking is great fun but not without its dangers.

▲ Do not put personal information in online profiles that can be viewed by anyone.

Activity

Learning more about staying safe online

Here are some sites that offer lots of information about staying safe online. Feel free to try the games and quizzes – all the information on these sites will help you stay safe and also help you answer exam questions.

http://www.thinkuknow.co.uk/
http://www.getsafeonline.org/
http://yp.direct.gov.uk/cyberbullying/

Questions A

1 Explain **two** ways in which an image posted on a website or social networking site can be misused. *(2 marks)*

2 Personal data should never be disclosed on a network service that anyone can view.
   (a) Give an example of a network service that anyone can view. *(1 mark)*
   (b) Give **two** reasons why this piece of advice is important. *(2 marks)*

Extension activity

Imagine you are the parent of an 8-year-old boy or girl. They want to use the Internet but you are concerned about this. Write a list of the steps you would take in order to ensure their safety online.

Questions

 Test yourself

The following notes summarize this topic. The notes are incomplete because they have words missing.

Using the words in the list below, copy out and complete the sentences A to H, underlining the words that you have inserted. Each word may be used more than once.

| personal | inappropriate | paedophiles | attachments |
| website | photo editing | viruses | cyberbullying |

A You should never ever give out _____ information when you are online.

B _____ often lurk in chat rooms and social networking sites and are looking for their next victim to abuse.

C Bullying using the Internet and mobile phones is often referred to as _____.

D You should avoid posting images of yourself on the Internet as they might be misused by posting them on an inappropriate _____.

E Images can be misused by others using _____ _____ software to distort what the original image showed.

F _____ use school and athletic club websites to obtain images.

G When using a service that can be viewed by others, you need to make sure that you do not use any _____ language such as swear words or threats to others.

H You should never open any file _____ to emails from people you do not know or only know slightly as they may contain indecent images or contain _____.

Examination style questions

1 There are many different ways to meet people using ICT.
   (a) Give the names of **two** ICT facilities that would enable you to meet new friends. *(2 marks)*
   (b) Describe **two** possible dangers in meeting people in real life whom you have communicated with online. *(4 marks)*

2 The growth of social networking sites has meant people can find out a lot about you.
   (a) By giving a suitable example, explain an advantage of them being able to do this. *(2 marks)*
   (b) It is important not to divulge personal data on social networking sites. Explain **one** reason why not. *(2 marks)*

3 It is very easy to use photo editing software to change an image such as a photograph.

By giving a suitable example, explain how an image might be misused using photo editing software. *(4 marks)*

4 Many people like to use ICT to chat to others in chat rooms. Explain why young children should never be allowed to use chat rooms unsupervised. *(4 marks)*

5 When emails that contain inappropriate language are sent or received, they are captured by the network. The network manager will then look at them and take further action if needed.
   (a) Explain **one** reason why a network manager might do this. *(2 marks)*
   (b) The use of inappropriate language in a chat room might breach the code of conduct. What action might the organization who supplies the chat room service take? *(1 mark)*

END-OF-TOPIC REVIEW

Exam support

Worked example

Parents of young children are worried about them using the Internet.

(a) Explain, by giving examples, why their fears are justified. *(4 marks)*

(b) Explain **two** things a parent can do to protect their children from harm when using the Internet. *(2 marks)*

Student answer 1

(a) Their child may reveal a lot about where they live, where they go to school, their phone number.

They may go into a chat room and a stranger might ask them to meet up and this is really dangerous.

(b) They can make sure their child only uses the Internet when they are sitting with them.

They can use a special function of the software called parental controls that will only allow them access to certain parts of the Internet.

◀ Examiner's comment

(a) These are two good answers, but the student should have looked at the marks allocated. It is always a good idea to work on one point is worth one mark unless the question indicates otherwise. Only two marks are given here.

(b) Two good answers get both of the marks. *(4 marks out of 6)*

Student answer 2

(a) They might access inappropriate material such as violent video or pornography by accident.

They may chat to someone in a chat room and arrange to meet them without their parents' knowledge.

The images they send to a stranger could be misused.

They may reveal information in a chat room that could be used by a stalker to harass them.

(b) They can ban the child from using the Internet.

They can tell them that they must not ever go into a chat room.

◀ Examiner's comment

(a) Four points well explained get four marks here.

(b) Banning the child from using the Internet may seriously hinder their education as the Internet for the most part is a good thing. No marks for this answer even though it might be the choice of some parents. The second answer gains a mark.

(5 marks out of 6)

Examiner's answers

(a) One mark for each point to a maximum of four marks.

- They could reveal personal details such as name, address, school, age, phone number, etc., to a stranger.
- They could arrange to meet a stranger without their parents' knowledge.
- They may access unsuitable content (e.g. pornography).
- They may take part in or be a victim of cyberbullying.

(b) One mark for each point to a maximum of two marks.

- Only allow them to access the Internet at home when they are present.
- Do not allow Internet access in a bedroom.
- Set the parental controls so they can only access suitable material and enter certain sites.
- Ask them to report anything they are not happy with to their parents.
- Examine favourites, email, etc., to check there is no abuse.

END-OF-TOPIC REVIEW

Summary mind map

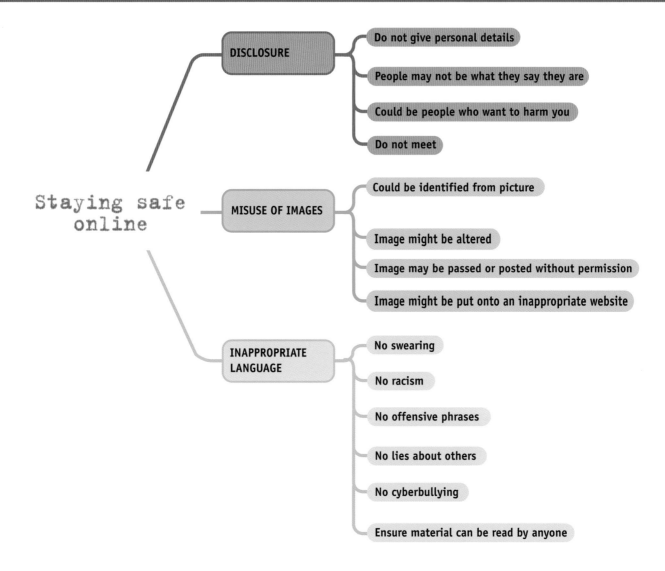

Staying safe online

DISCLOSURE
- Do not give personal details
- People may not be what they say they are
- Could be people who want to harm you
- Do not meet

MISUSE OF IMAGES
- Could be identified from picture
- Image might be altered
- Image may be passed or posted without permission
- Image might be put onto an inappropriate website

INAPPROPRIATE LANGUAGE
- No swearing
- No racism
- No offensive phrases
- No lies about others
- No cyberbullying
- Ensure material can be read by anyone

Topic 25

Data protection issues

The key concepts covered in this topic are:

- **How to protect data from accidental destruction**

- **How to protect data from deliberate damage (e.g., viruses and other types of malicious damage)**

- **How to protect stored or transmitted data from unauthorized access**

Hardware and software are easily replaced but if data is destroyed then it causes so much chaos that many companies that lose data soon go out of business. There are so many threats to data stored on computers that organizations must ensure that these threats are taken seriously. In this topic you will be learning about data protection issues and this includes the steps that organizations can take to protect their most valuable non-human resource (i.e. data).

Contents

Protecting data from accidental destruction, deliberate damage and unauthorized access

You will find out

▷ **About how to protect data from accidental destruction**

▷ **About how to protect data from damage caused by viruses and other types of malicious damage**

▷ **About how to protect stored or transmitted data from unauthorized access**

Data is valuable and needs to be protected from accidental destruction through equipment malfunction or destruction due to natural disasters such as floods, earthquakes, etc. Human error can also be responsible for accidental destruction.

In this section, as well as looking at accidental damage, you will also be looking at deliberate damage, how it is likely to occur and what can be done to prevent it and minimize any consequences should it occur. You will also be looking at the steps that need to be taken to prevent unauthorized access.

How to protect data from accidental destruction

Data can be destroyed accidentally in a number of ways such as:

- Equipment malfunction – for example, a hard disk drive might go wrong.
- Equipment destruction – if the computer or computer room is destroyed by fire, earthquake, flood then the data held on the computers, storage devices, etc., will be lost.
- User error – it is easy to make mistakes and we have all probably lost work. Training will help users be more aware of what they are doing in order to minimize the likelihood of this happening.

Here are some steps that can be taken to reduce the likelihood of permanently losing data accidentally:

- Train users – users should understand what they are doing. This will reduce the likelihood of them making mistakes such as copying an old file over a new file, deleting the wrong file, etc.
- Ensure backup copies are kept – if users do lose data then at least most or all of the data can be recovered from the backup copies kept.
- Thoroughly test software – software should be thoroughly tested before it is used with real data.

How to protect data from damage caused by viruses and other types of malicious damage

There are a number of different people around who present threats to data such as:

- Hackers who want to access your computer and view the data, alter the data or use the data to commit fraud.
- Disgruntled employees – these people may have a grievance with the organization and seek to do damage to it by destroying the data.
- People who produce and distribute computer viruses – it is illegal to produce and distribute computer viruses but this does not put some people off. Viruses can cause damage to data by altering or even deleting it.
- Cyber terrorists – it has become known to terrorists that they can cause as much damage as by a bomb by rendering certain sites and data unusable. They hack into the computer systems of large organizations to do this.

There are various ways to protect data from deliberate damage:

- Use a firewall to prevent hackers – a firewall is hardware, software or both that works in a network to prevent communication that is not allowed from one network to another. The firewall looks at each packet of data trying to pass from one network to another to see if it is allowed. If it isn't, the network rejects it.
- To protect against disgruntled employees destroying data – ensure that you carefully select the staff and if they leave they should not be allowed to work their notice.
- Virus attack – install virus checking software, do not open file attachments unless you know who they are from, train staff on the problems caused by viruses, do not allow staff to attach portable drives or memory sticks unless they are scanned first and do not allow employees to download games and other unauthorized software onto their computers.
- Virus scanning software should be kept up-to-date and scans should be scheduled so that they are performed automatically on a regular basis.

How to protect stored or transmitted data from unauthorized access

Here are some ways of protecting stored or transmitted data from unauthorized access.

Use of passwords and user-IDs/usernames

A user-ID/username is a name or number used to identify a user of a network. Once the network knows who is using the network, it can allocate resources such as storage area and access to certain files. You can also use a password to prevent access to a stand-alone computer.

Passwords are strings of characters kept secret by the user and are used to access the ICT system. The password makes sure that the person who gives the user-ID/username is the person who they say they are.

Passwords must be changed on a regular basis and users must remember to log-out when they are away from their computer.

Encryption

Encryption scrambles data as it is passed along communication lines or wirelessly so that even if it is intercepted, it makes no sense to

the interceptor. Encryption is also a feature of the latest operating systems where the data stored on the hard drive is automatically encrypted so that if the computer is stolen or the data copied it cannot be understood.

Physical methods

You can also use:

- locks to computer rooms and computers
- keyboard locks
- biometric access restrictions.

© Randy Glasbergen.
www.glasbergen.com

— GLASBERGEN —

"You caught a virus from your computer and we had to erase your brain. I hope you've got a back-up copy!"

Questions A

1 (a) There are a number of ways in which data can be destroyed accidentally.
Give **two** ways accidental destruction of data can occur. *(2 marks)*

(b) Give **two** ways in which data can be deliberately destroyed. *(2 marks)*

2 Data is often more valuable to an organization than the hardware and software.
Explain why this is so. *(4 marks)*

Questions

✔ Test yourself

The following notes summarize this topic. The notes are incomplete because they have words missing.

Using the words in the list below, copy out and complete the sentences A to H, underlining the words that you have inserted. Each word may be used more than once.

tested	training	firewall	scanner	download
	file attachments	passwords	accidental	

A _____ reduces the likelihood of users making mistakes such as copying an old file over a new file, deleting the wrong file, etc.

B Equipment malfunction, for example a hard disk drive going wrong, might cause _____ destruction of data.

C In order to prevent system crashes software should be thoroughly _____ before it is used with real data.

D To protect data from deliberate damage caused by hackers illegally gaining access to a computer network via the Internet, a _____ should be used.

E In order to prevent viruses entering an ICT system, a virus _____ should be used to search for and destroy viruses.

F Users should be told not to open _____ _____ attached to emails unless they know who they are from.

G Users should also be told not to _____ music and games off the Internet as these are often infected with viruses.

H To protect the data stored in networks, user-IDs and _____ should be used to prevent unauthorized access.

Examination style questions

1 For each of the following threats, outline **two** steps that an organization can take in order to reduce the seriousness of the threat.
   (a) Fire. *(2 marks)*
   (b) Theft of hardware. *(2 marks)*
   (c) Theft of data. *(2 marks)*

2 Enabling all employees of an organization to access the Internet can bring many benefits to an organization. It does, however, increase the number of threats to ICT systems.
   (a) Give the names of **three** types of threat that will have increased owing to connection to the Internet. *(3 marks)*
   (b) For **one** of the threats outlined in part (a) explain why the risk has increased with access to the Internet. *(1 mark)*

3 Data is often encrypted when being stored or sent over the Internet.
   (a) Give the names of **two** items of data a user may send over the Internet that are often encrypted. *(2 marks)*
   (b) What is meant by the term encryption? *(2 marks)*

4 One way to protect data from malicious or unauthorized access is to make use of usernames and passwords. These usernames and passwords are entered using the keyboard before the user is allowed access to the data and programs.
   (a) Give **one** purpose of a username. *(1 mark)*
   (b) Give **one** purpose of a password. *(1 mark)*
   (c) Users have to make up their own passwords. One guideline is that the password should be a minimum of 6 characters long.
   Write **three** additional guidelines for users when creating their own passwords. *(3 marks)*

END-OF-TOPIC REVIEW

Exam support

Worked example

Computer viruses are a threat to computer systems.

(a) Explain what is meant by a computer virus. *(2 marks)*

(b) Give **one** thing that a computer virus might do on a computer system. *(1 mark)*

(c) Give **one** way of preventing computer viruses entering a system. *(1 mark)*

Student answer 1

(a) A program that does damage.

(b) Destroy the computer.

(c) Use McAfee to stop viruses getting into your computer.

◀ **Examiner's comment**

(a) This is a bit vague because it is not specific about what it does damage to. Only one mark is given for this answer.

(b) This is a typical answer given by a weak pupil. Viruses can be removed and therefore cannot be said to 'destroy' the computer. No marks for this.

(c) Brand names should never be given. So instead of McAfee they should have said 'virus checking software or virus scanner'. No marks are given for this answer.

(1 mark out of 4)

Student answer 2

(a) A mischievous program that copies itself onto your computer and does harm by messing up settings or deleting data.

(b) It can start to make your computer run slow and can also cause it to crash unexpectedly.

(c) Use virus scanning software to scan for viruses and remove them if they are found.

◀ **Examiner's comment**

(a) A good answer which makes it clear that it is a program that copies itself so this answer is worth two marks.

(b) Again another good answer which gains one mark.

(c) This answer is correct and gains one mark.

(4 marks out of 4)

Examiner's answers

(a) Two marks allocated in the following way:
Program that copies itself automatically *(1)* and causes damage to data or causes the computer to run slowly *(1)*.

(b) One mark for an answer such as:
- Can erase files which means the operating system software cannot be loaded *(1)*.
- Can cause the deletion of data *(1)*.
- Can cause the computer to crash *(1)*.

- Can cause the changing of settings, which causes annoyance to the user *(1)*.
- Can copy passwords and usernames and transmit these to another person *(1)*.

(c) One mark for one of the following:
- Don't open file attachments unless you know who they are from.
- Install virus scanning/checking software.
- Keep virus scanning/checking software up-to-date.
- Don't download files from unknown sources.

Summary mind maps

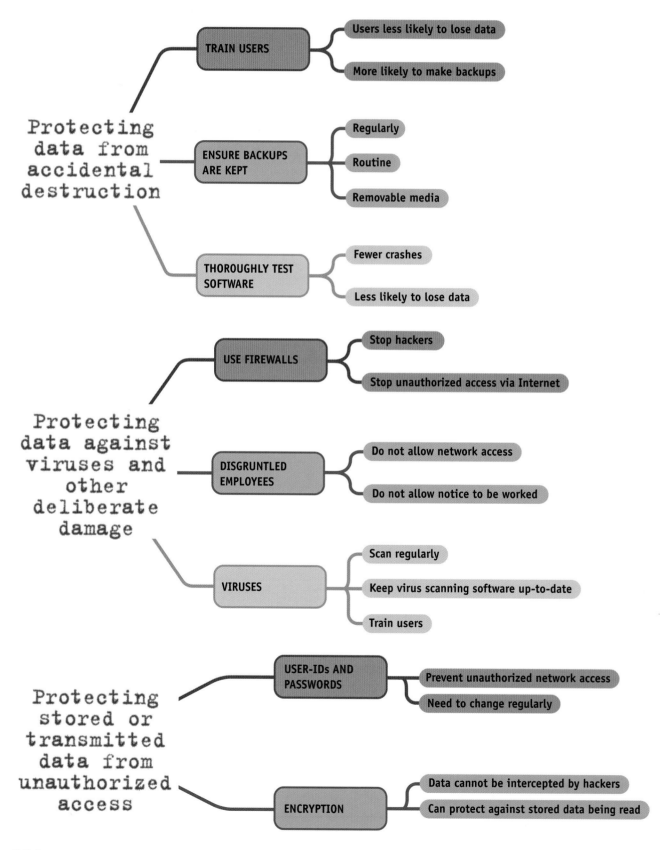

TRAIN USERS
- Users less likely to lose data
- More likely to make backups

Protecting data from accidental destruction

ENSURE BACKUPS ARE KEPT
- Regularly
- Routine
- Removable media

THOROUGHLY TEST SOFTWARE
- Fewer crashes
- Less likely to lose data

USE FIREWALLS
- Stop hackers
- Stop unauthorized access via Internet

Protecting data against viruses and other deliberate damage

DISGRUNTLED EMPLOYEES
- Do not allow network access
- Do not allow notice to be worked

VIRUSES
- Scan regularly
- Keep virus scanning software up-to-date
- Train users

USER-IDs AND PASSWORDS
- Prevent unauthorized network access
- Need to change regularly

Protecting stored or transmitted data from unauthorized access

ENCRYPTION
- Data cannot be intercepted by hackers
- Can protect against stored data being read

Topic 26

Health issues

The key concepts covered in this topic are:

- **Potential health hazards when using computers**

- **Methods for prevention or reducing the risk of potential health hazards**

Working with ICT equipment is mainly a safe occupation but there are a number of health hazards that can cause some health problems over time.

In this topic you will be looking at what the health hazards are and what you can do to lessen or even eliminate them.

It is important to note that there is a difference between using a computer now and again and using one all the time as the main part of your job. Many of the health problems do not usually occur overnight but instead they build up over the years.

Contents

Potential health hazards when using computers

You will find out

▷ **About the potential health hazards when using computers**

As there are potential hazards when using computers and other ICT equipment, you need to be aware of what the hazards are. You also need to be aware of the symptoms of the medical conditions they cause. In this section you will be looking at both of these aspects.

Health hazards

The main health hazards are:

- Repetitive strain injury (RSI) – this is caused by typing at high speed or using a mouse over a long period of time. RSI is a painful illness that causes swelling of the joints and is similar to arthritis. It can get so bad that many sufferers are unable to use their hands.
- Eye strain – looking at the screen all day can give you eye strain. Many of the people who use computer screens for long periods have to wear glasses or contact lenses. The symptoms of eye strain include blurred vision and headaches.
- Back ache – is a painful condition that prevents you from sleeping properly and doing many activities such as playing sport.
- Stress – computers can cause situations that are very stressful, such as losing your work, getting a virus, being unable to connect to the Internet and so on. All these things tend to go wrong at the worst possible time; for example, when you have an important piece of work to hand in. Stress is also caused by too much work to complete in too little time.

Stress can produce headaches and can affect a person's behaviour towards others. Stress can cause depression and mental illness.

▲ Back ache is a common ailment in computer users.

KEY WORD

RSI repetitive strain injury. A painful muscular condition caused by repeatedly using certain muscles in the same way.

Questions A

1 (a) What do the initials RSI stand for. *(1 mark)*
  (b) Describe what the symptoms of RSI are and how the condition is caused when using ICT. *(2 marks)*

2 (a) Give the names of **two** health problems that may be caused through prolonged computer use. *(2 marks)*
  (b) One computer worker said that using computers can be stressful. Describe **one** situation in which using a computer is stressful. *(1 mark)*

Extension activity

Repetitive strain injury (RSI) has become a major worry for those people who use computers continually throughout their working day.

You are required to use the Internet to find out more about this condition. You need to find out:

- What are the symptoms?
- Can you make it better?
- What is the likelihood of getting it?
- What can you do to prevent it?

Methods of preventing or reducing the risks of health hazards

▷ **About the methods of preventing or reducing the risks of health hazards**

In the last topic you were introduced to the health hazards and their symptoms. As you will be using computers throughout your life you need to ensure that you do as much as possible to avoid these problems. In this topic you will looking at the causes of the health problems and what you can do to prevent or reduce the risk of them occurring.

Back ache

The following can cause back ache:

- Not sitting up straight in your chair (i.e. incorrect posture).
- Using a laptop on your knees for long periods.
- Working in cramped conditions.

To help prevent back problems:

- Use an adjustable chair (NB in workplaces this is a legal requirement but your chair at home should be adjustable too).
- Always check the adjustment of the chair to make sure it is suitable for your height. Use a foot support, called a footrest, if necessary.
- Sit up straight on the chair with your feet flat on the floor.
- Make sure the screen is lined up and tilted at an appropriate angle.

Repetitive strain injury (RSI)

The following can cause RSI:

- Typing at high speed.
- Using a mouse for long periods.
- Not adopting correct posture for use of mouse and keyboard.
- Not having properly arranged equipment (e.g., keyboard, mouse, screen, etc.).

To help prevent RSI:

- Adjust your chair to the correct seating position for you.
- Make sure there is enough space to work comfortably.
- Use a document holder.
- Use an ergonomic keyboard/mouse.
- Use a wrist rest.
- Key in with your wrists straight.
- Position the mouse so that it can be used keeping the wrist straight.
- Learn how to type properly – two finger typing has been found to be much worse for RSI.

Eye strain

The following can cause eye strain:

- Using the screen for long periods.
- Working without the best lighting conditions.
- Glare on the screen.
- Dirt on the screen.

To help avoid eye strain:

- Keep the screen clean, so it is easy to see characters on the screen.
- Use appropriate lighting (fluorescent tubes with diffusers).
- Use blinds to avoid glare.
- Give your eyes a rest by focusing on distant objects.

- Have regular eye-tests (NB if you use a screen in your work, then your employer is required by law to pay for regular eye-tests and glasses if they are needed).

Stress

The following can cause stress:

- The pace of work (e.g., too much to do in too little time).
- Worry about using the new technology – older people feel they cannot cope.
- Software that is frustrating to use because it has not been designed properly.
- Losing work, problems with viruses and technical problems.

To help prevent stress:

- Have a help-desk to help with user problems.
- Train users fully in all the ICT systems they use so they do not get stuck.
- Ensure that all software is thoroughly tested so that it does not crash.
- Design the software so that it is easy to use.
- Ensure that users do not have an unreasonable workload.
- Take regular breaks to avoid stress.

KEY WORD

Ergonomics an applied science concerned with designing and arranging things people use so that the people and things interact most efficiently and safely.

Methods of preventing or reducing the risks of health hazards *continued*

Questions B

1 The use of ICT systems has been associated with a number of health problems.

(a) State **three** health problems that have been associated with the prolonged use of ICT systems. *(3 marks)*

(b) In order to avoid computer-related health problems certain preventative actions can be taken. Describe **six** such preventative actions that can be taken to alleviate the health problems you have identified in part (a). *(6 marks)*

2 An employee who spends much of their time at a keyboard typing in orders at high speed is worried about RSI.

(a) What do the initials RSI stand for? *(1 mark)*

(b) Give **one** of the symptoms of RSI. *(1 mark)*

(c) Write down **two** precautions that the employee can take to minimize the chance of contracting RSI. *(2 marks)*

3 Copy the table and tick (✓) the correct column to show whether each of the following statements about health risks in using ICT is true or false. *(5 marks)*

	True	False
The continual use of keyboards over a long period can give rise to aches and pains in the hands, arms and wrists		
RSI stands for repeated stress injury		
Wrist rests and ergonomic keyboards can help prevent RSI		
Back ache can be caused by slouching in your chair when using a computer		
Glare on the screen can cause RSI		

Activity

Investigating the equipment available to reduce health risks in using ICT

Computer equipment manufacturers and office equipment manufacturers produce many different pieces of equipment to minimize health risks in using ICT.

For this activity you have to produce a handout on the equipment available and how it reduces certain health risks. In this handout you will need to:

- find pictures of the piece of equipment/furniture
- identify which health problem(s) the piece of equipment reduces
- explain how it reduces the health problem
- list the web address(es) where you found the picture and information.

Extension activity

The Health and Safety Executive (HSE) is a government body responsible for enforcing health and safety in the workplace. Further information about health and safety aspects of using computer screens can be found at:

- http://www.hse.gov.uk/pubns/indg36.pdf
- http://www.direct.gov.uk/en/Employment/ HealthAndSafetyAtWork/DG_10026668

Use both these sites for information in order to produce a short leaflet (you decide which software to use), outlining the health and safety issues, to be given to Year 7 students when they start senior school.

END-OF-TOPIC REVIEW

Questions

 Test yourself

The following notes summarize this topic. The notes are incomplete because they have words missing.

Using the words in the list below, copy out and complete the sentences A to K, underlining the words that you have inserted. Each word may be used more than once.

headaches	blinds	eye strain
stress	easy	back ache
eye-tests	repetitive strain injury	

A _____ _____ _____ is caused by typing at high speed or using a mouse over a long period of time.

B Looking at the screen all day can give you _____.

C The symptoms of eye strain include blurred vision and _____.

D Working in cramped conditions and not adopting the correct posture when using computers can lead to _____.

E An adjustable chair should be used in order to prevent _____.

F Working in poor lighting conditions can lead to _____.

G Adjustable _____ should be used on windows to prevent glare on the screen and the screen should also be kept free from dirt.

H It is important to have regular _____ and use glasses or contact lenses when working with computers if needed.

I _____ is a medical condition caused by too much work to do or things not working out properly when using computers.

J To reduce _____ regular breaks should be taken and the managers/ employers should ensure that the amount of work given to employees is reasonable.

K To reduce stress software should be developed that is _____ to use.

Questions *continued*

Examination style questions

1 (a) What do the initials RSI stand for? *(1 mark)*

(b) RSI is a health problem that may be caused by prolonged computer use.
Write a sentence to show how RSI is caused. *(2 marks)*

(c) Write down **one** precaution that a computer user can take to minimize the chances of contracting RSI. *(1 mark)*

2 Here is a list of health problems. Write down the names of those that can be caused by prolonged computer use: *(4 marks)*

Back ache
Toothache
Stress
Sprained ankle
RSI
Eye strain

3 People who work with computers for long periods may experience some health problems. These health problems include eye strain and RSI.

(a) Give the names of **two** health problems other than eye strain and RSI that a user may experience. *(2 marks)*

(b) Explain **two** things a user should do when sitting in a chair at a desk and using a computer in order to prevent future health problems. *(2 marks)*

END-OF-TOPIC REVIEW

Exam support

Worked example

There are a number of health hazards associated with the use of computers.

(a) Give the names of **three** health hazards, outlining the health problems they create. *(6 marks)*

(b) For each of the health hazards described in part (a) describe what a user can do to help reduce the risk of their occurrence. *(3 marks)*

Student answer 1

(a) *People who use computers a lot get fat and this can cause a heart attack.*

You can get eye strain when using computers.

You can get repetitive strain injury which causes aches in your hands and wrists.

(b) *Fatness – do not snack while you are using your computer.*

Eye strain – have regular eye-tests.

Repetitive strain injury – use a wrist rest when using a keyboard or mouse.

◀ Examiner's comment

(a) Getting fat is not really directly caused by computers because this is caused by overeating or lack of exercise so no mark is awarded here.

The second answer is OK but it fails to explain what the symptoms of eye strain are (i.e., headaches, tiredness, etc.). Only one mark for this.

The third answer is fine and both the health hazard and the symptoms are made clear. Three marks are given for part (a).

(b) The answer about 'Fatness' gains no marks but the other answers are good and gain full marks. Two marks for this part.

(5 marks out of 9)

Student answer 2

(a) *Back ache which causes aches and pain in the lower back and meaning you cannot get a good night's sleep.*

Too much change in the workplace causing stress, meaning you cannot sleep because you are worried all the time.

Incorrect lighting causing headaches which give migraine and blurred vision.

(b) *Back ache – use an adjustable chair and make sure you adjust it to suit your height. You can use a footrest if there is one.*

Stress – make sure that users get good training so they are not stressed by the changes they have to cope with.

Headaches – make sure that fluorescent tubes are used with diffusers on them to spread out the light.

◀ Examiner's comment

(a) Here the hazards have been identified and it is clear what discomfort they cause the user. Full marks, so six marks for this part.

(b) Again an excellent answer. Notice how it is clear which health hazard is being referred to. Full marks again for this section so three marks.

(9 marks out of 9)

Exam support *continued*

Examiner's answers

(a) One mark for the health hazard and one mark for an explanation of how it affects the user.

- Eye strain – causing headaches, migraines, blurred vision.
- Back ache – pain in back or shoulders.
- Stress – loss of sleep, tiredness, changes in personality, etc.
- RSI – pains in fingers, hands, wrists, etc.
- Neck strain – unable to move head without it hurting.
- DVT (deep vein thrombosis) – can cause a stroke or heart attack.

(b) One mark for each prevention method. For the mark it should be clear which health problem the prevention refers to.

Here are some of the many possible answers:

- Eye strain – have regular eye-tests/focus on distant objects/keep screen clean/eliminate glare on screen.
- Back ache – use adjustable chair/sit upright using correct posture.
- Stress – employers to provide adequate training on new systems/have regular breaks/employers to give reasonable workload.
- RSI – use wrist rests or supports; use systems which minimize keyboard and mouse use; use an ergonomic keyboard.
- Neck strain – use a copy holder; ensure the screen is level with your eyes.
- DVT (deep vein thrombosis) – do not sit in the same position; get up and walk around every now and again.

EXAM TIPS

It is generally best to err on the side of caution by adding more information to an answer than you think you might need. For example, if you are asked to state a health problem, do not just write a one-word answer (unless it says in the question that a one-word answer is acceptable) or the word 'give' is used. Write a short sentence such as: 'Back ache is caused by slouching in a chair whilst surfing the Internet.'

The Health and Safety (Display Screen Equipment) Regulations 1992 are the regulations that refer to the use of ICT equipment. Refer to these when talking specifically about ICT equipment.

Summary mind maps

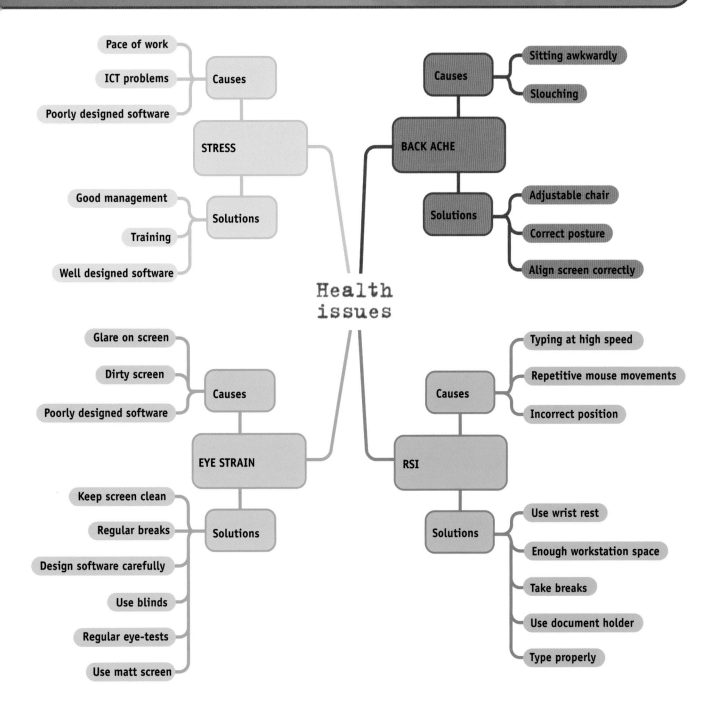

END-OF-TOPIC REVIEW

Summary mind maps *continued*

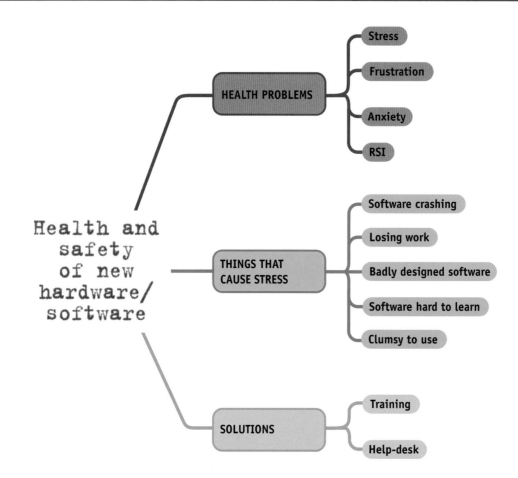

Emerging technologies

The key concepts covered in this topic are:

- Emerging technologies in the home, school, business and commerce

In this topic you will be looking at some emerging technologies. Predicting the future is very difficult. Some of the technologies discussed here are being used already, whilst others are still at the research stage. It is certain that ICT devices will be capable of carrying out many more tasks and that they will become faster and more portable.

One area in which we will all benefit will be in the use of home robotics. These will hopefully take away the drudgery of doing certain tasks like mowing the lawn and so on.

Contents

Emerging technologies in the home, school, business and commerce

You will find out

▷ **About the improvements in mobile devices**

▷ **About emerging technologies such as flexible screens, nanotechnology, Bokodes, robotics and smart cars**

ICT is evolving all the time and there are improvements to existing systems as well as completely new ones. In this section you will be looking at some devices and technologies that have brought about improvements in our lives as well as some which are set to do so.

The improvements in mobile devices

You will have noticed that mobile phones have many more functions than they used to have. They can be used to surf the Internet but their use is restricted by the size of the screen. Another factor is that if a keyboard is included, it becomes harder to use. You can of course have a touch screen but even then the keys are not much bigger.

If people want to work and make calls they have to carry two devices: a laptop/PDA and a mobile phone.

The problems with laptops are:

- They are heavy (although notebooks are lighter).
- They have a short battery life.
- They are hard to use (small keys and screens that are hard to see).

Here are some emerging technologies that will help solve these problems:

- Low power chips – these will not use the power up as fast.
- Longer life batteries – a whole day would be an ideal battery life.
- Able to use applications from the Internet – rather than have software on your computer, it would be stored on a server that you can access at high speed.
- Flexible screens – computer screens that fold out would mean devices could be portable yet still have a large screen.

Flexible screens

Flexible screens are set to make a huge impact on portable devices such as mobile phones, laptops, PDAs and notebooks.

What about these ideas based on flexible screens for the future:

- A 50-inch screen that you can unfold from your bag and use to give presentations.
- Electronic wallpaper. You can change the wallpaper at the press of a button.
- Reusable electronic newspapers that you can fold. They can update themselves from the Internet each day and even have interactive advertisements.

"Stop using the tiny keyboard on your PDA and see if they grow back to normal."

Nanotechnology

Nanotechnology is a scientific technology that is still in its infancy and is set to transform our lives like electricity or the internal combustion engine. New materials can be invented where standard-sized particles can be reduced to sizes as small as a nanometre. A nanometre is about one-hundred-thousandths the thickness of a human hair. At these sizes materials start to exhibit strange properties. For example, gold melts at room temperature and carbon is 100 times stronger than steel.

Nanotechnology will have the following uses in ICT:

- Personal computers with the power of today's computer centres.
- Chips containing films with over 1000 viewing hours.
- Miniaturized data storage systems with capacities equivalent to a whole library.
- Flexible display technologies and e-paper.
- Printable electronic circuits.

A replacement for bar codes

Bar codes in supermarkets are used to hold certain information. For example, part of the bar code is the product number, which can be looked up in a product database. Another part of the number gives the country of manufacture.

The replacement for the barcode, called a Bokode, can hold thousands of times more data and can be read by the camera in an ordinary mobile phone. Normal striped bar codes can only be read from a distance of no more than one foot but a Bokode can be read at distances from 12 to 60 feet. They can also be read from a greater range of angles.

These Bokodes will probably start being used to keep track of objects in factories but they could be used in supermarkets where the customer could read data about the product on their mobile phones.

▲ The Bokode is the circular light dot at the centre of the image.

Robotics

Robots have been widely used in manufacturing for years, especially for painting and welding in car factories. Robots are also used for picking and packing goods in large warehouses.

Robots have been developed that will do some of the tasks humans hate to do such as mowing the lawn or vacuuming the floors.

▲ Robots have been developed for use on farms and these robots can perform a variety of farm tasks such as planting, weeding in-between crops, crop spraying and picking crops.

▲ Robots will eventually be seen in all homes. This vacuuming robot is already in the shops.

There are robots available for the home that will wash floors, clean gutters and clean swimming pools.

The robots that are available at the moment in the home are usually capable of performing one task. In the future you will probably buy a single multifunctional robot capable of carrying out a range of different tasks.

Smart cars

Traffic accidents are mainly due to human error. Intel, the company who have a huge share of the market in the manufacture of microchips, are working on an ICT system for a smart car that will hopefully prevent many accidents.

▲ A smart car will use computer vision to recognize and track objects on the road for driver assistance and safety.

EXAM TIP

When you are asked to discuss a topic in a question, you should not simply produce a list of bullet points. You must write your answer in proper sentences and in continuous prose.

▲ Mowing the lawn is a chore for many people, so this robot lawnmower is a useful device.

Emerging technologies in the home, school, business and commerce *continued*

Activity

Finding out about robots at home

Do some research using the Internet to find out about robots being used to perform tasks in the home.

Produce a mind map that summarizes what you have found.

Activity

Finding out about emerging technologies

There are many emerging technologies that may shape the future. Some of these we may never see, but there is no doubt than some of them will be used by everyone in a few years time.

For this activity, you are required to work in small groups (your teacher will tell you about the details of this) and research two future technologies that are not mentioned in this topic.

You are required to produce a group presentation on your two emerging technologies.

Your presentation needs to be a group effort and each member of the group should produce an equal amount of work.

Here is more detail on what you are required to do:

- Gather your research materials (mainly using the Internet), which should include text, images and any other media you think are suitable.
- Remember you should acknowledge the sources of any copyright material you use.
- You will need to put the text into a series of easily digestible bullet points using presentation software.
- Ensure that your presentation is as exciting as it can be.
- Give your presentation, which needs to be no longer than five minutes.

Tips

Stories about emerging technologies often make the news, so a good place to start looking for material is the BBC website. YouTube can be a good place to find video of the latest technologies and gadgets but you will probably be prevented from accessing it at school.

Also useful are the online newspapers whose website addresses are shown here:

http://www.telegraph.co.uk/
http://www.dailymail.co.uk
http://www.guardian.co.uk
http://www.timesonline.co.uk/tol/news/

Questions A

1. Many devices have revolutionized the way we work and play. Mobile phones are one such device.
   - **(a)** Other than mobile phones, describe how a device or system has changed the way people work or play. *(3 marks)*
   - **(b)** Briefly describe an emerging technology that is likely to change society. *(2 marks)*

2. **(a)** Discuss the developments in ICT that have enabled remote and mobile working. *(6 marks)*
   - **(b)** Despite advances in ICT there are still limitations in remote and mobile working. Describe **two** such limitations. *(2 marks)*

Extension activity

Finding out about the interesting world of nanotechnology

Nanotechnology is one of the newest and most interesting technologies and opens up lots of interesting and new ICT-based inventions.

You will cover nanotechnology in your GCSE Science lessons.

Look at the following site and pick out the parts that relate to ICT and write a couple of sentences about each development you think offers possibilities for the future.

http://www.nano.org.uk/news/newsarchive.htm

END-OF-TOPIC REVIEW

Questions

 Test yourself

The following notes summarize this topic. The notes are incomplete because they have words missing.

Using the words in the list below, copy out and complete the sentences A to H, underlining the words that you have inserted. Each word may be used more than once.

packaging	nanotechnology	mowing
paint	voice	vacuuming
storage	accidents	mobile	welding

A Robots are currently used in factories for the assembly and _____ of goods.

B Robots are also used in car factories for the _____ of panels on cars and also the spraying of _____ .

C Robots are used in homes for the _____ of floors and the _____ of lawns.

D _____ is a new technology which uses materials with very small particles.

E This material can be used to mark chips with huge _____ capacities.

F New interfaces to control devices such as _____ recognition will mean that devices can be controlled by human speech.

G Smart cars will be safer because they will be controlled by a computer in order to prevent _____ .

H Flexible screens are an emerging technology that will make _____ devices easier to use.

Examination style questions

1 Give **two** examples of tasks that are completed by robots. *(2 marks)*

2 Give **one** example of a robot being used in the home and explain why the task is suited for a robot. *(2 marks)*

3 Explain how emerging technology has enabled many more people to work whilst on the move. *(3 marks)*

END-OF-TOPIC REVIEW

Exam support

Worked example

Discuss briefly **three** emerging technologies that are going to have an effect on home, school, business or commerce. For each of the technologies you describe, you need to say what their main benefit is. *(9 marks)*

Student answer 1

Robots will be able to do all the jobs around the house for you such as clean your bedroom, put all your magazines away, clean up the empty drinks bottles.

They will be able to do all sorts of stuff.

Social networking sites as you can find out about your friends and where they live.

You can also find out about the friends of your own friends and so on. It is great if you are a nosey parker like me!

You will be able to talk to your mobile phone like you talk to other people. You will be able to ask it to dial a certain number or play a certain music track for you. It will be great as you do not have to bother with those tiny keyboards that drive you mad.

◀ Examiner's comment

The specification says that students need to learn about emerging technologies. Some leeway either side is needed so technologies that are with us now and are slightly into the future are acceptable. Wildly futuristic prophecies are not what is required.

This means this student's idea of the capabilities of robots is way into the future, so this is not an acceptable answer. If the student had mentioned about robots vacuuming their bedroom floor, then this would have been an acceptable answer.

The section on social networking sites is a possible answer because some of these are relatively new and more are developed all the time. However, this chatty style of writing is not really appropriate in an examination and should be avoided.

The third part to the answer is better with clear benefits being explained.

If you look at the range of marks with their criteria in the Examiner's answers you will see it falls into the 4–6 mark range. The examiner considers it only worthy of the lower end of these marks.

(4 marks out of 9)

Student answer 2

Identifying people from behind will help businesses because there will be fewer robberies. People will not be able to put on a mask as when they walk away the database will look for someone with the same walk. Because this is distinctive, it can be used as evidence. The businesses insurance premiums will go down as robberies will decrease as they are more likely to be caught.

Flexible screens will be great. You don't have to look at tiny screens especially when you are surfing the Internet on your mobile phones.

I think there will be a huge increase in the use of voice recognition systems. You will be able to talk to your phone and instead of dialling numbers you will be able to just say 'ring Amy at home'. This will mean people will not have to struggle using tiny keyboards or keyboards on touch screens.

◀ Examiner's comment

The first part of the answer is of technology that is currently being used and they have explained it clearly.

The second answer is a little brief especially on the benefits. Students should always be specific in their answers.

The third part to this answer is very clearly explained.

(6 marks out of 9)

Examiner's answers

The students can give answers which discuss any fairly new or developing technology for their answer. Wildly futuristic new uses for ICT should not be awarded marks as the technology must be recent or emerging.

Some of the following may be cited by students:

- The use of flexible screens
- The use of server technology (where programs and storage are not on the device itself)
- The use of portable devices with more power (i.e., greater storage, processing speed, etc.)
- The use of voice recognition
- Multifunctional devices (e.g., phones, digital TV, movie players, laptops all rolled into one)
- The use of robots
- The use of artificial intelligence
- The use of biometric methods (especially in schools).

Mark scheme

9–7 Candidates give a clear, coherent answer identifying three emerging technologies.
They use appropriate terminology and accurate spelling, punctuation and grammar.

4–6 Candidates identify some of the emerging technologies but their responses lack clarity.
There are a few errors in spelling, punctuation and grammar.

1–3 Candidates simply list a range of points or give a very brief explanation.
The response lacks clarity and there are significant errors in spelling, punctuation and grammar.

0 Response not worthy of credit.

EXAM TIPS

In longer questions, the mark you get will not only depend on the content of your answer (i.e., the number of correct points you make) but also on the way you write your answer. You will also be marked on your correct use of spelling, punctuation and grammar.

You will not have the ICT facilities such as an online thesaurus and spellchecker in the exam, so you will need to ensure that you use the correct words.

Proof reading (i.e. visual checking) is not just restricted to working on a computer. When you have completed your answer to a question, you need to read through the answer carefully to check that it makes sense and that you have used the correct spelling and punctuation.

Summary mind map

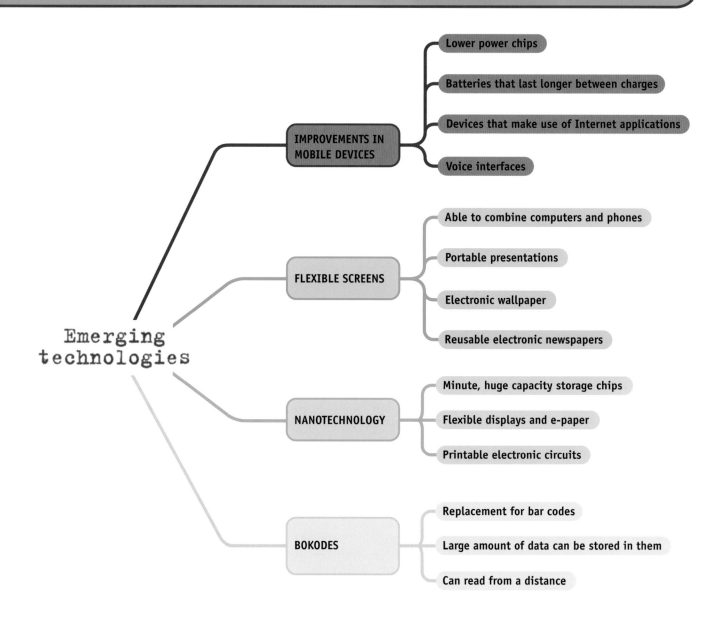

Glossary

Absolute reference A reference to a cell used in a formula where, when the formula is copied to a new address, the cell address does not change.

Access rights Restrictions of a user's access to only those files they need in order to perform their job.

Address book The names and email addresses of all the people to whom you are likely to send email, stored as a file.

Application software Software designed to do a particular job.

Artificial intelligence (AI) Creating computer programs or computers that behave in a similar way to the human brain by learning from experience.

Bandwidth A measure of the amount of data that can be transferred per second over the Internet or other network.

Batch total A meaningful total that is used to check that the computer has input all the data.

Biometric A property of the human body such as fingerprints or pattern on the retina that can be used to identify a person.

Bitmap graphic A graphic or image that is stored as a map showing the position and colour of individual dots of light called pixels.

Blog A website that allows comments to be posted.

Bluetooth A method used to transfer data wirelessly over short distances from fixed and mobile devices.

Character Any symbol (letter, number, punctuation mark, etc.) that you can type from the keyboard.

Check digit A decimal number (or alphanumeric character) added to a number for the purpose of detecting the sorts of errors humans normally make on data entry.

Client–server A network where several computers are connected to a more powerful computer that controls the operation of the network.

Compression Storing data in a format that requires less space. Bitmapped graphics such as photographs are usually compressed to a fraction of their normal file size.

Computer Misuse Act 1990 An Act that makes illegal a number of activities such as deliberately planting viruses, hacking, using ICT equipment for fraud, etc.

Content The actual text, images, etc.

Control total A meaningful total (e.g., the total of a batch of invoices) that is entered to check that all the data has been entered/processed.

Copyright, Designs and Patents Act 1988 A law making it a criminal offence to copy or steal software.

Data Raw facts and figures, e.g. readings from sensors, survey facts, etc.

Data capture Term for the various methods by which data can be entered into the computer so that it can be processed.

Data integrity The correctness of data stored.

Data logger A device that collects readings from one or more sensors. The time interval between each reading can be varied (called the logging rate) and the total time over which the data is logged (called the logging period) can also be varied.

Data logging The process of using an ICT system to collect data from sensors at a certain rate over a certain period of time. Remote weather stations use data logging.

Data Protection Act 1998 A law that restricts the way personal information is stored and processed on a computer.

Digital camera A camera that stores a picture digitally.

Digital signature A way of ensuring that an email or document sent electronically is authentic. It can be used to detect a forged document.

Download To copy files from a distant computer to the one you are working on.

Encryption The process of coding files before they are sent over a network to protect them from hackers. Also the process of coding files stored on a computer/storage device so that if the computer/storage device is stolen, they cannot be read.

Ergonomics An applied science concerned with designing and arranging things people use, so that the people and things interact most efficiently and safely.

Expert system An ICT system that mimics the decision-making ability of a human expert.

Extranet An external network that can be used by the customers, suppliers and partners of an organization as well as the organization itself.

Favourites Storage area where the URL (i.e., the web address) of a website can be stored so that it can be accessed later using a link.

Feedback Where the output from the system directly affects the input.

Field A space in an information handling system or database used for inputting data. For instance, you could have fields for surname, date of birth, etc.

File attachment A file that is attached to an email.

Firewall A piece of software, hardware or both that is able to protect a network from hackers.

Footer Text placed at the bottom of a document.

Format checks Checks performed on codes to make sure that they conform to the correct combinations of characters.

Gateway The device/software that translates between two different kinds of computer networks (e.g., between a WAN and a LAN).

GIGO Abbreviation for garbage in garbage out. It means that if you put rubbish into the computer then you get rubbish out.

GIS An ICT system used to capture, manage, analyse and display geographically referenced information.

GUI (graphical user interface) Interface that allows users to communicate with the computer using icons and pull-down menus.

Hackers People who try to break into a computer/computer network.

Hardware The physical components of a computer system.

Hash total Meaningless total of numbers such as order numbers used to check that all the data has been entered.

Header Text placed at the top of a document.

Hotspot An image or piece of text used as a link. When you click on the image or text, you are taken to another part of the same page, a different page or a different site, or it may open a new file or a new window.

Hyperlink A feature of a website that allows a user to jump to another webpage, to jump to part of the same webpage or to send an email message.

HyperText Markup Language (HTML) A computer programming language used to create documents on the World Wide Web. You use it to specify the structure and layout of a web document.

Image map An image that contains more than one hotspot.

Information Data that has been processed by the computer.

Information Commissioner The person responsible for enforcing the Data Protection Act. They also promote good practice and make everyone aware of the implications of the Act.

Input device The hardware device used to feed the input data into an ICT system such as a keyboard or a scanner.

Interactive Where there is a constant dialogue between the user and the computer.

Internet A huge group of networks joined together.

Internet service provider (ISP) A company that provides users with an Internet connection.

Intranet A private network used within an organization that makes use of Internet technology.

Kilobyte (KB) A measure (1024 bytes) of the storage capacity of disks and memory.

Knowledge Derived from information by applying rules to it.

LAN (local area network) A network of computers on one site.

Magnetic ink character recognition (MICR) Input method making use of numbers printed onto a document, such as a cheque, in a special magnetic ink that can be read by the magnetic ink character reader at very high speed.

Mail merge Combining a list of names and addresses with a standard letter so that a series of letters is produced with each letter being addressed to a different person.

Management information system (MIS) An ICT system that supplies information that helps give managers and others the information they need to make effective decisions.

Megabyte (MB) One million bytes.

Megapixel One million pixels (i.e. dots of light).

Memory cards Thin cards you see in digital cameras used to store photographs and can be used for other data.

MIDI (Musical Instrument Digital Interface) Used mainly to communicate between electronic keyboards, synthesizers and computers. MIDI files are compressed and the files are quite small.

Mind map A hierarchical diagram with a central idea or image at the centre of the map surrounded by branches that extend from the central idea.

MP3 Music file format that uses compression to reduce the file size considerably, which is why the MP3 file format is popular with portable music players such as iPods and mobile phones.

Multimedia Making use of many media such as text, images, sound, animation and video.

Network A group of computers that are able to communicate with each other.

Networking software This is systems software that allows computers connected together to function as a network.

Notification The process of letting the Information Commissioner's Office know that an organization is storing and processing personal data.

OCR (optical character recognition) This is a combination of software and a scanner that is able to read characters into the computer.

OMR (optical mark reader/ recognition) Reader that detects marks on a piece of paper. Shaded areas are detected and the computer can understand the information contained in them.

Online shopping Shopping over the Internet, as opposed to using traditional methods such as buying goods or services from shops or trading using the telephone.

Online tutorial Using ICT to help in the learning process.

Operating system The software that controls the hardware and also runs the programs.

Operating system software Software that controls the hardware of a computer and is used to run the applications software. Operating systems control the handling of input, output, etc.

Optical mark recognition (OMR) The process of reading marks (usually shaded boxes) made on a specially prepared document. The marks are read using an optical mark reader.

Output The results from processing data.

Parity check Check to make sure that the data sent is the same as that received when data is transmitted from one computer to another.

Password A series of characters chosen by the user that are used to check the identity of the user when they require access to an ICT system.

Peer-to-peer network Arrangement where each computer is of equal status.

Personal data Data about a living identifiable person that is specific to that person.

Piracy The process of illegally copying software.

Pixel A single point in a graphics element or the smallest dot of light that can appear on a computer screen.

Process Any operation that transfers data into information.

Processing Performing calculations or arranging the data into a meaningful order.

Program The set of step-by-step instructions that tell the computer hardware what to do.

Range check Data validation technique that checks that the data input to a computer is within a certain range.

Real-time processing Type of processing where data received by the system is processed immediately without any delay.

Relative reference When a cell is used in a formula and the formula is copied to a new address, the cell address changes to take account of the formula's new position.

Rollover button/image A button/image that changes its appearance when a cursor is moved over it.

Router Hardware device that is able to make the decision about the path that an individual packet of data should take so that it arrives in the shortest possible time.

RSI (repetitive strain injury) A painful muscular condition caused by repeatedly using certain muscles in the same way.

Sensors Devices that measure physical quantities such as temperature, pressure, humidity, etc.

Social networking site A website that is used to communicate with friends and family and to make new friends and contacts.

Software The programs used by computers.

Spellchecker Program usually found with a word-processor and most packages that make use of text, that checks the spelling in a document and suggests correct spellings.

Stand-alone computer If a computer is used on its own without any connection (wireless or wire) to a network, then it is a stand-alone computer.

Style sheets A document that sets out fonts and font sizes for headings and subheadings, etc., in a document. Changes to a heading need only be made in the style sheet and all the changes to headings in the document will be made automatically.

Swipe card Plastic card containing data stored in a magnetic strip on the card.

Tags Special markers used in HTML to tell the computer what to do with the text. A tag is needed at the start and end of the block of text to which the tag applies.

Templates Electronic files that hold standardized document layouts.

Thesaurus Software that suggests words with similar meanings to the word highlighted in a document.

Transaction A piece of business, e.g. an order, purchase, return, delivery, transfer of money, etc.

Transcription error Error made when typing data in using a document as the source of the data.

Transposition error Error made when characters are swapped around so they are in the wrong order.

Update The process of changing information in a file that has become out of date.

URL (uniform resource locator) A web address.

User A person who uses a computer.

Username or User-ID A name or number that is used to identify a certain user of the network or system.

Validation checks Checks a developer of a solution sets/creates, using the software, in order to restrict the data that a user can enter so as to reduce errors.

Vector graphic A graphic that is expressed mathematically as an equation and can be resized without loss in quality.

Verification Checking that the data being entered into the ICT system perfectly matches the source of the data.

Videoconferencing ICT system that allows face-to-face meetings to be conducted without the participants being in the same room or even the same geographical area.

Virus A program that copies itself automatically and can cause damage to data or cause the computer to run slowly.

WAN (wide area network) A network where the terminals/computers are remote from each other and telecommunications are used to communicate between them.

Web browser Software program you use to access the Internet. Microsoft Internet Explorer is an example of a web browser.

Webcam A digital camera that is used to capture still images and video images (i.e. moving images).

Wi-Fi A trademark for the certification of products that meet certain standards for transmitting data over wireless networks.

WIMP (Windows Icons Menus Pointing devices) The graphical user interface (GUI) way of using a computer rather than typing in commands at the command line.

Index

Acknowledgements

Background – Coloured swirls © Bocos Benedict/Fotolia
Background – Question mark © Stephen Coburn/Fotolia

p.v © Nmedia/Fotolia; p.4 © GreenGate Publishing Services; p.4 © kmit/Fotolia; p.4 © GreenGate Publishing Services; p.5 © Don Bayley/iStock; p.5 © Marlee/Fotolia; p.7 © GreenGate Publishing Services; p.8 © BlueMiniu/Fotolia; p.9 © Monkey Business/Fotolia; p.16 © Tan Kian Khoon/Fotolia; p.17 © Yuri Arcurs/Fotolia; p.17 © Glasbergen; p.18 © ilumin8/Fotolia; p.18 © Viktor Gmyria/Fotolia; p.18 © Nikolai Sorokin/Fotolia; p.19 © Denis Dryashkin/Fotolia; p.19 © Clifford Farrugia/Fotolia; p.19 © Aleksandr Ugorenkov/Fotolia; p.20 Kodak; p.20 © Glasbergen; p.21 © xdominant7/Fotolia; p.22 © Glasbergen; p.23 © Glasbergen; p.25 © Glasbergen; p.25 © Glasbergen; p.27 © camdoc3/Fotolia; p.32 © cristimatei/Fotolia; p.32 © Metin Tolun/Fotolia; p.33 © Paulus Rusyanto/Fotolia; p.33 © OrdinaryLight/Fotolia; p.33 © Sean MacLeay/Fotolia; p.33 © Alex White/Fotolia; p.34 © ta_samaya/Fotolia; p.34 © Petar Atanasov/Fotolia; p.35 The AA; p.40 © treenabeena/Fotolia; p.43 Thomson; p.55 www.data-harvest.co.uk; p.57 © Iglira/Fotolia; p.57 © Arvind Balaraman/Fotolia; p.57 © kapp/Fotolia; p.58 © Yakov Stavchansky/Fotolia; p.59 © Pierre-Emmanuel Turcotte/iStock; p.59 © Zoe/Fotolia; p.60 © Naum Bogdan/Fotolia; p.60 © Kostyantyn Malinovskyy/Fotolia; p.61 © Harvey Hudson/Fotolia; p.71 © Edyta Pawlowska; p.72 © www.techno-vision.co.uk; p.72 © Hooleon Corporation; p.72 © diego cervo/Fotolia; p.72 © Andres Rodrigo Gonzalez Buzzio/Fotolia; p.72 © overthehill/Fotolia; p.81 © Vieloryb/Fotolia; p.81 © Graça Victoria/Fotolia; p.81 © Milan Surkala/Fotolia; p.94 © cameraman/Fotolia; p.95 © Nikolai Sorokin/Fotolia; p.104 © Sean Gladwell; p.105 © Glasbergen; p.106 © Jaimie Duplass/Fotolia; p.106 © beaucroft/Fotolia; p.106 © Hedgehog/Fotolia; p.132 © BVDC/Fotolia; p.133 © KonstantinosKokkinis/Fotolia; p.136 © lionel Valenti/Fotolia; p.142 © Guy Erwood/Fotolia; p.142 © lookata/Fotolia; p.145 © abdulsatarid/Fotolia; p.146 © Glenn Jenkinson/Fotolia; p.153 © Glasbergen; p.163 © Ronald V/Fotolia; p.163 © Glasbergen; p.164 © carlosseller/Fotolia; p.166 © Albo/Fotolia; p.166 © Kwest/Fotolia; p.172 Stephen Doyle; p.172 Stephen Doyle; p.175 © GreenGate Publishing Services; p.178 © logomaster; p.184 © Adam Hart-Davis/Science Photo Library; p.184 © Losevsky Pavel/Shutterstock; p.186 © Pictorial Press Ltd/Alamy; p.188/9 © James Quine/Alamy; p.189 © Lev Dolgatshjov/Fotolia; p.189 © Surkov Vladimir/Shutterstock; p.189 © nyul/Fotolia; p.189 © 7artman/Fotolia; p.189 © Galina Barskaya/Fotolia; p.189 © Eric Isselée/Fotolia; p.190 © Sharpshot/Fotolia; p.190 © DeanMurray.com/Fotolia; p.191 © ioannis kounadeas/Fotolia; p.196 © Glasbergen; p.196 © Viktor Gmyria/Fotolia; p.197 © Renewer/Fotolia; p.197 © bertys30/Fotolia; p.197 © Kwest/Fotolia; p.197 © chrisharvey/Fotolia; p.198 © streetphotoru/Fotolia; p.199 © Milan Surkala/Fotolia; p.200 © dundanim/Fotolia; p.200 © kolesn/Fotolia; p.206 © alphaspirit/Fotolia; p.207 © titimel35/Fotolia; p.209 © ktsdesign/Fotolia; p.209 © Nmedia/Fotolia; p.210 © Ew Chee Guan/Fotolia; p.210 © Georgios Alexandris/Fotolia; p.210 © RTimages/Fotolia; p.210 © Alexander/Fotolia; p.211 © Sean MacLeay/Fotolia; p.213 © Dmitrij Yakovlev/Fotoli; p.213 Retail Systems Technology; p.221 © Sean Gladwell/Fotolia; p.222 Thomson; p.223 © Kirill Roslyakov/Shutterstock; p.223 © Photosani/Fotolia; p.233 © palms/Fotolia; p.233 © OneO2/Fotolia; p.233 © patrimonio designs/Fotolia; p.234/5 © robynmac/Fotolia; p.235 © Daisy Daisy/Fotolia; p.236 © Dragan Trifunovic/Fotolia; p.237 © Small Town Studio/Fotolia; p.237 © AlienCat/Fotolia; p.238 © DX/Fotolia; p.239 © Marcin Balcerzak/Shutterstock; p.240 © Glasbergen; p.240 © Sean Gladwell/Fotolia; p.241 © Helder Almeida/Fotolia; p.241 © Christopher Walker/Fotolia; p.241 © Helder Almeida/Fotolia; p.241 © Glasbergen; p.241 © Glasbergen; p.242 © Photosani/Fotolia; p.242 © cphoto/Fotolia; p.243 © io/Fotolia; p.248 © icing/Fotolia; p.249 © Nabil Biyahmadine/Fotolia; p.250 © Elenathewise; p.253 © tetrex/Fotolia; p.254 © Stephen Finn/Fotolia; p.260 © ktsdesign/Fotolia; p.263 © OneO2/Fotolia; p.263 © Hao Wang/Fotolia; p.264 © Kheng Guan Toh/Fotolia; p.268 © Sean Gladwell/Fotolia; p.268 © Sorin Popa/Fotolia; p.274 © rmarinello/Fotolia; p.275 © kentoh/Fotolia; p.275 © WebButtonsInc/Fotolia; p.275 © Willee Cole/Fotolia; p.280 © Thaut Images/Fotolia; p.281 © Glasbergen; p.286 © bilderbox/Fotolia; p.296 © Glasbergen; p.296 © Nmedia; p.297 Hortibot; p.297 Neusoft; p.297 © Baloncici/Shutterstock; p.297 www.Mowbot.com.

Adobe product screen shot(s) reprinted with permission from Adobe Systems Incorporated.

Microsoft product screenshots reprinted with permission from Microsoft Corporation.

Every effort has been made to contact copyright holders of material used in this publication. If any copyright holder has been overlooked, we should be pleased to make any necessary arrangements.